Overcoming Panic Disorder

A Woman's Guide

LORNA WEINSTOCK, M.S.W., AND ELEANOR GILMAN

Foreword by Una D. McCann, M.D.,
National Institute of Mental Health

CB
CONTEMPORARY BOOKS

Library of Congress Cataloging-in-Publication Data

Weinstock, Lorna.
  Overcoming panic disorder : a woman's guide / Lorna Weinstock, and
Eleanor Gilman.
     p.   cm.
  Includes index.
  ISBN 0-8092-3102-6
    1. Panic disorders—Popular works.   2. Panic disorders—Patients—
Rehabilitation.   3. Women—Mental health.   4. Self-care—Health.
  I. Gilman, Eleanor.   II. Title.
  RC535.W45   1998
  616.85'223—dc21   97-42182
                                                                          CIP

Please see page x for permissions to reprint previously published material.

The instructions and advice in this book are not intended as a substitute for
medical or psychological counseling. Consult a professional before determining the
nature of your problem. The authors and the publisher disclaim any responsibility
or liability resulting from the application of procedures advocated or discussed in
this book.
    Names, locales, and other identifying characteristics of women used in the
cases have been changed to protect privacy and confidentiality.

Cover design by Monica Baziuk
Cover illustration copyright © Linda Montgomery
Interior design by Amy Yu Ng

Published by Contemporary Books
A division of NTC/Contemporary Publishing Group, Inc.
4255 West Touhy Avenue, Lincolnwood (Chicago), Illinois 60712-1975 U.S.A.

International Standard Book Number: 0-8092-3102-6
99 00 01 02 03 04 MV 19 18 17 16 15 14 13 12 11 10 9 8 7 6 5 4 3 2

Dedicated to women everywhere
struggling to overcome panic disorder

Contents

Foreword

*T*hose of you who are reading this book because you believe that you may have panic disorder or another anxiety disorder should consider yourselves among the fortunate. The majority of people with anxiety disorders remain undiagnosed and untreated. Anxiety disorders are the most common mental illnesses in the United States, affecting more than 23 million Americans each year. Of those 23 million, approximately 2.4 million have panic disorder, a serious and potentially debilitating anxiety disorder. Only one-third of people with panic disorder are treated for their illness.

Lorna Weinstock and Eleanor Gilman have compiled an enormous amount of information in an easy-to-read format, tailored specifically for women who have panic disorder. For reasons that are not known, women are twice as likely as men to suffer from panic disorder. As is reviewed herein, panic disorder frequently co-occurs with other anxiety disorders, including social phobia, post-traumatic stress disorder, and generalized anxiety disorder. In addition, approximately 50 percent of women with panic disorder will develop major depression at some point in the course of their illness and one-third will develop agoraphobia, the avoidance of situations associated with previous panic attacks. This book will help readers to recognize the symptoms of panic disorder and common comorbid illnesses, and it will provide them with useful information regarding treatment options.

Panic disorder, like most mental illnesses, is unfortunately associated with stigma and shame. As readers will learn, research conducted with patients having panic disorder has led to a greater understanding of the causes of panic disorder and the brain areas responsible for symptoms of panic attacks. Studies have demonstrated that heredity and environment both play a role in the development of panic disorder, and that people with panic disorder are no more responsible for their symptoms than people with diabetes or heart disease. While tremendous progress has been made toward educating society about the causes and treatments for panic disorder, there is still much work to be done. As illustrated in several of the case studies reviewed in the book, it is not uncommon for patients with panic disorder to be misdiagnosed, patronized, or even improperly treated. In today's health care environment, with increasing emphasis on cost- and time-saving measures, there is a real danger that the numbers of improperly diagnosed cases of panic disorder will rise unless patients and consumers become better informed. This book provides a service to women who are no longer willing to passively await diagnosis, but seek to take control of their own health care.

As reviewed in this book, there are two forms of treatment that have been shown to be effective for the treatment of panic disorder using controlled research methods. Cognitive Behavioral Therapy (CBT) and certain types of medication, either alone or in combination, can lead to significant symptom improvement in 70 to 90 percent of patients with panic disorder. When properly administered, these treatments should begin to work within six to eight weeks. The authors of this book review the principles of both of these effective forms of treatment and provide guidelines for consumers who want to ensure that they are being treated appropriately. In addition, they review several types of adjunct therapy (e.g., other forms of psychotherapy) that can be useful for some women with panic disorder.

If there is a single message conveyed by this book, it is "Take action." Clearly, panic disorder can be serious, debilitating, and even fatal for those who go untreated. Conversely, when panic disorder is properly diagnosed and treated, secondary complications such as agoraphobia, depression, and suicidality can be circumvented. For those of you who recognize yourselves in any of the case studies described in this book, let this be your first step toward recovery. Become one of the multitudes of women who have regained control of their lives by seeking and obtaining treatment for panic disorder.

Una D. McCann, M.D.
Chief, Unit on Anxiety Disorders
Biological Psychiatry Branch, NIMH

Permissions

Acknowledgments

*M*any people deserve our appreciation. Sincere thanks to the women whose courageous contributions to this project will provide hope to millions of other women suffering from panic disorder.

We are extremely grateful to David H. Barlow, Ph.D.; Judith Beck, Ph.D.; Edmund Bourne, Ph.D.; Stephen Josephson, Ph.D.; Donald Klein, M.D.; Una McCann, M.D.; Katherine Shear, M.D.; Elke Zuercher-White, Ph.D.; and Manuel Zane, M.D., for their invaluable contributions.

Special thanks to Kenneth A. Frank, Ph.D., for extensive time spent reviewing the manuscript and for his many excellent suggestions. Thanks also to Michael Milano, M.D., for his encouragement and insightful comments.

We're grateful to Jean Baker Wunder, Leslie Schwartz, Lynda Santoro, M.S.W., and Bob Jones, Ph.D., for their generous assistance.

Thanks to our agent, Agnes Birnbaum, for making this book a reality; to our editor, Kara Leverte, for advice and guidance; and to project editor Gerilee Hundt, for meticulous attention to our manuscript.

Special gratitude to our families—George, Pamela, and Andrea Weinstock and Arthur, Stephanie, and Eric Gilman—for their love and support.

Ms. Weinstock would also like to thank her patients for enriching her life.

Introduction

*W*hen we began collecting information on panic disorder, we wondered why women are so much more vulnerable than men to this illness. Indeed, out of more than three million Americans who have or are likely to develop panic disorder, two-thirds are women, according to the National Institute of Mental Health.[1]

As we reviewed the research and listened to the women whose stories we recount, some of the pieces of the puzzle fell into place. We discovered that certain characteristics—low self-esteem, dependency, separation anxiety, a fear of what others think, perfectionism, and sensitivity to criticism, among others—make women more vulnerable to the disorder.

What's more, many women are enormously stressed. They often attempt the extremely difficult task of balancing home and family with full-time careers; often, they must care for aging parents, too. The stress leads to anxiety: anxiety in turn can place one at risk for developing panic disorder.

In addition, there is a link between panic disorder and depression, agoraphobia, and anxiety disorders such as generalized anxiety disorder and obsessive-compulsive disorder, all of which appear more frequently in women. A relationship also exists between panic disorder and PMS, eating disorders, childhood sexual abuse, and physical abnormalities such as mitral valve prolapse—all more likely to occur in women.

Contributing further to the vulnerability are genetic factors (women with mothers or sisters who have the disorder are more at risk) and hormonal changes, such as those that may cause PMS.

We are well aware that researchers and the medical profession have, until recently, given inadequate attention to illnesses suffered by women. Neglect of heart disease in women is just one example. The experiences of the women to whom we spoke underscore society's failure to take women's health issues seriously.

Complicating the situation are problems involving diagnosis. Panic disorder often mimics physical ailments, so people spend much time and money rushing to hospital emergency rooms, consulting doctors, and taking tests. Indeed, half of all unnecessary angiograms, at $2,000 each, are ordered based on symptoms of panic disorder.[2] One study found that among patients who were referred for coronary evaluation and found normal on several tests of heart function, 58 percent had panic disorder.[3]

A survey of a group of panic disorder patients found that on average they made 37.3 medical visits a year, as compared with about 5 a year for the general population.[4] It is not at all unusual for panic disorder sufferers to see 10 or more doctors before being properly diagnosed.[5]

One of the women you will read about saw nearly 200 different doctors in the 10-year period before she was finally diagnosed. Many other women with panic disorder told us about frustrating experiences in their attempts to find a diagnosis— and relief.

Today, however, we are witnessing progress in the area of women's health: some real advances are being made with regard to diagnosing and treating panic disorder. After years of lumping panic disorder together with other anxiety disorders, the American Psychiatric Association officially recognized the diagnostic category of panic disorder in 1980. A decade later, the National Institutes of Health concluded that "panic disorder is a distinct condition, with a specific presentation, course, and family history, for which there are effective pharmacologic and cognitive behavioral treatments." [6]

Researchers are placing increasing emphasis on finding the causes, risk factors, links to other conditions, and treatments for panic disorder. In 1990 research was scant; over the past few years several dozen studies have been conducted.

Because of the new awareness about panic disorder, women are discovering that they are not alone, that others are living with the same terrifying, life-altering symptoms. You'll read about some of these women in the pages that follow.

We found some of our case study subjects through panic disorder support groups or self-help groups. We have made an effort to include women of different ages and backgrounds. Our selection was also based on the types of methods used in their recovery; we wanted to show the wide variety of help available today. What all the women had in common was their determination to overcome panic disorder, despite setbacks and disappointments. All of them learned to cope better with their illness and are functioning in a healthier way. They were eager to talk to us, knowing that their stories would be included in a book that would help other women with panic disorder.

In Part I, you will meet these women who refused to submit to defeat. You will understand the reasons behind each woman's vulnerability to panic disorder, the ways in which she coped, and her road to recovery. The stories clarify the relationship between panic disorder and depression, anxiety, and agoraphobia. In this section you'll learn what causes panic disorder, how it is diagnosed, and the scope of the problem.

Part II will take you on the path toward healing. You will learn different relaxation techniques and cognitive techniques. In this section we explain the role of medication, discuss how psychotherapy can help, and talk about the use of exposure and contextual therapy for agoraphobia. We tell you how support groups and the alternative approaches of humor and spirituality can be part of your treatment plan. We offer tips for choosing and working with a therapist. And we explain the latest research and give you an opportunity to listen to the comments of researchers and experts in the fields of anxiety and panic disorder.

The information is encouraging. New discoveries about panic disorder and the variety of options available today translate to good news. As you embark on this adventure toward recovery, you have every reason to feel hopeful.

Two caveats, however, are in order here.

Before turning the page, you need to be certain that your symptoms are not due to a physical ailment. Because the symptoms of panic disorder are so similar to those of some physical illnesses, it's important to see a physician before considering a diagnosis of panic disorder.

We also recommend that you use this book along with the help of a professional in the mental health field who will identify and treat all the factors contributing to your illness.

Part I

Women and Panic

The Misdiagnosed Woman

Before a problem can be treated, it must first be identified. But for panic disorder sufferers, that's no easy matter. For them, obtaining the right diagnosis is often a major hurdle. Much of the difficulty stems from the way that panic disorder frequently mimics physical ailments; in fact, it is considered one of medicine's great imposters.

Unless the patient has done some reading, met others with the same condition, or been fortunate enough to find a doctor who recognizes panic disorder, she probably is wondering why she feels so terrible when the doctors assure her that she is healthy. She may worry that she has some rare, mysterious physical ailment or, even worse, that she is "crazy."

In Chapter 1, we meet Jane, a widow who remarried. Though Jane suffered from panic attacks for many years, it was just three years ago that she finally learned her problem had a name. While trying to discover the cause of her suffering, she saw nearly 200 different doctors who thought she had physical conditions ranging from anemia to a tooth abscess. She had all her teeth pulled, endured surgery, and took a variety of medications. Unhappily, many panic disorder patients, in their attempts to find a diagnosis—and relief—have experiences similar to Jane's.

Jane's difficult search for a solution ended when she began treatment in therapy.

Jane's Story

I was the baby of seven children and was always a shy and anxious child. I had to sleep with the light on, and sometimes I demanded to sleep with my mother. I was very attached to her.

My father drank. When he was drunk, my mother would argue with him. I remember them fighting and screaming at two in the morning, many times. That always left me in a dither. I was very upset with the fighting. Sometimes, to get away from it, I would go outside and sit on the dark porch.

When I was 17, my father was murdered. As he was leaving work at eight in the evening, someone mugged him and left him on the street with a fractured skull. My family dwelled on the murder. "Why did it have to happen to Pop?" we said over and over. We weren't able to drop it.

I got married at 21 and had three children—the first when I was 23, the second at 28, and the third at 30. I was content to stay close to home and had no desire to socialize much. I crocheted and kept the house clean. That was my palace and if someone messed it up, I got upset.

The panic attacks began when I was 26. I would wake up in the middle of the night unable to breathe, with my heart pounding. I was scared that something was terribly wrong physically and thought I was dying. The next day I would be very weak and shaky.

Sometimes I would go to bed and feel that an attack was going to occur that night. Then, an hour and a half later, I would wake up with the usual symptoms.

For 10 years, the attacks continued on and off both during the day and at night. For a while they were occurring once every two months; then they started coming closer together, about once a week. All that time, I tried to figure out why they were happening. I thought, maybe, that something I was eating was giving me heartburn. So I propped my pillows up and took Tums, but that did no good. No one knew about the attacks, not even my husband sleeping next to me. Once I ran out of the house during the night and he ran after me. "What's wrong with you?" he said. "You're talking like a robot."

I went to bed each night worrying that I would have a panic attack. The fear would build up before the attacks started. I wasn't sleeping well, and I was light-headed much of the time. I didn't feel much like eating and went down to 80 pounds.

I called doctors in the middle of the night. They would come over, stay for a while, and give me something to help me sleep. Once I called the police and asked them to take me to the hospital.

The attacks were leaving me worn out and depressed. A family doctor thought they were coming on because I was nervous. He gave me shock treatments twice in the hospital, "to clear my mind," he said. They did nothing for me and left me crying and even more depressed. He was treating my problem as if it were a severe mental illness, and that scared me to death. Was I really crazy?

Other doctors also thought they knew what was wrong. An internist said I was anemic and gave me vitamin B_{12} shots. One doctor thought, because I had difficulty swallowing during the panic attacks, that something was wrong with my throat. He said I had globus hystericus and gave me some kind of electronic treatment for my throat three times a week. An endocrinologist said that I had thyroid trouble. Another doctor took my tonsils out. In another operation, a surgeon removed part of my palate. It was so ridiculous.

During this 10-year period, I saw about 200 doctors. An eye doctor told me to get eyeglasses; an ear, nose, and throat doctor thought it was an inner-ear problem and prescribed Dramamine; a dentist thought I had an abscess draining throughout my system and pulled all my teeth. One doctor said I was suffering from "house nerves" because I had told him how my house had to be immaculately clean.

The doctors prescribed all kinds of medication over the years. An internist gave me Xanax. Not only did it not help, it nearly killed me. I was also on Inderal, Klonopin, Elavil, and Tofranil. Recently I took Zoloft, which gave me hallucinations. One time I was given a pill—I forget the name—and didn't get up for two days. Nothing worked except for Valium, which helped me feel calmer. That was given to me by a psychiatrist who knew I was anxious.

Nobody could give me an answer for what was wrong. The doctors said I was in good physical health but I thought I was dying. I've got cancer, I thought. My husband didn't know what to do, and I felt bad that he had to go through such a difficult time with me.

I was so upset that I didn't want to see anyone. In fact, as the children got older, my need to stay home became stronger. I can recall a time when my husband drove me to the grocery store. Halfway into the store, I felt like passing out and had to go back to the car.

Bowling nights were terrible. I would have to walk outside. I needed air. Other times, too, I felt claustrophobic. I couldn't lock the bathroom door or go into elevators.

My husband liked to visit friends, but when we did my face would turn beet red and I would feel hot, as if I had a fever. So I began to avoid seeing people. I was afraid I would embarrass myself.

Once while I was in the supermarket carrying a basket

filled with groceries, the floor seemed to move under me. Someone got me a chair. I felt immobilized and terrified. I left the groceries in the store and my husband took me home. After that, I stayed in bed for a month, leaving only to go the bathroom or to get something to eat. My life was miserable.

When I was 37, I lost my husband to a heart attack. But instead of having more panic attacks, the attacks subsided. I was busy raising my children and working as an office manager. When I felt insecure, I would get busy.

At 42, I remarried and found that I could do everything I had once done before—go grocery shopping, go to parties, see people. I flew all over the world. I was a different person.

Then my husband started drinking. I began having feelings of insecurity and fears of going back to how I felt as a child. One night I felt my heart pounding and racing. I had terrible palpitations. I was terrified. I called my son. This happened twice more and after all three incidents, I landed in the hospital. Each time I was put in intensive care for three days.

When I was discharged, I still didn't know what was wrong. The EKG tests were negative all three times. The last time I was in the hospital, the doctor said that he had gone as far as he could, physically, and suggested that I go somewhere for therapy.

I went into a decline. I was weak. My legs felt like jelly and I couldn't walk.

Understanding Jane

The Roots of Panic

As we began examining the lives of women with panic disorder, we noticed a pattern. Women with this illness were often anxious children, overly attached to their mothers. In fact, there appeared to be a correlation between anxiety during childhood and the manifestation of panic attack symptoms as an adult.

Research supports our findings. Studies of patients with panic disorder have concluded that separation anxiety (a fear of separating from a parent and being alone) is a possible cause of panic disorder. A group of psychoanalysts at the Payne Whitney Clinic in New York asserts that panic disorder arises from a "bad fit" between an inhibited child and a parent who can't ease the child's fear of new experiences. The child clings to the parent, they say, in an attempt to ensure the child's and the parent's safety.[1] Children who cling to their mothers are usually shy; according to researchers at Harvard Medical School, shy youngsters have a heightened risk of anxiety problems later in life.[2]

Fighting between parents, alcoholism in the family, and major changes are other factors that are frequently present in the childhood of panic disorder patients. A recent Duke University study found that adult children of alcoholics showed a significantly higher tendency toward panic disorder than the general population.[3] It also concluded that daughters of alcoholic fathers have a higher rate of generalized anxiety disorder, a condition that is linked to panic disorder.[3]

Jane had to cope with an alcoholic father, tension between her parents, and a major change—her father's death. The murder marred her childhood, and she had to live with its aftermath. In healthy grieving, survivors eventually accept the loved one's death, so they can go on with their lives. But Jane's father was an alcoholic who fought with her mother and caused much anguish. The family's ambivalent feelings about him interfered with the grieving process. Whatever relief they felt because of his death created guilt. They couldn't mourn appropriately and didn't work through their grief. The result was a lot of anxiety, vulnerability, and anger.

The Illness Develops

Most women with panic disorder begin to have panic attacks in their teens or mid-twenties. Jane, at 26, started to experience common symptoms of the illness—heart palpitations; shortness of breath; and fear of losing control, fainting, having a heart attack, or dying. Many panic disorder sufferers don't eat or sleep well, complain of exhaustion, and often lose weight or become ill. Jane's weight dropped to 80 pounds.

Depression, fear of recurring attacks, and agoraphobia (an anxiety about being in places or situations from which escape might be difficult or embarrassing) frequently develop as the illness progresses. Some women turn to alcohol or drugs.

In many cases, panic attacks increase after a major change, such as the birth of a child. Stress caused by new responsibilities, changes in lifestyle, exhaustion, and strain in the couple's relationship can result in greater risk for panic attacks in someone who is prone to them. On the other hand, symptoms sometimes abate during comparatively tranquil periods. While Jane's illness was severe when her children were very young, it subsided while they were growing up and she was busy working.

Jane had made her home her haven, her "safe place." Her focus on cleaning her "palace" and getting upset if someone messed it up could be interpreted as evidence of obsessive-compulsive disorder. It is possible for overly anxious women to cope better with their anxiety by engaging in repetitive behaviors such as excessive hand washing or compulsive housecleaning. Although they recognize that these are time-consuming compulsions, they can't do anything to stop them. Jane also obsessed over having more panic attacks and over the way her father died.

Nocturnal Attacks

Some of Jane's panic attacks were occurring in the middle of the night—a particularly disturbing pattern. It is extremely startling to wake up with such intense symptoms. Yet nocturnal attacks aren't unusual. According to David Barlow, Ph.D., director of the Center for Anxiety and Related Disorders at Boston University, 25 percent of people with panic disorder have experienced at least one nocturnal panic attack.[4]

The question of why some attacks occur during the night is one that research has begun to answer. Nocturnal panic attacks occur during light sleep when the body is relaxed and heart rate and respiration have slowed. Some researchers think that a sensitive person might react to a change in her body, such as muscle twitches, during this period of relaxation.[5] These alien sensations feel strange and cause alarm. Thus, Jane's pounding heart, reacting to some internal change, could have awakened her.

Another theory, known as "false-suffocation alarm," was proposed by Donald Klein, M.D., a professor of psychiatry at Columbia University, College of Physicians and Surgeons. Klein's theory suggests that panic disorder patients suffer from a respiratory dysfunction in which a false signal to the brain causes them to believe they are suffocating. This sensation leads to panic.[6] The false signal usually occurs when one is relaxed or sleeping.

Jane might have felt that nighttime was unsafe—a reaction rooted in the past, since her parents had argued during the night and her father was murdered in the dark. Her feeling of vulnerability at night easily could have led to thoughts that caused her heart to pound.

Not all panic attacks have warning signals; some come out of the blue. In Jane's case there was some warning. However, the knowledge that an attack was imminent didn't help her. With her heart pounding, unable to breathe, and thinking she was dying, Jane was too startled and overwhelmed with fear to attempt anything that might have calmed her down. She had no strategies to rely on when she suspected that an attack was coming. Had she done deep breathing, for instance, she might have felt more in control of the situation. Not knowing what to do, she ignored the warnings.

Living with the Terror

Jane was frightened and anxious as the attacks began to permeate her life. At first, she looked for a simple explanation and, suspecting an intestinal problem, tried to find a solution.

The attacks occurred on and off for 10 years, a pattern that is fairly typical of the disorder. While panic attacks have some predictability, they don't necessarily have any particular rhythm. Over a period of time, the severity of attacks, the time of day they occur, and the interlude between them can vary.

Symptoms may not be identical. A lot depends on what is going on in the person's life at a particular time.

Unless they are very young, panic disorder patients usually suffer alone, keeping the problem to themselves, since they don't want to be thought of as crazy. From the onset, they feel embarrassed. It would have been a big relief—and very helpful—if Jane could have shared what was happening to her.

Instinctively, people try to help themselves, reverting to coping skills that worked in the past when they were stressed. So, after one attack, Jane ran out of the house during the night, just as she had done as a child trying to cope with her parents' fighting.

She talked without expression after that incident, unconsciously distancing herself from the terror she felt. People who become very frightened sometimes have a flat affect (meaning they show no emotion). Their actual mood—what they feel deep inside—is disconnected from what they show the outside world. Had Jane been able to talk to her husband about what was making her so scared, she might have been able to deal better with her fear.

Searching for a Solution

Jane's family doctor gave her shock treatments. But it was an inappropriate choice, since shock treatments are used for depression, not panic disorder. Though she might have been somewhat depressed because of her problem and the frustration she experienced in dealing with the medical profession, Jane's condition didn't warrant treatment for depression. Today, doctors are more prudent about giving shock treatments, and the treatments themselves have become more refined.

Panic disorder is also often misdiagnosed as a physical illness, with specialists sometimes viewing patients' problems in the context of the particular ailment that they treat. This is especially understandable when one considers that the symptoms of panic disorder are so ambiguous. Had Jane seen a cardiologist—in addition to all the other specialists from whom she sought help—he or she most likely would have suspected a heart ailment, while a gastroenterologist might have thought something was wrong with Jane's digestive system.

Nobody was able to define Jane's problem. Each doctor looked at it from a different orientation and subjected her to an enormous amount of trial and error and medical misdiagnosis. All the doctors she saw were guessing.

Prescriptions for medications, as well as treatment, were the result of all this guesswork. (Many doctors are not familiar with the variety of help available and their first choice is to prescribe drugs.) Jane took tranquilizers (Valium, Xanax, and Klonopin), antidepressants (Zoloft, Elavil, and Tofranil), and a beta-blocker for palpitations (Inderal), as well as other drugs whose names she can't recall. Some of the medications had bad side effects. Nothing worked except Valium.

Because panic disorder is as puzzling to family members as it is to patients, Jane's husband didn't know what to make of her problem. Some people become frightened and feel helpless when they watch their loved ones deteriorate. They want to help and be supportive, but they don't know how.

The Illness Worsens

As typically happens, Jane began to develop agoraphobia, which is brought on by fear of the fear. But, because people with panic disorder test themselves out occasionally, Jane tried to go to the grocery store, visit friends, and go bowling—all with disastrous results. Jane was extremely shy; when thrown into a group, she would become anxious. Her shyness and the fear of panic attacks made her reluctant to socialize. At times she felt claustrophobic. This was additional evidence of her anxiety.

Yet another example of her extreme anxiety was the incident in the supermarket. She had a particularly frightening time there, experiencing derealization, a feeling that something in the environment had changed. Derealization is a disassociative state, similar to the depersonalization that some panic disorder patients experience when they feel removed from the people around them.

With no prior therapy, Jane lacked tools, such as relaxation techniques, that she could depend on when she felt panicky. Instead, she just wanted to rush home where it was safe.

Finally, an Answer

Then Jane's life turned around. She became stabilized and able to function like everyone else during the years when she focused on work and raising her children. Sometimes when one is busy, panic disorder symptoms dissipate. (At other times, symptoms can disappear for no discernible reason.) What's more, a good job raises self-esteem. People are usually less anxious when they feel better about themselves.

Insecurity once more plagued Jane when her second husband started drinking. It might have reminded her of the terrible times she had when her father drank and, once again, she began having night panic attacks.

Fortunately, her doctor suggested that she go somewhere for therapy. It had taken years and years, exhaustive tests, and a barrage of treatments and medications before Jane found the right direction. She needed informed doctors and therapy to realize that nothing was physically wrong with her, that her problem was psychological. Yet this acknowledgment, rather than bringing relief, distressed her. The implications were frightening and included worries about others' perceptions of her as crazy and a strong fear of being locked up. But she could no longer deny the truth; she had to face reality. And she did.

Jane's Recovery

Treating Panic Disorder with Cognitive Therapy

*C*urrently the most useful approach in the treatment of panic disorder appears to be a combination of cognitive therapy, behavioral therapy, and medication. All of these treatments make the illness more manageable and facilitate recovery. In some cases, the attacks become less intense. Some patients find that, with treatment, their attacks occur less frequently; with other people the attacks disappear completely.

Most people with panic disorder are treated with cognitive therapy and behavioral therapy—usually in a combined treatment referred to as cognitive-behavioral therapy (CBT). When someone is so overwhelmed that she can't function, medication can be a useful adjunct. The majority of patients we talked to, however, say they prefer approaches that don't involve medication. Many of them, like Jane, tried various medications, but complained that they weren't useful or caused side effects.

The therapist Jane found used the three basic techniques, but it was cognitive therapy that helped Jane most. In this chapter we will tell you exactly what cognitive therapy is and how it helps heal panic disorder. In Part II we will explain how cognitive therapy can help you, too, recover from panic disorder.

Distorted Ideas

Cognitive therapy involves the correction of distorted ideas about oneself and one's environment. People with distorted ideas view the world in an unrealistic way; as a result, they experience emotional and behavioral disturbances.

Jane believed, *without question*, that certain places were unsafe—that she would *definitely* have a panic attack in a store or at a bowling alley. That belief was a distortion in her thinking; in actuality there was no certainty that she would have a panic attack in a particular place, even if she had had one there before. The fear was a disturbance in her emotions, and her reluctance to venture out of the house was a disturbance in her behavior.

Another woman, a bank officer prone to panic disorder, worried about a speech she had to give to colleagues. She remembered having had a panic attack the last time she had given a speech and was terrified about having the same experience again. The terror comprised the emotional disturbance while avoiding the speech was the behavioral disturbance.

Many panic disorder patients worry about what will happen during an attack. They are afraid of fainting, having a heart attack, choking, losing control, or embarrassing themselves in myriad ways.

Lisa, a computer programmer, personified this kind of distorted thinking. Her first panic attack occurred on the second-floor walkway of the atrium of her office building. It was a routine walk, one that she had made three or four times daily for four years, in order to get from one side of the building to the other. But this time her walk was filled with terror. It would be the last time, for years, that she would cross the atrium.

This is her account of the experience:

About a third of the way across, I suddenly felt as if the walkway was moving. I knew it couldn't move; I knew it was stable. But it seemed that it was swaying like an unsteady bridge or like a plank held up by ropes. I sensed that it was swinging. I thought it would collapse.

I felt nauseated and dizzy. My legs started to shake, and I thought that I would jump out of my body. I was desperate to get to the other side, to get out of there, but I couldn't move my legs. My body felt frozen.

I was terrified. Terrified because I thought I would pass out and terrified because I was afraid of the way I was feeling. I knew there was something wrong with me and not the walkway. The walkway wasn't collapsing. I just stood there and cried. About five minutes passed. No one came by during that time. Actually, I was relieved that no one was around because I really thought I was going crazy and I didn't want anyone to see me in that state.

I talked to my feet and my knees, saying "Come on, let's get through this." I used a lot of brainpower, hoping that my brain would tell my body how to move. I prayed to God that my legs would listen to my brain. I was working so hard to make myself do what should be done.

I was finally able to run to the other side. When I got there, I opened the door and walked through the hall to the computer room, where I froze again for a few minutes. Then I ran outside.

For a month I used the stairs. I couldn't go through the atrium. Then, I became afraid to walk through the enclosed stairwell and use the stairs. So I couldn't go to work because I had no way of getting to my office. I couldn't fight my fears.

Lisa's thinking demonstrated some distortions common to women with panic disorder: thinking she was jumping out of her body, thinking she would pass out, and thinking she was going crazy.

How Does Cognitive Therapy Correct Distorted Ideas?

Cognitive therapy corrects distorted ideas by helping the frightened patient understand that her fears won't become reality. True, she may feel nervous, scared, even terrified under certain situations. But she won't make a fool of herself. In fact, she is probably the only one aware of the emotional and physical changes in her body. The chances that she'll faint are practically nil. So is the likelihood that she'll have a heart attack.

Keeping in mind the following concepts can help prevent distortions in thinking and perception.

- There is little evidence that you will faint; you have probably never fainted.

- Your last physical showed that you have no heart problems.

- You are not going crazy, you are not psychotic, and you are not having hallucinations.

- You have had panic attacks before and have never lost control. Panic disorder patients usually don't lose control.

- You can always continue your task even if you are having a panic attack.

- Panic attacks are time-limited; they are usually over in 10 minutes. You will recover from them.

When patients understand that their thinking is distorted, they begin to think more logically. The results are calming and reassuring. And, with the distortions corrected, emotional and behavioral changes can follow.

Once they know that their worst fears won't be realized, that they won't faint or humiliate themselves, patients can begin to function. The bank officer knew that she could get through her speech and manage to do a satisfactory job, even if she did have a panic attack while standing at the podium. Because her distorted ideas were corrected, she was actually calmer while speaking. Lisa was able to return to work once she understood that she could get there and function on the job without anything disastrous happening. And, Jane, as you will see, was eventually able to drive, go to stores, and visit friends.

How Cognitive Therapy Helped Jane Recover

For most people, going to a supermarket, a party, or a shopping mall is pretty routine. Most people can drive. They enjoy leaving home periodically. But not Jane. Her distorted thinking prevented her from living a normal life.

Yet Jane had a list of things she wanted to do. She wanted to go shopping, to go to the hairdresser, and to visit friends. Desperate for help, she asked her doctor to recommend a therapist. Jane was lucky: the therapist she contacted asked many questions, listened carefully to the description of her symptoms, and diagnosed her as having panic disorder.

What helped enormously was the correction of her distorted thinking. Jane realized that what she feared wasn't real: the pounding in her heart wasn't a heart attack and the funny feeling in her head wasn't a stroke. Her illness wasn't physical and she wasn't dying. With her therapist's help, she began to understand that, because of distortions in her thinking, she had declared certain places off limits.

She accepted the fact that panic attacks would occur— often quickly and without warning—no matter what she did. Gradually she became confident that she could handle them.

One night, sitting home alone, she had a strong urge to go somewhere. "I had this crazy feeling that I had to get out," she recalls. "I remembered that the church was having a fair and I decided to go."

After being virtually housebound for two years, Jane got into the car and went off by herself, thinking, "I can do it now. I don't need a pill. Isn't this marvelous? Now I can go places, make trips."

"I had reached the point of accepting my illness and knowing that I could cope with it better," she says.

Although Jane has made much progress, she continues to set goals for herself. "It gives me something to work on," she says. The last time we spoke to her, she had just attended her niece's wedding. When she first received the invitation, she wasn't sure she could make it. But she was determined to find a way.

She got through the ceremony by clasping in her hand an index card with some calming thoughts written on it. From time to time, she looked down and read them. They said:

- It won't last forever.

- Let it roll over me.

- Let it go; let it run its course.

- Live with it.

- I will do my best to get through it.

"I couldn't dance but at least I went to the wedding," she says with pride.

For Jane, the path to healing was long, circuitous, and punctuated by wrong turns and detours. In contrast, your recovery will be smoother because you will be armed with the information and suggestions that you need. In the next chapter we provide facts about this illness we call panic disorder and explain how it is diagnosed.

What Is Panic Disorder?

Panic Attack and Panic Disorder

What is a panic attack and how exactly does it relate to panic disorder? According to the revised fourth edition of the American Psychiatric Association's *Diagnostic and Statistical Manual of Mental Disorders (DSM-IV)*, a panic attack is a discrete period of intense fear or discomfort in which four (or more) of the following symptoms develop abruptly and reach a peak within 10 minutes.

- palpitations, pounding heart, or accelerated heart rate

- sweating

- trembling or shaking

- sensations of shortness of breath or smothering

- feeling of choking

- chest pain or discomfort

- nausea or abdominal distress

- dizziness, unsteadiness, light-headedness, or faintness

- derealization (feelings of unreality) or depersonalization (being detached from oneself)

- fear of losing control or going crazy

- fear of dying

- numbness or tingling sensations

- chills or hot flushes

To satisfy the criteria for panic disorder with or without agoraphobia, the attacks must be recurrent and unexpected. At least one of the attacks must be followed by one month (or more) of one (or more) of the following:

- persistent concern about having additional attacks

- worry about the implications of the attack or its consequences (e.g., losing control, having a heart attack, going crazy)

- a significant change in behavior related to the attacks

Panic attacks resulting from panic disorder are not due to the direct physiological effects of a substance such as a drug, a medication, or a general medical condition like hyperthyroidism. The attacks are not better accounted for by another mental disorder, such as social phobia, obsessive-compulsive disorder, post-traumatic stress disorder, or separation anxiety disorder.[1]

Because the physical symptoms of panic disorder are so intense, many patients feel that the next step must be death. They often wind up in hospital emergency rooms—and are usually sent home still wondering what is wrong!

Many patients fear that the attack will last indefinitely, that they will never recover. In reality, most panic attacks peak within 10 minutes, and then quickly subside. However, the patient feels so overwhelmed while in the midst of the attack that the few minutes it lasts feel like forever.

Afterward the question "Will it happen again?" haunts patients. Because the attacks are such horrible experiences, most panic disorder patients develop anticipatory anxiety, also known as fear of the fear. They fear not only the actual panic attack, but also the anticipation of it. They think they will experience the fear that produces the attack, and then obsess over the idea that they will have more attacks. "What will I do if it happens again?" they ask themselves. In a vicious circle, this rumination over the possibility of another attack increases their anxiety level. The slightest physical symptom can set off waves of anticipation and cause fear of the fear.

The Scope of the Problem

In any one month, 0.5 percent of the population, or one million people, will exhibit symptoms of panic disorder.[2] This debilitating condition will affect at least one out of every 75 people worldwide during their lifetime.[3] Two-thirds of these sufferers are women.[4]

Panic disorder typically begins in the late teen years or the early to mid-twenties. The median age of onset is 24 years, but the disorder can also develop in childhood, middle age, or the later years.[5] Panic disorder appears to run in families; 15 to 17 percent of patients who have close relatives with panic disorder also have the disorder themselves.[6] Studies involving twins confirm the possibility of a genetic predisposition to panic disorder.[7]

The first attack is often preceded by a stressful event—the death of someone close, an illness, a move to a new place, or the breakup of a marriage. However, any event that causes stress—even a positive event such as marriage, the birth of a child, or graduation from college—can trigger an attack.

Following the first attack, the frequency of the attacks can range from several times a day to once or twice a week to just once a year. Some people never have a second attack. But no matter how often or seldom the attacks occur, patients typically develop fear of the fear.

One-third of people with panic disorder also have agoraphobia.[8] Panic disorder with agoraphobia is diagnosed about twice as frequently in females as in males.[9]

One-half of those with panic disorder will have an episode of clinical depression at some time in their lives; 20 percent of people with panic disorder have attempted suicide.[10]

People with panic disorder often turn to alcohol and drugs to alleviate their mental and physical symptoms. Thirty-six percent have a history of alcohol or other drug abuse.[11] Other anxiety disorders may also develop.[12] Physical ailments associated with panic disorder include mitral valve prolapse, irritable bowel syndrome, migraines, and asthma.

Most patients seek help; antidepressants supplemented by tranquilizers seem to relieve symptoms. Best results occur when patients take medication in conjunction with cognitive-behavioral therapy. Long-term psychotherapy helps patients deal with issues related to panic attacks, such as low self-esteem, dependency, and separation anxiety.

A small study that we conducted of women whose average age was 26 yielded results that are similar to those of the general population. The first attack generally occurred at age 16 and in most cases came "out of the blue," while the subject was grieving over a loss or while giving a speech. The most prevalent symptoms were shortness of breath, dizziness, shaking, nausea, sweating, and chest pain. Frequency of attacks ranged from one a year to every day. Most of the subjects experienced attacks twice to five times a week. Fear of the fear was reported often. Other illnesses noted were premenstrual syndrome (PMS) followed by respiratory difficulties. A sizable number of the subjects had a history of verbal abuse and family and relationship stress. Most of the respondents didn't smoke or use alcohol or drugs, though a significant number reported that they were depressed and, at times, suicidal. None reported agoraphobia, but this phenomenon is probably due to the fact that we were assessing women in an environment away from home, in self-help groups and college classrooms. Many said that someone else in the family, most often their mothers, suffered from panic attacks or panic disorder. Most had sought help that included relaxation training, behavior therapy, psychotherapy, and cognitive therapy. The most-used medications were tranquilizers, which most respondents said they found moderately helpful.

What Causes Panic Disorder?

No one knows the exact cause of panic disorder, although theories abound. Many researchers believe that a combination of factors is to blame. Furthermore, there are a variety of viewpoints within each discipline.

Behavioral and Cognitive Views

Behaviorists say people become conditioned to panic whenever they are in a situation similar to the one that caused an initial attack. For instance, if someone has a panic attack in a car, she may fear she will have another panic attack the next time she gets into a car. Behaviorists believe that, since panic attacks develop through conditioned learning, treatment involves relearning or reconditioning.

Cognitive theorists believe that incorrect thinking can trigger panic attacks. They say that some people focus on anxiety-provoking thoughts, assuming the worst possible outcome. These people misinterpret harmless bodily sensations as danger signals, fearing a heart attack when their heartbeat speeds up, for instance. Cognitive theorists think that people with panic disorder have a system of erroneous beliefs about themselves and the world. The goal, these theorists say, is to recognize the distortions and to correct them.

Biological Views

Some experts think that panic attacks are caused by a disturbance in neurotransmitters, which regulate the transmission of impulses between neurons, the pathways along which impulses travel from various parts of the body to the brain.

Other experts say that some people may have nervous systems that are hypersensitive, responding excessively to stimuli. They react physically and emotionally to perceived threats as if to actual dangers.

Another theory, involving the respiratory system suggests that hyperventilation is excessive in patients with panic disorder. Still another theory maintains that panic attacks come from an unusual sensitivity to fluctuations of carbon dioxide in the body.

Evidence supports a genetic basis for panic disorder, with some experts contending that an abnormal gene is involved. Research shows that panic disorder runs in families. There is a much higher incidence of panic disorder among twins, and a significant number of first-degree relatives of panic disorder sufferers are similarly afflicted. Family members frequently have the same fears—which could be an inherited trait.

Researchers interested in biological causes of panic disorder have been conducting research into brain-imaging studies, mitral valve prolapse, and tests involving sodium lactate, a substance that produces panic attacks in vulnerable people.

Biological theories have been supported by the use of antidepressant medications, which have been shown to have a beneficial effect on panic disorder.

Psychoanalytic Views

Psychoanalytic theorists believe that unconscious conflicts may cause panic attacks. For example, when someone represses anger because she feels that it is unacceptable or inappropriate for her to experience this anger, she may have panic attacks instead. Panic may also result from other unconscious conflicts, such as that between dependency and autonomy.

These theorists also contend that difficult separations when a person is young may create more susceptibility to anxiety when separations occur in adulthood.

Another view maintains that being overwhelmed by stress and loss may put one more at risk for panic. Many researchers believe that panic disorder occurs when someone with a hereditary or biological vulnerability to the illness experiences a stressful life event that strains her or his coping mechanisms.[13] (For an interesting explanation of causes of panic disorder, see *The New Psychiatry* by Jack Gorman, M.D.)

Because causes are not specific, a varied approach to them may be appropriate. Accordingly, Dr. Kenneth A. Frank, a psychologist who has treated many panic disorder patients, proposes the following.

Many patients find it helpful to think in terms of a "biopsychosocial" model of panic. This model points out that panic has three types of causes—biological, psychological, and social. Each cause requires a particular approach. Using this three-pronged model, the therapist teaches that the *biological* reactions (of racing heart or dizziness, for example) act as a trigger for anxiety that the patient can learn to manage with relaxation and breathing techniques. The *psychological* source of panic involves ways of thinking that are anxiety-arousing. Negative thinking is an enormous source of distress. For example, if when your heart starts racing you tell yourself, "Oh my God. Here comes another panic attack," or "Oh-oh. I know this will be the big one" (heart attack, that is), then, in a sense, you're causing your own panic. But if that racing heart becomes a signal for self-calming statements such as "I know I can handle this," or "This will pass in a minute," then instead, the patient can settle down. That is just what the therapist helps the patient learn to do—to call on a variety of self-calming techniques at the first hint of distress. When we refer to the *social* sources of panic we refer to the settings that are associated with panic—a shopping mall or supermarket checkout line, for example. These social sources can be mastered through exposure therapy which gradually builds the patient's confidence in her ability to use self-calming techniques to face them. Of course, in reality, these three causes—biological, psychological, and social—all interact with one another in complicated ways. But for laying out the problem and the treatment simply and effectively to patients, this model is very useful.

Finally, experts have suggested the following panic attack profile:

- people who were fearful, nervous, and shy as children

- people whose parents who were angry, frightening, critical, or controlling

- people who have discomfort with aggression

- people who have low self-esteem

- women married to men who are passive and kind

- people who have stresses that cause frustration and resentment preceding the onset of panic[14]

Diagnosing Panic Disorder

Why Is Diagnosis Such a Problem?

Panic disorder is an extremely difficult illness to diagnose because its symptoms are so diffuse; they run the gamut from palpitations, dizziness, and irregular breathing to loss of balance, gastrointestinal disturbances, and difficulty swallowing. Sufferers experience problems in multiple parts of the body including the heart, circulatory system, thyroid, and respiratory system.

Other emotional illnesses are easier to diagnose because they don't affect the body as pervasively as panic disorder does. And, as we mentioned earlier, panic disorder is often complicated by depression, generalized anxiety disorder, obsessive-compulsive disorder, or alcoholism, making the diagnosis even more difficult.

It's impossible for panic disorder patients to ignore their wildly beating hearts, labored breathing, or choking sensations. The symptoms of this illness are so intense and alarming that many sufferers, like Jane, scurry from one doctor to another in an effort to discover the cause of their problem and learn that, with regard to a physical diagnosis, the possibilities are enormous.

The search for an answer translates to excessive doctor and emergency room visits. According to NIMH director Frederick K. Goodwin, M.D., undiagnosed and untreated panic disorder accounts for a large proportion of the inappropriate overutilization of the general health care system.[15]

Every year, millions of people seek help for anxiety (panic disorder belongs to the anxiety-disorders category). In fact, doctor visits for anxiety rank ahead of visits for colds and bronchitis.[16]

Sometimes patients don't know they are suffering from anxiety; they just know something is wrong. A recent report found that about 20 percent of patients seeking help from primary-care physicians suffer from anxiety or depression. It added that in those patients who complained of a mixture of vague symptoms, such as tiredness and headaches, "the rate of underlying anxiety disorders or depression is 40 to 50 percent if there is no medical explanation for the complaints."[17]

Is It All in My Head?

Undiagnosed panic disorder patients often worry that doctors will think they are hypochondriacs or that their illness is psychosomatic. They are fearful that doctors will view their symptoms as unimportant and fail to give their problem the validity it deserves.

Their concerns are realistic since, even today, it is well known that some doctors tend to take women's symptoms less seriously than they do those of men. When tests and examinations turn out negative, as they often do in cases of panic disorder, doctors tend to believe that, with no physical basis for the symptoms, the cause is psychosomatic or hypochondriacal. Being told that their symptoms are not treatable or are insignificant intensifies the suffering of panic disorder patients. They feel helpless and/or patronized.

It's important here to distinguish between psychosomatic problems and hypochondriacal ones. Psychosomatic symptoms are real symptoms with a psychological basis; they are usually related to stress. The connotation—that the patient is fabricating her illness—is, obviously, a negative one.

A hypochondriac is someone who is preoccupied with her or his own health. Hypochondriacs think that at any moment they might imminently be sick or die; or they worry that they will contract some illness. Any change in bodily sensation causes them immediately to fear that they are coming down with something. Hypochondriasis is a diagnosable illness, according to the *DSM-IV.*

Although not being taken seriously is a real concern for many panic disorder patients, in recent years doctors have become somewhat more adept at diagnosing panic disorder because of the specific criteria established by the American Psychiatric Association. The cluster of symptoms and the profile of panic disorder patients are now clearer and more widely recognized.

The best way for patients to help themselves is by becoming educated about panic disorder. That's happening more frequently due in part to a three-year panic disorder education campaign launched by the National Institute of Mental Health in 1991. It is also important to find a doctor who is familiar with the symptoms of the illness and sensitive to patients' suffering. Collaborative efforts of patients, their families, and clinicians bring more timely diagnoses and treatment of panic disorder.

Is It Really Panic Disorder?

Before making the assumption that you have panic disorder, it is essential to make sure that organic problems are not, in fact, responsible for the symptoms. While we've emphasized how panic disorder can be mistaken for a physical illness, the opposite situation can also occur. Sometimes what appears to be panic disorder is actually a physical illness. For example, researchers have found that people with a common kind of heart arrhythmia were misdiagnosed more than half the time and treated for emotional problems.[18]

The following are some other physical ailments that are commonly confused with panic disorder and need to be ruled out. To make matters more complicated, diagnosis of these illnesses can be difficult because many of their symptoms are similar.

Mitral Valve Prolapse

This condition involves the malfunctioning of a heart valve. Symptoms are palpitations, chest pain, headaches, and arrhythmia. Screening is handled through echocardiogram. Mitral valve prolapse is very common, occurring particularly in women.

Hypoglycemia

This condition causes low blood sugar. Symptoms are tremors, palpitations, sweating, dizziness, and weakness. Patients are screened through a blood test for blood sugar levels. The condition is very common.

Hyperthyroidism

This condition involves an overactive thyroid caused by excessive production of thyroid hormone. Symptoms include shortness of breath, palpitations, tremor, sweating, rapid pulse, feelings of anxiety, and nervousness. Patients are screened through a physical examination and a blood test. The condition is eight times more frequent in women. The age of onset is similar to that of panic disorder.

Cushing's Syndrome

This disorder of the adrenal gland is caused by excess production of steroid hormones produced by the cortex of the adrenal gland or by prolonged treatment with such hormones. Emotional symptoms are acute anxiety, panic, and depression. Patients are screened through blood test and x-rays.

Temporal Lobe Epilepsy

Symptoms are dizziness and vagueness. Patients are screened through electroencephalogram.

In some cases a physical illness can exist along with panic disorder and one illness can exacerbate the other. When panic disorder patients also have a physical illness, the resulting bodily changes or sensations can lead to anxiety. The more anxious the patient is, the more susceptible she will be to a panic attack. Moreover, when people have panic disorder and an illness, symptoms can be difficult to differentiate.

At this point, you are no doubt beginning to see why there is so much confusion about diagnosing panic disorder. But no one understands how you feel better than you do. If doctors have been unable to attribute your symptoms to a physical illness, reread the beginning of this chapter. It may be time for you to make some suggestions to your doctor—or even switch doctors if need be.

The Sad Woman

The fact that half the people with panic disorder will also experience clinical depression may seem striking until one considers the toll that the illness takes. Panic disorder virtually paralyzes its victims so that they cannot engage in the activities or follow the lifestyles that unafflicted people do. Things that most people take for granted—driving a car, traveling, shopping, going to school, or even leaving the house—can be a nightmare or simply impossible for the panic disorder sufferer. The disorder can interfere with forming relationships, marrying, and raising a family. Fear of the fear keeps these people in a state of anxiety and rules their lives like a malicious tyrant. No wonder such a high number of those with panic disorder become depressed.

When depression reaches extreme depths, some women consider suicide. Studies indicate that when depression accompanies panic disorder the suicide rates are significantly higher than for the general population.

In this section we will explore the relationship between panic disorder and depression, and the potential for suicide. The case that follows is a classic example. Distraught by family strife, Carol developed a depression, which eventually led to thoughts of suicide. She felt she would rather die than continue living the way she had been. But she was a survivor: when her life seemed completely hopeless, she turned it around. Today she is married and expecting her second child. She is, she says, 90 percent cured.

Carol's Story

When I was 11, my parents got divorced. My mother didn't deal well with the divorce and had problems managing my two older brothers. There was a lot of arguing in the house.

A couple of years later, I began having terrible fights with my mother about staying out late, drinking, and partying. She didn't like my boyfriend or the kids I was hanging around with. So at 15, I decided to move in with my father.

Within one week, my whole life changed—I was living in a different house in a different town and attending a new high school. That's when the panic attacks began. During class, my vision blurred, I couldn't breathe, my palms were sweaty, and I had palpitations; my heart felt as if it was coming out of my chest.

I thought someone was putting something, maybe acid [LSD], in my food. I tried eating a different breakfast. I temporarily eliminated juice and coffee. But the attacks continued.

If the door to the classroom was shut, I felt panicky. If I was in the back of the room, far from the door, I felt like I was going to lose it in front of everyone. I had to know that I could leave the room. I couldn't sit through a class.

After a couple of weeks of this, I went to my family doctor, who prescribed phenobarbital, but that didn't do anything so I stopped it almost immediately. My heart would pound from the second I woke up in the morning. I had some anxiety all the time. When the attacks came, they were so severe that I thought I was going to die. They were making me so physically exhausted that all I could do was sleep when I came home from school.

I had to think carefully about everything I did, so I wouldn't be trapped in a situation where an attack could occur. I had to think about which people to be with—who I was comfortable with and who I wasn't comfortable with. My life was not normal and I was very depressed about my situation.

About this time, I began smoking a pack of cigarettes a day and drinking six-packs with my friends. But, after a night of drinking, the panic attacks would be even worse the next day. I would wake up with my heart racing. The drinking escalated. My father appeared not to notice; he overlooked my drinking because he was an alcoholic.

At this time, I became more and more uncomfortable about leaving the house. It was a feeling I had had before; even as a small child I had had anxiety about leaving home. I remember being at a fair in my hometown when I was seven or eight years old and insisting to my baby-sitter that I had to go home.

Now, with the increased anxiety, I started cutting classes so I could stick close to home. If my father had been more lenient, I wouldn't have left the apartment at all. But I had to get away from his attempts to control me.

Things started getting really bad between my father and me. We fought more and more. He didn't like the way I lived— my late hours, my smoking, or my clothes that he thought were too wild.

After being away from my mother for a year, I thought I'd give another try to living with her again, so just after my Sweet Sixteen party, I moved back in. I was hoping the return to my old school and neighborhood would make me calmer. But the panic attacks continued and I felt even more depressed. When I was 17, the family doctor prescribed Valium.

Thinking about my problems, I decided I would rather die than live life the way it was. I am a people person. I like to travel, to do things. I felt that everything was an effort. I wasn't living. I was frustrated with having no life. If this was it, I didn't want it. My only consolation was the idea of suicide, which I had thought about every day since I was 15. I felt that I had an option. If I can't take it anymore, I thought, I'll end it. Thinking about how to kill myself was my salvation.

My mother took me to see a therapist who diagnosed me as clinically depressed. My father felt that I was pulling an attention stunt, and my mother didn't know what to think. I was at the breaking point. I had had it. My life was on hold. I felt that the therapist would either help me or I would end it. Life was a living hell.

During one session with the therapist, I cried and cried and told her that I wanted to kill myself. She called my mother and told her that she couldn't let me go home, that I would have to be admitted to the hospital right away. In the psychiatric unit of the hospital, I was given an antidepressant, Tofranil, but it didn't make me feel any better.

Toward the end of my two-week hospital stay, there was a turning point. I attended a sermon in the chapel where the chaplain talked about a butterfly coming out of its cocoon. That made an impression on me; it was something I could relate to. I decided that I could also change and that I would have to be the one to make that change, to make something positive happen in my life.

Before that, being a New York kid, I always pretended I had a tough exterior. Now, I told myself, I didn't have to pretend to be tough anymore, that I could allow the real me—the scared me—to emerge, just as the butterfy emerges from the cocoon. I could relax and not have to put on a front.

At that point, I felt that I had become strong enough not

to accept my situation. If I had been a more passive person, it would have done me in.

When I was released from the hospital, I made a drastic move: I went cross-country with my boyfriend. I felt that if I was going to drop dead, it might as well be in California.

Before I left on my trip, I stopped taking the Tofranil because it hadn't worked. But I continued to take Valium; I took 60 milligrams a day. I made sure I had the pills with me whenever I left home.

I did some reading during this time and realized that the panic attacks I had been having meant that I had panic disorder. I also discovered that I wasn't the only one with panic disorder. Others had the same thing I did. I felt that my illness was validated. I wasn't crazy. I had something very real.

At the end of August, I came back home to live with my mother and finished my last year of high school. After graduation, I returned to California. Because I had felt better there, the West Coast had pleasant memories for me. I found a roommate and got a job as a receptionist.

From the ages of 18 to 24, the attacks became less intense. At 24, I stopped taking Valium. At this time I joined the Navy and became more hopeful. I had decided that I would no longer accept life as it had been, but I still couldn't leave the house without my bottle of 100 Valium, each one 10 milligrams, just in case.

During the year in boot camp, the panic attacks increased. I had blurry vision, felt weak, and would hyperventilate. I felt as if my body was giving out.

I kept wishing that my problem was something physical like a brain tumor that could be removed. If it was something physical, then I could have medication or an operation and be cured. Since I was 15, I had been searching for some medical reason for my problem. I didn't want it to be mental.

At 26, I got married and had a daughter a year later. Right after my daughter was born, I wound up in the emergency room after having a severe panic attack, unable to speak.

Another time, I remember making formula for my baby and feeling as if I were going to pass out. I was terrified. I lit a cigarette and my body collapsed. I couldn't speak or answer questions. I couldn't fight the panic attack.

By the time I was 27, the attacks were coming four to six months apart. I could sense them coming a day or two before they actually hit.

I had recently started working for a women's clothing manufacturer when one day I had an intense panic attack in my office. A colleague drove me to the emergency room. This scenario began to occur more and more. But I was still in denial, partially convinced that something physical was wrong.

When I was 28 or 29, I was working 10 hours a day and going to school at night to learn textile design. I was climbing the corporate ladder and loved being in the garment business, but there was a certain amount of stress. Business trips could involve flying to Arkansas, working until two or three in the morning when I got there, and getting up the next day to give a presentation. Also, there was the difficulty of getting the baby to day care every day. If I drank coffee or had PMS, that would increase the possibility of a panic attack.

One day, when I was 29, I was sitting at my desk. My heart started pounding and racing. I asked someone to call an ambulance. When the paramedics came, they gave me oxygen and brought me to the hospital. I had an EKG and other tests, but the doctors failed to come up with any diagnosis. They put me back on Valium, and also prescribed Prozac and Inderal.

Though the medication helped me cope somewhat, I felt that my body was collapsing. I couldn't fight it anymore. I was very weak all the time and I often felt that I would pass out.

Understanding Carol

A Turbulent Childhood

Carol had a childhood that was rife with the seeds of panic disorder—alcoholism in the family, fighting between parents, and major lifestyle changes. Not only did she have to cope with the breakup of the family when her parents divorced, but a few years later when she moved in with her father, she had to adjust to a different house, town, high school, and to new friends. Within a week, her whole life changed. These changes would certainly cause tremendous stress. If the changes had been fewer or more spread out, she might have managed better. The profuse anxiety that she experienced made her vulnerable to panic attacks.

Carol experienced typical symptoms of panic disorder: sweaty palms, dizziness, heart palpitations, blurred vision, and hyperventilation. The feeling of suffocation that she experienced is one of the most common symptoms of panic disorder. The victim feels as if she can't take in enough air.

When someone is in a threatening or anxiety-filled situation, she reverts to the primitive fight-or-flight state. Her body prepares itself as if it were gathering resources to flee or fight off the physical danger, such as an attack by a wild animal, that our ancestors faced. The autonomic nervous system (the part of the nervous system that regulates involuntary action) responds to the psychological threat as if it were a physical threat, with sweating; quick, shallow breathing; and heart palpitations. The panic increases if the person fears that she can't escape from the anxiety-provoking situation.

It is frightening when the body goes out of control, as it does in someone with panic disorder. The sufferer attempts to find some rational reason for the problem, to make sense out of the chaos and terror inside her. In Carol's case, because drugs like LSD were part of her culture, she thought a classmate might be putting drugs in her food, so she eliminated juice and coffee.

In the 1970s, when Carol sought help, the treatment of choice was phenobarbital, which doctors prescribed to sedate their patients. Carol's family doctor probably thought she was nervous and needed something to calm her down. Phenobarbital wasn't the right medication for the problem, but at that time, doctors not only didn't know what to do for panic disorder, they didn't even know what panic disorder was.

Exhaustion and Depression

The panic attacks were making Carol so physically exhausted that all she could do was sleep when she came home from school. The heightened anxiety she experienced was enervating, leaving her with little energy to deal with anything else. To cope, she tried to avoid anxiety-producing situations.

Panic disorder sufferers typically attempt to avoid situations that may cause an attack. They start to back off in what becomes the beginning of an agoraphobic reaction. Carol had to be constantly vigilant, thinking carefully about where it was safe to go and who it was safe to be with. Monitoring her life this way certainly was stressful and added to the drain on her energy.

As Carol thought about the abnormal, constricted way she was living, she became depressed. She was discouraged that her situation wasn't getting any better.

She began smoking a pack of cigarettes a day. Like many smokers, she enjoyed the relaxing effect of nicotine. Interestingly, studies of young adults who smoke show that people with a history of depression are more likely to become dependent on nicotine.[1]

At this time, Carol also was drinking to get some relief. As studies indicate, there is a correlation between drinking and panic disorder. But drinking has a rebound effect. Carol felt more anxious after a night of drinking. Then, in a vicious circle, she would drink again to feel better. Both her anxiety and her drinking escalated.

Coming from a home in which there was an alcoholic parent, it was easy for her to have a drink. Children of alcoholics often drink because liquor is so available and because they see their parents drinking. For Carol, drinking was an easy way to feel better, to self-tranquilize.

Staying Home

At this point, Carol became more uncomfortable about leaving home. Like many other women with panic disorder, she'd had antecedents for this discomfort earlier in her life; she reports that even as a young child she had anxiety about leaving home.

Children whose parents fight a lot worry about whether their parents will stay together. Most likely, Carol had this concern and was anxious when she left the house, fearing that one or both parents wouldn't be there when she got back.

Yet, during high school, she couldn't be at home as much as she wanted to, because she was trying to escape her father's strict control. She was trying to break away by behaving like her peers. At the same time, staying away from home and keeping late hours tended to make her more anxious. And that intense anxiety made her more dependent on her father's support and help. Her suffering drew her back home, where it was safe. The desire for freedom clashing with the need to race home created conflict, inflamed her anxiety, and increased her panic attacks.

The Depression Deepens

Before she had left her mother's house to go and live with her father, Carol had had no attacks, so she must have hoped to return to that state of normalcy by going back to her mother. But her panic attacks continued and escalated; soon Carol's anxiety couldn't be contained even with the help of Valium.

Her hopes were dashed. What she had thought would help—the return to familiar surroundings—failed to ease her distress. At this point, her depression began to deepen. People who have this disorder naturally hope that it will get better and when it doesn't they become despondent.

Carol's life was turning out entirely different from the way she had hoped and thought it would. She became so discouraged that she began thinking seriously of suicide, an idea that had been with her every day since she was 15.

Some parents of depressed or suicidal teens don't take their children's problems seriously. But Carol's mother did the right thing by taking her to a therapist. It's important to note that threats of suicide are cries for help that must be taken seriously.

A Turning Point

Carol was in despair and desperately needed to talk to a trained professional. The therapist she met with listened to her problems and tried to help her. During the session in which Carol cried and talked about suicide, the therapist recognized the extent of her depression and arranged for her hospitalization. By doing so, she may have saved Carol's life.

The inspirational sermon in the hospital's chapel proved to be a serendipitous event that had a profound effect on Carol. Sometimes people find something they didn't realize they were looking for, something that turns their lives around. For Carol, the sermon's message was the first ray of hope, a meaningful symbol that things could get better. It's interesting to note that this source of inspiration occurred away from her family, school, and peers, each of which had been a source of conflict and anxiety for her. The hospital was a safe place for her, a place where she was in good hands, where she felt taken care of. Removed from the constant stress, she was calmer and could consider her life more clearly. The realization that she didn't have to maintain her tough exterior anymore had the effect of liberating a lot of Carol's energy.

The doctor in the hospital prescribed the antidepressant Tofranil. Carol became discouraged when the medication didn't work immediately; she failed to give it time to take effect. (Antidepressants usually take from several weeks to several months to help.) A number of antidepressants are available and doctors can prescribe different ones until the right one is found.

Valium did work at this point in Carol's life and she relied on it. When she left for California, she was taking 60 milligrams of Valium a day just to remain somewhat stable; the typical therapeutic dosage is much smaller. It's clear that she was self-medicating. Some people with panic disorder abuse drugs to this extent because they are so anxious. Often the medications are not monitored correctly, making it easier for patients to take more and more pills until, eventually, they become addicted.

People with this disorder frequently need to know they have something that they can use in case they need it. Like Carol, they make sure they have the pills with them whenever they leave home. They may not have needed the medication for years. Still, knowing that it is in their possession provides a sense of security and makes them feel better.

Carol also felt comforted when she began to discover that other people suffered from panic disorder. It was reassuring, normalizing, and stress-reducing to know that she wasn't the only one with the problem.

It's for this reason that patients join support groups where they hear from others who have the same symptoms. They feel less abnormal, less different, and less isolated. It's a relief for them to listen to people who understand what they are going through and who are dealing with the same problems. They feel as if they are rejoining the human race. Especially for teenagers—many of whom think it's very important to be like everyone else—feeling different can be devastating.

From the ages of 18 to 24, Carol was relatively more serene. There was no particular stress in her life at this time; she had a job and a roommate and lived in an area that she liked. Her new hopefulness—the result of the sermon she had heard in the hospital—gave her new determination. And, Valium was available in case she became anxious.

Setbacks

She then embarked on a major transition. When she joined the Navy and entered boot camp, she set herself up for new experiences that were extremely strenuous and demanding. It comes as no surprise that Carol's attacks increased; people who are exhausted are often more prone to panic attacks.

Because it's much more frightening and unsettling for people to think that they have a mental rather than a physical condition, Carol found herself wishing that the source of her illness was physical, even if it meant something serious. A physical condition is much more acceptable because it's more real to others, more treatable, and it doesn't involve a question of one's sanity. A mental condition, on the other hand, has an alarming connotation.

Carol's anxieties piled up as more changes, including motherhood, followed the stint in the Navy. She couldn't cope with the stress and responsibility of caring for a child. For a person who is anxious, the transition to having a family of one's own can be overwhelming.

Right after her daughter's birth, Carol had a severe panic attack. Her inability to speak during this incident might be consistent with depersonalization, a common symptom of panic disorder. Sometimes the sufferer becomes so terrified that she copes by psychologically removing herself from a situation. She enters a state where she has an out-of-body experience and sees herself as if from the outside looking in. When looking at another person, some patients say they feel as if there is something between them, as if they are looking through gauze. Patients who experience this have difficulty speaking or answering questions, and that provokes even more terror.

Although the therapist had taught Carol some relaxation techniques that helped when she felt an attack coming on, at this point those techniques weren't enough. Carol needed once again to get back into psychotherapy.

Carol was under extreme stress from several sources: caring for a new baby, traveling, working 10-hour days, going to school, and giving presentations. PMS and caffeine exacerbated the symptoms. People with panic disorder need to modify their lifestyles. Yet Carol, in an attempt to live a normal life, kept adding stresses. Carol's body was telling her that she was exhausted and depressed, but she wasn't paying attention.

In the hospital, she was tested for a physical problem. As we've noted, the symptoms of panic disorder mimic symptoms of physical ailments, so patients who have panic disorder are often misdiagnosed. As typically happens with panic disorder patients, Carol at first appeared to be suffering from a heart problem, but the tests came back negative.

Trying to Cope

To relieve Carol's symptoms, the doctors once again prescribed Valium. They also prescribed Prozac, an antidepressant that is now commonly used for panic disorder. Patients report good results and fewer side effects than with other antidepressants. Inderal, the third drug prescribed, is a beta blocker. It slows the heart rate and prevents tachycardia or rapid heartbeat. Carol would take Inderal as needed, perhaps before giving a speech.

Carol began doing somewhat better. The medication helped her cope by calming her and making her feel less hopeless, but her exhaustion persisted and she still had occasional panic attacks.

After a number of good years, the attacks reoccurred (panic disorder patients sometimes experience setbacks), and there was no reassurance that they would stop. Though Carol now knew what her illness was, she wasn't sure what to do about it. Eventually, she realized that the treatment that had saved her life once before—psychotherapy—was the route she had to take again.

Carol's Recovery

Treating Panic Disorder with Psychotherapy

When panic disorder patients suffer from depression, the usual treatments for panic attack—cognitive therapy, behavioral therapy, and medication—while very helpful, may not be enough. Certain patients may also need psychotherapy to relieve the depression.

Psychotherapy helps the patient understand and work on problems such as poor relationships, dependence, low self-esteem, separation anxiety, deep-seated anger, and other difficulties that may contribute to the depression. Some of these issues can be dealt with in short-term therapy; others may require long-term treatment.

Depressed patients are angry. Or, to put it another way, depression is anger turned inward. A therapist helps her patient understand the dynamics of her anger, exploring why she is angry and what she does with the anger. The more patients understand about their emotions, the better they can deal with them. Psychotherapy helps the patient become healthier, stronger, and less likely to slip into a deeper depression. When depression is alleviated, the patient has more energy to deal with the panic attacks.

Carol exemplifies a patient with tangled relationships, turbulent feelings, and panic disorder. Depressed to the point that she considered suicide, Carol found that psychotherapy saved her life. In this chapter you'll learn what psychotherapy entails and how it can help. In Part II, you will learn whether you are a candidate for psychotherapy and, if so, how you can benefit. We'll also explain how to choose the right therapist.

What Happens During Psychotherapy?

During therapy sessions, the therapist helps by listening in a nonjudgmental way, clarifying issues, and providing support. The importance of having an empathetic and nonjudgmental listener cannot be overemphasized. If you are depressed, talking to a psychotherapist can help you deal with the following feelings which are prevalent in panic disorder.

- Guilt because you are suffering from panic disorder. It is difficult not to feel guilty for having an illness that interferes with a normal lifestyle and family functioning.

- Fear of losing control, having a nervous breakdown, or going crazy because of the illness. The disassociative feelings of depersonalization and derealization commonly experienced during panic attacks exacerbate feelings of losing control or fears of never feeling normal again.

- Shame because of the thought that something is wrong with you and that you will do something foolish.

- Anger over having an illness so overwhelming that it interferes with your life, not understanding why you have it, and not knowing how to cope with it.

- Anxiety about leaving the house, about what will happen in various situations.

When you can express these feelings and can understand (with the help of the therapist) why you have them, their intensity is reduced and they are no longer so powerful.

Consider how a patient named Linda gained an understanding of her anger. An administrator in an advertising agency, Linda prided herself on her high-powered job that required a lot of travel. But because she had once had a panic attack while on a plane, she feared flying. Linda began to see that she was angry because her attacks interfered with her ability to function on the job. Her self-esteem, which was connected to her work, was being destroyed by her illness.

People often know that they are angry, but they don't understand why. The therapist helps them put the pieces together and might also:

- provide education about the illness, so the patient can understand how it is triggered

- bring in family members for family therapy sessions so they can learn to be supportive

- help the patient to decide on goals and make lifestyle changes

- work with the patient on changing her environment so as to minimize stressors such as constant arguing, job pressures, or overprogramming

- help the patient cope with relationship problems by improving communication

How Psychotherapy Helped Carol Recover

In addition to the normal, anxiety-producing adolescent issues with which she was dealing, Carol also had to cope with panic disorder. But she had no healthy, close relationships with family or friends. She felt isolated. She desperately needed someone to talk to about her relationships with her family and her typical teen problems.

Carol described her therapist as a sounding board and her therapy sessions as a safe place to get into her feelings. When she talked about the "living hell" that was her life, she felt that her therapist cared about her and that the therapist didn't judge her the way others did. Carol discussed the aspects of her life that were causing her stress and pain; she also talked about her fear of going crazy.

Her therapist listened empathetically and acknowledged that the panic attack symptoms were a real illness and not just something conjured up in Carol's mind. She clarified the difficulties between Carol and her mother, and the problems Carol was having in school. Her mother didn't like Carol's friends, felt she was hanging out with a bad crowd, and thought that she wasn't taking school seriously enough. Carol, on the other hand, felt that her mother was too intrusive and that she didn't trust her judgment. She wanted to break away and become more independent.

The therapist provided help by walking Carol through the steps needed to make the changes that would reduce her anxiety and depression: explaining her feelings to her mother, telling her that she didn't like being treated like a baby; writing a letter to her mother about how she felt; and sitting down with her mother to agree on expectations about nights out and telephone use.

To help reduce the constant arguing between Carol and her mother, Carol's therapist brought them in together for some sessions and had a few sessions with Carol's mother alone about parenting skills. After Carol's mother kicked Carol out of the house for coming home drunk, the therapist immediately scheduled a session for the two, so that they could talk things out and get back together again quickly.

She even provided long-distance support, when Carol, traveling across the country to California, called her collect from Nevada with fears about what she was doing.

"She was a strong figure in my life," Carol said of her therapist. "I trusted her." How fortunate Carol was to have this caring, stable person as a sounding board and role model.

Therapy later in life again helped Carol deal with her stressors. Carol is improving now; she has some understanding of her illness and accepts the fact that attacks will come and go. She has attacks only about twice a year now, whereas years ago, she might have experienced them several times a week. "If I look back on what it was, this is great," she says. "There's no way I would want to live my life the way it was. My illness no longer interferes with my life. I no longer have a fear of panic attacks. I function, I have a regular job, I travel, I can get on a plane. I am thankful that I finally know what I have. Many people out there don't know what's wrong."

Nina: Another Example of How Psychotherapy Can Help

Nina, another patient, has a history of mild episodes of depression. She is the mother of two teenage boys, one of whom has Down's syndrome. Her relationship with her husband was unhealthy. Throughout their marriage, her husband increasingly abused her verbally with belittling, demeaning, and insulting remarks. What's more, he lost his job and was unable to support the family. Nina was working as a salesperson in a department store, but her small income didn't help much and the family had enormous financial difficulties. The bank foreclosed on their house and the family had to make plans to relocate to a less expensive area.

When she gets anxious, Nina tends to have physical symptoms such as headaches and stomach cramps; moreover, her alarmist nature causes her much anxiety when she experiences these symptoms.

Two years ago, she began to have panic attacks. "I was at a party when the first one came on with no warning," she recalls. "My fingers started to tingle and my heart pounded. I felt as if my throat was closing. I couldn't breathe; I gasped for air. I felt as if the room was spinning around me and I had to sit down."

Pale and frightened, she called an ambulance. At the hospital, the doctors gave her an EKG (which turned out negative) and told her that she had experienced a panic attack.

From then on, she experienced attacks periodically. As the panic attacks became more frequent, she became depressed, apathetic, and withdrawn. "For six months, whenever I wasn't working, I stayed in bed," she says. "I didn't sleep or eat well, and I cried on and off."

Finally, she saw her internist, who recommended psychotherapy. In therapy, she expressed her guilt about her inability to care for her children. She had always been a good parent, she said, but now she was so overwhelmed by the panic attacks, that she didn't have the energy to cope with the children, her husband, or the ever-worsening financial problem.

Therapy provided a safe environment where Nina could talk freely about fears of the future and about losses she had endured or was facing—possible loss of a marriage that had started out well; loss of her home, the area in which she lived, and friends who would soon be too far away to visit regularly. Perhaps most of all she mourned her loss of control. The panic attacks had robbed her of the ability to make day-to-day decisions and to function normally.

To keep herself from being so overwhelmed, Nina had to learn to prioritize what needed to be dealt with first. It seemed that she needed to decide first where she wanted to move and what jobs she wanted to consider. "I felt better once I made decisions about those important issues," she says. "Then I felt I could tackle other problems like finding a good school for my handicapped son and dealing with my marital situation."

Therapy also helped Nina acknowlege her anger toward her husband. With the therapist's help, Nina analyzed some dependency issues that related to her ambivalence about leaving her abusive husband. She examined why she stayed in the marriage instead of striking out on her own. "I was terrified of leaving and being a single parent like my own mother, who divorced my father," she remembers. "I was frightened of being the only one responsible for my children, and I was also worried about how I would manage financially if I left my husband."

In therapy, Nina learned to cope better with her panic attacks through the use of relaxation techniques. (She found deep breathing particularly helpful and used it often.) In addition, she learned how to reduce the stress in her environment by being more direct about her needs in asking for help from her husband and persuading him to get help with anger management, so he would be less abusive. She also did something good for herself by enrolling in an exercise class.

Nina learned not to be so alarmist when she felt slight anxiety. Once her depression lifted, she had the energy to apply for—and get—a job as a buyer in the children's section of a department store in the area where she would relocate. The higher salary she earns plus the reduced living expenses in the smaller home and less expensive area relieve some of her family's financial strain. Though Nina continues to have tremendous conflicts about her marriage, her mood is elevated, and she feels more in control of her life. Her self-esteem has improved and she no longer tolerates her husband's abuse. She still has panic attacks, but with less frequency and intensity. When they come, she is no longer overwhelmed by them.

Nina, Carol, and countless other women suffer from depression and panic disorder that respond to psychotherapy. In the next chapter, we explain why panic disorder and depression are so often related.

The Connection
Between
Panic Disorder and
Depression

Panic disorder is a chronic illness that interrupts life and interferes with previous ways of functioning and enjoying oneself. It is all-encompassing: much of one's energy and thought processes focus on the anticipation and prevention of attacks, and coping with them when they occur.

When the sufferer finds that her condition is not improving, she begins to feel hopeless. She believes that she will never get better, that there is no way out, and that she will always have to deal with the attacks. These feelings often lead to depression.

The illness can be a deceptive one. Periods where the patient is better bring a sense of hopefulness that is quickly turned into despair if the symptoms return. Disappointment and discouragement follow.

In some instances, panic disorder is progressive, not only continuing but getting worse as time goes on. Attacks can, over time, become more frequent and more intense.

If agoraphobia develops, the patient becomes increasingly withdrawn, participating less and less in things that were once an important part of her life. The resulting isolation, with its restricted movement and lessened contact with other people, contributes to depression.

Also adding to the depression is the panic disorder patient's poor self-image. She often feels demeaned and demoralized. She thinks that something is very wrong with her and believes she is weird or different from other people. Still, she needs to depend on others. This dependency is especially difficult for young adults who are trying to break away. Their self-esteem, already low, becomes even lower.

Panic disorder is an illness that is not easily ameliorated; there's no quick fix. Patients eager for an immediate cure and a quick return to a normal life can become depressed.

Symptoms of Depression

Everyone has low periods that they get over in a day or two. But clinical depression, which is much more profound and much more prolonged than occasional sadness, comprises definite symptoms and lasts longer. Nearly everyone suffering from depression has pervasive feelings of sadness. In addition, depressed people may feel helpless, hopeless, and irritable. If you are experiencing four or more of the following symptoms continually or most of the time for longer than two weeks, you need to seek professional help.

- noticeable change of appetite, with either significant weight loss (not attributable to dieting) or weight gain

- noticeable change in sleeping patterns
- loss of interest and pleasure in activities formerly enjoyed
- loss of energy; fatigue
- feelings of worthlessness
- feelings of hopelessness
- feelings of inappropriate guilt
- inability to concentrate or think; indecisiveness
- melancholia
- disturbed thinking
- physical symptoms
- recurring thoughts of death or suicide; wishing to die; or attempting suicide (People with this symptom should receive treatment immediately!)[1]

Suicide Warning Signs

The depressed person often is not aware of the extent of her depression. However, if you are reading this book because you want to help a family member with panic disorder, it's important to be knowledgeable about the following warning signs of suicide:

- serious depression
- increasing isolation
- giving away prized possessions
- sudden drop in school or work performance

- making statements about wanting to die
- acting in a violent fashion
- taking unnecessary risks
- threatening to commit suicide
- acting in a strange manner
- suddenly happy, for no reason, after a long depression
- abusing drugs or alcohol[2]

The Anxious Woman

These are stressful times, particularly for women. Many women must work, care for their families, and, despite strides made during the women's movement, do most of the housework. A large number of them are single mothers. What's more, because people are living longer, it's not unusual for middle-aged women, often dubbed the sandwich generation, to shoulder the responsibility for aging parents, as well as for their children. Exhaustion and frustration frequently lower the tolerance for stress at home and in the workplace.

Much has been written about causes and effects of stress and the ways to cope with it. Our task here is not to amplify what has already been said, but to explore the relationship between stress and panic disorder.

We know that prolonged stress can lead to various physical ailments, and contribute to depression and anxiety. And, as we'll see in this section, anxiety and panic disorder are linked.

The idea, often implied by the media, that it's easy to conquer stress may be a bit simplistic. Just about everyone experiences stress to some degree. Stress is related to change, and change is a part of life.

Certainly some people have more profound stress in their lives than other people; but what's more significant is how one reacts to stress. One's reaction depends on many factors including temperament, personality, life experiences, resiliency, strengths, coping abilities, and outlook on life.

In addition, stress is related to the degree of control one has over one's life. Surprisingly, it's not high-level executives who suffer more from stress; it's lower-level

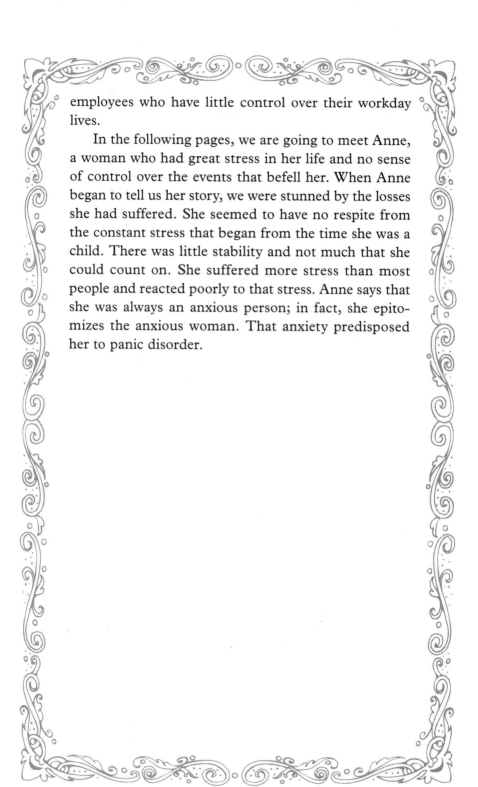

employees who have little control over their workday lives.

In the following pages, we are going to meet Anne, a woman who had great stress in her life and no sense of control over the events that befell her. When Anne began to tell us her story, we were stunned by the losses she had suffered. She seemed to have no respite from the constant stress that began from the time she was a child. There was little stability and not much that she could count on. She suffered more stress than most people and reacted poorly to that stress. Anne says that she was always an anxious person; in fact, she epitomizes the anxious woman. That anxiety predisposed her to panic disorder.

Anne's Story

I came from an anxious family. There was always stress and tension in the house caused by my parents screaming and yelling at each other or at me and my three younger brothers.

My parents were undemonstrative and the atmosphere was cold and unloving. No one hugged or kissed and conversation was practically nonexistent. We children learned early on not to express our feelings, to keep our mouths closed. "Children should be seen and not heard" was the maxim we lived by.

I was angry and resentful that my parents weren't there for me emotionally. I worried about being abandoned, about winding up alone.

I was always an anxious child. For instance, when teachers called on me in school, I got very nervous. My body trembled and my hands and feet tingled. I would get a headache and a dry mouth, my vision would blur, my breathing became shallow, and I would have palpitations. Because my body would be doing all these things, I felt that it was out of whack. I was so anxious and withdrawn that I had no friends and felt very isolated.

At 17, I got married and, the next year, I had a son, Kevin. But my husband and I fought all the time. When he got angry, he would call me names and hit me.

Two years after my son was born, I had a little girl. My husband didn't want another baby and he talked me into giving her up for adoption. I decided not to see her or hold her. The day after I gave birth, I flew out of the hospital with no socks or shoes on and took the bus home in the middle of a snowstorm. I didn't tell anyone, not even my parents or my brothers, that I had given the baby up. Everyone thought she had died.

By the time Kevin was five, the fighting got worse, and I knew that the marriage wasn't going to work. I left, moved into a rooming house, and got a job as a salesgirl in a women's clothing store. I wanted to start a new life, so I allowed my husband's mother to have custody of my son; I knew that she would raise Kevin better than I possibly could. I promised my mother-in-law that I would never visit, and I didn't. But I remember feeling a lot of guilt as I stood outside my mother-in-law's house, watching my son play. I never tried to go inside.

At 31, I remarried. I had three more children with my second husband—twin boys and a daughter—four years later. One of the boys was born deaf and the other had diabetes.

But I couldn't forget about the children I had given up. I kept thinking about them both and missing them terribly. I was plagued by flashbacks of the day I ran from the hospital after giving birth to my daughter.

I did everything I could to see Kevin at that time. I wrote and called a lot; sometimes he'd answer, but most of the time he didn't. When he was 18, he came to see me and a year later he moved in with me and my family for six months. My ex-husband had died when Kevin was 16 and I guess it was important for him to have a connection to one parent. I tried to make amends and tell him that I wasn't the same person I had been, but he made me feel very guilty about leaving. He was angry that I had remarried and had a new family. He chose to hold on to his anger. When he said, "I don't hate you but I can't deal with it," I felt like the big bad wolf.

While Kevin was living with me, I introduced him to my girlfriend's daughter. They fell in love and decided to live together. A few months later, they got married. I wasn't invited to the wedding. He had cut off all ties with me. For years, I thought about him and about not going to the wedding. My girlfriend showed me pictures from the wedding and, from time to time, told me what was going on in his life. I felt abandoned, left out. It was very hard.

My life was filled with anxiety. In addition to the pain of thinking about the children from my first marriage and hoping someday to see them both again, I was also dealing with other problems. My son who is deaf required special attention, and I had financial problems which were caused partially by my husband's gambling. Several years later, things got worse, when the diabetic twin starting taking drugs. I once found him passed out on the bathroom floor. I knew that he was stealing to buy drugs.

When stress built up during the day, my chest became tight, my breathing became shallow, and I would become disoriented.

I always had a feeling of restlessness, of being keyed up or on edge. I had to be on the go. "Shake 'n' bake" is the best way I can describe my body. I always felt like a jumping bean, as if I were going to jump out of my skin. I didn't know how to relax; both my body and mind, especially my mind, were restless.

I believe that my need to be in constant motion stemmed, in part, from my childhood. I never knew when my father or mother would yell or scream at each other or at us; I couldn't relax. The only time I didn't feel restless was at work. There I was calmer, more in control.

Because of both the restlessness and the stress, I was easily exhausted and needed a lot of rest. But I had a hard time going to sleep.

Right after Kevin got married, I had my first panic attack.

It came out of the blue, with no warning. I was waiting on a customer in the clothing store when I started hyperventilating. Another saleswoman gave me a brown bag to breathe into and had me put my feet up. She told me that my face was white. My hands and feet tingled and I felt distant, as if I were under anesthesia. Everyone seemed far away from me. Someone called the police and the ambulance came. After an hour in the hospital, the doctors said that everything was fine, that it was just an anxiety attack.

But I couldn't stop thinking about the attack and was afraid that it would happen again. About a week later, I was in church and had to run out because I had another attack. The symptoms were exactly the same. I thought, "Maybe I have a brain tumor, maybe I'm going to die." The attacks came on about once a week after that.

I saw my doctor; he said I had anxiety and put me on Ativan, an antianxiety drug. He also told me to cut down on coffee (I always drank a lot of coffee) because he thought I might be sensitive to caffeine.

Ativan worked, but it it gave me an upset stomach. So the doctor tried Desyrel, an antidepressant, but that caused a panic attack. I was on every antidepressant you can name. I was a guinea pig. I would take the medications for three days and then go off them. The pills made me feel too jumpy.

I went to many other doctors besides my family doctor. One of them said that I had manic depression and put me on lithium, but it made me feel very blah. I couldn't focus on anything. Anyway, I didn't know why he thought I was depressed.

I took Xanax for two years, but it actually caused a panic attack after I went off it suddenly because I heard it was addictive. I took Ativan again and found a support group through a newspaper ad. Both helped me cope.

During these years, I hadn't forgotten about my two oldest children. There wasn't much chance that I would reunite with Kevin, but I still kept hoping. And I hadn't given up on meeting the daughter I had never seen. In fact, I had kept in touch with the agency that arranged for her adoption and wrote a letter, which they kept for me. In case I died, I wanted her to know something about her mother—what I liked, what I didn't like.

Finally, for the first time, after 25 years, I saw her! I had watched a TV show featuring people who located children given up for adoption. I called the number on the screen and they helped me find my daughter. We arranged to meet in a restaurant near her home. I drove one hour to get there even though driving terrifies me. But the will to see her was greater than my fear. I felt the usual tightness in my chest and the shallow breathing. As I got closer to the restaurant, my eyes began tearing and I had a fluttery feeling in my chest. I was scared and happy at the same time. The only way I could cope on that long ride was by using some techniques I had learned from my support group.

My daughter and I talked for six hours and showed each other pictures. It's hard to believe she's married now and has two children. I was happy but numb. I wanted so much for her to know who I was. "I want to be your friend," I told her. But she said that she needed a couple of months to digest everything we had talked about. I cried. I felt anxious and sad.

After that, I had this great anxiety most of the time. I felt depressed when I thought of how I had lost out on seeing my daughter grow up. I was uncertain about having any relationship with her in the future. All the old symptoms, which had lessened somewhat because of the Ativan and the support group, came back in full force. I tried to get my body under control, hoping my mind would follow, but the tension and panic attacks just increased. So did the fear of attacks. The anticipatory anxiety was the hardest part. Although I was so happy to see my daughter, the feelings that it brought caused a lot of stress, and I felt like I was back to square one.

10

Understanding Anne

Anxious Parents/Anxious Child

Anne's anxiety is best understood if we consider the losses she suffered. As a child, she missed the love of nurturing parents. Her mother and father were undemonstrative and argued all the time. The atmosphere was cold.

The frequent screaming and yelling to which she was exposed made her feel frightened and threatened. She never knew when an argument would erupt. Because of the arguing, she was undoubtedly concerned that her parents would separate or divorce.

Uncertainty about the stability of one's family is very unsettling; naturally, a sense of anxiety pervaded Anne's early life. Clearly, she fits the pattern of a woman prone to anxiety disorder—she had been an anxious child of parents who fought.

Anxious parents create stress in their children and will usually produce an anxious child. The pattern is perpetuated in generation after generation.

Anne was angry about her parents' behavior, yet she had no way to express that anger. She had been taught that children should be seen and not heard. She knew she must keep all her feelings bottled up.

It's a very difficult situation to have no way to ventilate feelings, to have no one to listen to you. She couldn't talk to anyone at home and reports having no friends. The lack of a support system—someone to confide in—added to Anne's anxiety.

An Unsatisfying Marriage

In marrying at a young age, Anne was probably running away from her bad family situation. But she had no role model for a good marital relationship; all she had seen was fighting. She didn't know how to relate to a partner and must have felt isolated. Like her parents, she and her husband didn't get along.

Giving up her baby was a dramatic example of the horror her life had become. Anne, already an anxious person, was under severe stress because of her marital situation and wasn't thinking clearly. She was overwhelmed and couldn't cope well; she needed to simplify things. She did so in an extreme way: under pressure from her husband, she caved in to his demand to give up their child. The act demonstrated that her self-esteem was very low.

The decision to give up the daughter she had carried for nine months was an agonizing one. It caused tremendous conflict. How ashamed she must have been. She wasn't able to tell the truth to anyone—not even her family. She was too embarrassed to ask for help or sympathy. Lying increased the stress.

Anne experienced additional trauma and loss when she left her marriage and gave up her son. Relinquishing custody of her remaining child was more evidence of Anne's low self-esteem; she thought that her mother-in-law could rear her child better than she could.

But she couldn't forget about the children she had given up. She was feeling guilty and conflicted about her son as well as her daughter. Had she felt less guilty, she might have made more of an effort to visit Kevin.

As we've seen, any kind of change causes stress and, at this point, Anne was experiencing many changes in her life, including the move to a rooming house and a new job.

Remarriage Doesn't Help

More changes came when she remarried. Her problems increased after she had three more children; two of the three had serious handicaps.

Meanwhile, she kept having flashbacks about running away from the hospital. Sometimes flashbacks can reoccur for years; most of the time they last over a period of several months.

By now, Anne had endured the lack of a nurturing family while growing up, the loss of her first two children, the divorce of her first husband, and, later, his death.

Hope and Despair

When Kevin moved in for six months, her hopes of a reunion were raised and then quickly dashed. He couldn't deal with his anger, and Anne's feelings of guilt intensified. Having no therapy and no friend who cared about her made life tough.

Once again, Anne felt a sense of loss, similar to the way she had felt as a child. Her feelings of disappointment, like her feelings of loss, contributed to her stress.

Anne's tension manifested itself in a restlessness, a feeling of being keyed up or on edge. When stress built up, she would experience a tight chest, shallow breathing, and disorientation—typical symptoms for someone with anxiety.

Because of her turbulent background, the continued stress, and the constant chaos, she had no sense of being in control of her life. The only time she felt in control was at work.

All the turmoil in her life left her exhausted. Constantly thinking about her problems created worry, which made sleep difficult. Then, in a vicious cycle, lack of sleep caused anxiety about not sleeping. Also, as we saw in Carol's case, exhaustion—among other things—makes someone with panic disorder more prone to panic attacks. According to researchers at Johns Hopkins University, "The occurrence of panic attacks may be related to the degree of stress in the environment."[1]

Considering all the stressors and constant losses, it might have been helpful for Anne to seek counseling, but she didn't know where to turn.

The Attacks Begin

Right after Kevin got married, Anne had her first panic attack. During this attack, Anne was hyperventilating and someone gave her a bag to breathe into. Hyperventilation disturbs the balance of carbon dioxide in the body; breathing into a bag helps reestablish the proper balance.

Anne also experienced depersonalization, a vague, spacey feeling akin to being drugged. She felt as if she were under anesthesia.

For the first time, a doctor recognized the fact that Anne was suffering from generalized anxiety disorder (GAD): excessive anxiety and worry that interferes with social or occupational functioning. At this time, doctors were becoming more familiar with GAD; they were beginning to realize that it can overlap with panic disorder. Studies have found that people with GAD are more prone to panic disorder.

Like many other people with panic disorder, Anne began to obsess about her panic attack and feared that she would have another one. We saw this phenomenon with many women we met. Like them, Anne also started to obsess about having a physical illness. She was afraid that she had a brain tumor and was going to die.

When Anne saw her own doctor, he confirmed the diagnosis of anxiety and suggested that she cut down on caffeine. Some people have to be careful about drinking too much coffee because they have a sensitivity to caffeine. For them, caffeine causes physical reactions like palpitations, racing heart and pulse, or dizziness. These bodily changes are similar to symptoms felt at the onset of a panic attack.

The following anecdote illustrates the confusion that can occur between panic disorder and problems with caffeine. Melissa was drinking 30 cups of coffee a day. Her symptoms were similar to those described above, and she went from doctor to doctor searching for a diagnosis. The results of all the tests and examinations were negative, and they couldn't understand the source of her problem. She was convinced that she was having panic attacks. That is, until one of the doctors thought to ask her how many cups of coffee she drank a day.

The symptoms caused by caffeine consumption can create anxiety and precipitate a panic attack in someone predisposed to the disorder. One recent study shows that caffeine may induce panic attacks in those with a history of such attacks.[2] That's why it's a good idea for someone who has panic disorder to avoid caffeinated drinks, especially if she knows that she is sensitive to caffeine. Carol, as you may recall, was also more likely to have a panic attack after drinking coffee.

In addition to advising her to cut down on coffee, Anne's doctor prescribed the tranquilizer Ativan (which is similar to Valium and Xanax) for panic attacks. Placed under the tongue, it works quickly and patients can take it if they feel an attack coming on.

But because of the side effects it caused, Anne's doctor switched her to the antidepressant, Desyrel. Anne says it caused a major panic attack, an unusual reaction for an antidepressant. But she was taking medications incorrectly, going off them abruptly after three days because she couldn't tolerate the jumpy feeling they caused. Some people with panic disorder are supervigilant to any minor change in their bodies. Nevertheless, it's unwise to go off an antidepressant suddenly.

Anne says she was a guinea pig for every medication. One doctor prescribed lithium, a drug used only for manic depression, which he thought she had. Although it is unclear whether or not Anne was manic-depressive, certainly anyone contending with her problems would have a reason to be depressed. The loss of her children with no hope of reunion was certainly a factor in her depression. She was grieving and missing them. But her assertion "I don't know why they thought I was depressed" suggests that she might have unknowingly denied her depression.

There is a strong correlation between anxiety and depression. It is common for someone suffering from anxiety to also have depression, as we saw in Carol's case.

Anne stopped taking lithium because of the side effects she experienced. Lithium slows the patient down, producing lethargy and drowsiness. Anne says she felt blah and couldn't focus on anything.

Her doctor tried the tranquilizer Xanax next. After she stopped taking it, Anne had panic attacks, in what was most likely a rebound effect. This is a common occurrence when going off certain medications abruptly. According to a recent study, long-term use of antianxiety drugs such as Xanax may lead to withdrawal symptoms and increased anxiety when patients stop taking the drug. [3]

Again, Anne had attempted to be her own physician. It's

very dangerous to play doctor; medication must be carefully supervised.

Anne went back on Ativan because it had helped, whereas nothing else had. People tend to return to what they have found useful in the past. Different medications work for different people.

The Stress of Reunion

During all this time, Anne continued to think about her children. As she began to feel better because of the Ativan and the support group, her hopes of reuniting with her daughter grew. Anne wanted her daughter to know something about her in case she died. Because of the panic disorder, she was frightened and didn't know what the future held in store for her.

The trip to meet her daughter was a stressful one, but she coped by using techniques that she learned from her support group. While a lot of people with anxiety disorders feel that they can't function, the reality is quite the contrary. They actually find that they can do a fine job and still perform the task, albeit with some discomfort, even though they are anxious and sometimes terrified.

Anne's anxiety worsened after she saw her daughter. Again she had to deal with abandonment issues and enormous guilt. When someone has to deal with increased stress, anxiety symptoms return. Also, as we've noted, symptoms ebb and flow, getting better and worse over a period of time.

Anne tried to get her body under control, hoping her mind would follow. The reverse, getting the mind under control, hoping the body will follow, is also important for recovery.

But because of the increased stress in her life, whatever had helped her before failed to work this time. The tension and panic attacks increased. So did the anticipatory anxiety. Because Anne's problems were so complex and severe, she needed psychotherapy to deal with her issues of abandonment, guilt, and, loss. She found the one-to-one relationship valuable because it helped her concentrate on her particular problems. Her therapist also taught her behavioral techniques that she found extremely useful. The combination of individual therapy, the medication Ativan, and the support group was extremely beneficial and helped Anne through her recovery.

Anne's Recovery

Treating Panic Disorder with Behavioral Techniques

The mind-body connection, which plays a significant role in the treatment of many other illnesses, is clearly effective in the treatment of panic disorder. Both cognitive techniques and psychotherapy are useful in helping the *mind* calm down and letting the *body* follow. In this chapter we explore techniques that help the *body* calm down and let the *mind* follow.

Behavioral techniques are concrete, practical methods that have proved highly effective for reducing anxiety. They are regimented, repetitive, and easy to practice.

Unlike cognitive techniques, which result in changes in thinking, and psychotherapy, whose partial role is to effect changes in emotion, behavioral techniques involve external, not internal, change. As their name denotes, behavioral techniques result in changes in behavior. Therapists use behavioral techniques (in conjunction with cognitive techniques) as a first offense before trying the other possibilities. Patients like this approach and usually show improvement within six weeks or less. By taking an active part in their own recovery, they have a sense of control over their illness.

Patients with panic disorder need this feeling of control. They are alarmed by their symptoms and worry that they will become worse. As the fear of losing control increases, they become more and more anxious.

In some patients anxiety is a conditioned response to their environment. People become accustomed to the occurrence of certain phenomena and expect them to happen repeatedly. Consider the following analogy: if you trip on a particular segment of the sidewalk each time you walk over it, you may become conditioned to thinking you will trip again, even if the sidewalk has been repaired. Similarly, people react with anxiety from living in stressful environments. Every time they find themselves in a similar environment, they anticipate anxiety and then, in a self-fulfilling prophecy, they feel anxious.

Behaviorists believe that certain things in the environment provoke fear, and that certain behaviors—avoidance, flight, nervousness, reliance on alcohol and/or drugs, or inability to venture out alone—are reactions to that fear. Our environment usually can't be changed, but we can work on modifying our reactions to the environment with behavioral techniques.

How Behavioral Techniques Work

Behavioral techniques make the panic disorder patient feel more relaxed by reversing her rapid responses and her agitated physical state, helping her to take action, and distracting her from her symptoms.

- **Reversing the process.** Behavioral techniques slow down the body. In particular, they slow down the racing heart and fast breathing.

- **Taking Action.** Using behavioral techniques is a way of taking action. It's a good feeling to do something rather than to do nothing. Each of the women we have discussed is a fighter who went from helplessness to self-help. Fighters try to overcome their problems; they don't sit back and let life beat them. Because of their indomitable spirit, they prevail.

- **Focusing.** When patients focus on deep breathing, for example, they don't think about the possibility of going crazy or of having a heart attack. They have to concentrate on breathing in and out.

The Techniques

The following are some techniques that patients have found particularly useful.

- **Deep Breathing.** A person's breathing becomes shallow and fast when she or he is anxious. Deep breathing helps slow down respiration. Patients practice slowing down their breathing until the technique becomes so automatic that they can summon it whenever they need it.

- **Progressive Relaxation.** Hands, feet, and other parts of the body tighten with anxiety. Progressively relaxing the body is calming. The patient works on tensing and relaxing various muscle groups, one at a time. She learns how she feels when she is tense and when she is relaxed.

- **Visualization.** Patients learn to concentrate and visualize in great detail a familiar scene that is soothing and relaxing. Just as they do with deep breathing, they practice it at various times during the day, so they can use it when they are tense or anxious.

- **Systematic Desensitization.** The therapist may ask a patient with panic disorder to draw up a list of fears related to a certain stress—having to give a speech, for example. Working on the least frightening aspects of that fear first, the therapist teaches the patient to relax using visualization.

- **Meditation.** During meditation, instead of paying attention to the outward demands of one's environment, patients learn to turn their attention inward. They concentrate on a word or phrase, which they repeat while sitting quietly with their eyes closed. The result is a quieting and steadying of the mind.

- **Biofeedback.** While using a relaxation technique such as deep breathing, for example, the patient is hooked up to a monitor that allows her to see the changes in temperature or muscle activity. The feedback from the machine shows her that she has the ability to relax her body. The more she sees confirmation of her success, the more she is able to use the techniques without the machine to become calm.

    Behavioral techniques take a lot of practice. They have to become a way of life. In Part II, we'll explain more fully how behavioral techniques can be part of your treatment plan.

How Behaviorial Techniques Helped Anne Recover

Anne knew that she needed help, and, being resourceful, she found a support group, where she learned some behavioral techniques that started her on the road to recovery. Although the support group was helpful, it was not enough. She needed professional help. She called her family doctor, and he recommended a therapist who taught her additional relaxation techniques that included visualization, progressive relaxation, and deep breathing.

The therapist gave Anne a series of tapes with calming sounds that included soft music, raindrops, trains, and ocean sounds. She told Anne to listen to the tapes for 10 minutes a couple of times a day when she felt anxious. As Anne listened to the sounds, she was to visualize herself as calm and relaxed. Anne says she responded best to the ocean sounds. When her mind was racing, when she thought she was going to pass out, or when she worried that the end was coming, she would go to her bedroom and put on a tape. "It would quiet me," she says. "I found that I was less anxious and could cope with whatever was around me—noise, TV, the kids."

Anne's therapist also gave her tapes with instructions on deep breathing and progressive relaxation, and she alternated using the two techniques. As she breathed, she would say to herself, "I am breathing in calmness and breathing out anxiety." For unwinding before bedtime and whenever she felt anticipatory anxiety, she found the progressive relaxation tapes helpful. Now she says she can do visualization, deep breathing, and progressive relaxation without the tapes.

Another technique Anne found helpful came from a chiropractor she'd visited for an unrelated problem. The chiropractor, who was interested in holistic medicine, instructed Anne to picture warmth passing through her body from her eyes, ears, and neck down to her toes. Focusing on the warmth for 10 minutes at a time made her feel calm and tranquil. Because it's hard to concentrate on more than one thing at a time, she couldn't think about her anxiety when she focused on the warmth.

Driving was always difficult for Anne because she had once had a severe panic attack while she was at the wheel. Ever since then she had worried that she would have another attack while driving, that the car would crash, and the police would come. But she learned several behavioral tools from her support group. Before she gets into the car, she pictures herself driving, calm and relaxed. If she gets anxious while she is driving, she distracts herself—while always careful to keep her eyes on the road. She reads signs and names of streets; she spells words backward (*Walnut* becomes *Tunlaw*), and counts trees on a block. "There are 22 trees from my house to the library," she laughs. "You can't think about anxiety when you're counting trees." When she stops at a red light, she looks at the cars, people, or the cover of a magazine. She takes a sip of water from the bottle she always brings along, or sprays perfume on her wrist. She plays the radio and counts bumps on the steering wheel. "The anticipatory anxiety is always there," she says. "But I bring along my tools and tell myself 'I'm OK. I won't pass out. Just because I'm anxious when I drive doesn't mean I can't drive.'"

On her way to see her daughter, she distracted herself by snapping a rubber band that she kept on her wrist. (This technique isn't recommended, however, since it tends to make one associate pain with a palliative). She counted backward from 100 to keep from worrying about the meeting. She rubbed a fuzzy bear that she carried around with her and also alternated between turning on the heater and the air conditioner. (Some people also put ice on their face, believing that feeling the cold interrupts the anxiety.) She kept her mind on finding her way to the restaurant. "I thought about what I would say to my daughter," she recalls. "At times, I calmed myself with deep slow breathing either while I was driving or after I pulled over to the side of the road."

Always on hand in her big pocketbook are her tools: the mints, drinking water, perfume, magazines, holy stones to touch and feel, coins from which to read dates—all objects to focus outside herself and distract her mind from the anxiety. She may focus on something in a room—colors, pictures on the wall, frames around the pictures. In church, she counts how many men and how many women are in attendance, and how many are wearing dressy shoes and how many are wearing sneakers.

Determined to get better, Anne worked at using these and other behavioral techniques for nine years. While she was recovering, even everyday things like escalators were a challenge. Although she says she "always looked fine from the outside," when in public she was almost always using some technique or another—for example, slowing down her breathing while talking to herself in a calming way.

But after a while, the techniques became automatic and relaxing was easier. During our last conversation with Anne, she said that she can now make the 20-mile drive to visit her brother. And she told us excitedly that she was about to take her first plane ride.

"At first, the panic controlled me. I had no life; my world was getting smaller," she says. "The attacks still come out of the blue, but they don't frighten me as much because I have faced the fear and have control over it.

"We do survive. What we fear will happen doesn't happen."

The Connection
Between
Panic Disorder
and Anxiety

Anxiety Disorders

As Anne's story illustrates, GAD and panic disorder are related. They are both part of the category of anxiety disorders as listed in the *DSM-IV*.

A great deal of anxiety may put one at risk for developing panic disorder. And, conversely, panic disorder patients become more anxious because of their concerns about the attacks. Research supports this observation; studies indicate that more than 80 percent of people with GAD have had panic disorder and/or phobia at some time in their lives.[1]

To understand what abnormal anxiety is, you must first understand normal anxiety. When you face real danger or feel threatened, you experience normal anxiety—a desirable state since it spurs you to take the steps needed to cope with danger. For example, fear of public speaking can cause anxiety in someone who must make a speech. The speaker fears the threat of embarrassing herself or doing a poor job. A normal amount of anxiety is appropriate and even good, since it propels and motivates one to prepare properly and provides the energy to do a good job. Normal anxiety dissipates when the danger or threat is no longer there.

But abnormal anxiety is out of proportion to the danger being experienced. What's more, the anxiety doesn't go away. If the person giving the speech begins to get extremely anxious about the speech to the point of obsessing about it, having palpitations, diarrhea, sweatiness, shakiness, inability to concentrate or speak, or diminished appetite, her anxiety is abnormal. Anxiety is also abnormal if it doesn't dissipate after the speech or if the speaker begins to obsess about the next speech. Abnormal anxiety greatly affects thinking, perception, and learning because it produces distortions. It interferes with one's functioning on the job or personal life and contributes to physical symptoms such as back problems or migraine headaches.

People with GAD exhibit excessive anxiety and worry occurring on more days than not for at least six months, about a number of activities (such as work or school performance). They find it difficult to control the worry, which is associated with three or more of these symptoms: restlessness or feelings of being keyed up or on edge; fatigue, difficulty concentrating or mind going blank; irritability; muscle tension; and sleep disturbance (difficulty falling or staying asleep, or restless, unsatisfying sleep).[2] However, people with GAD usually don't have the extreme physical reactions that panic disorder sufferers do. Twice as many women as men suffer from GAD.[3]

Besides GAD and panic disorder, the anxiety disorders category in the *DSM-IV* also includes phobic disorders, obsessive-compulsive disorder, and post-traumatic stress disorder, as well as some less prevalent anxiety disorders. Between 10 and

15 percent of people in the United States will at some time in their lives experience one type of anxiety disorder.[4] As sufferers well know, these disorders can cause just as much pain and suffering as physical illnesses.

Patients can have more than one anxiety disorder. In fact, there is a substantial overlap in the anxiety disorders category, and not just between panic disorder and GAD. For instance, 30 percent of people with phobias report having panic disorder.[5]

Phobias include agoraphobia, specific phobia, and social phobia. Agoraphobia, which we have mentioned earlier in this book, will be described in detail in Chapter 16. As we've noted, a large number—one-third—of panic disorder sufferers develop agoraphobia. They avoid, or endure with marked distress or anxiety, certain places or situations; some fear leaving the house altogether.

Specific phobia, the most common of the anxiety disorders, is an excessive or unreasonable fear triggered by a specific object (animals, for example) or situation (flying, heights). Exposure to the object almost invariably provokes an immediate anxiety response.

Social phobia is a fear of being exposed to scrutiny by others, a fear of doing something to humiliate or embarrass oneself.

The first panic attack may lead to phobias. The more intense the panic attack, the more possible it is that a phobia will develop. Lisa, the woman we discussed in Chapter 3, became fearful of walking through the atrium of her office building. Other people with panic disorder fear being trapped in an elevator, a car, a closed room, or any place that feels unsafe.

Obsessive-compulsive disorder (OCD) can also be triggered by the first panic attack. Sufferers of panic disorder typically obsess about having attacks. They often act in compulsive ways in attempting to calm themselves down. Jane, as you remember, obsessed over having another panic attack and tried to calm herself by keeping her hands busy with cleaning and needlework. Some people with OCD engage in superstitious thinking, such as believing that walking only on the right side of the street will ensure safety from panic attacks.

Post-traumatic stress disorder occurs after a person has experienced a a traumatic event. The response involves intense fear, helplessness, or horror and is persistently reexperienced.

Some Facts About Anxiety

The category of anxiety disorders for which people seek the most help is panic disorder. Sufferers of panic disorder have a distorted sense of reality. When they are in the throes of a panic attack, they think they will faint or die; because 20 percent of them have some heart reaction (pain or palpitations), they may think they are having a heart attack.[6] They spend overwhelming effort and time trying to prevent the attacks.

All of the anxiety disorders have similar symptoms; the most common one is anxiety. Even so, it's important to determine which disorder or disorders a patient has, so she can be treated properly. Treatments can differ, depending on the disorder.

Although about 4 percent of the population has one anxiety disorder, the 20th century's fast-paced society can't take the rap for all this stress. Horace, writing in 65–68 B.C., said "At the rider's back sits dark Anxiety." John Dryden, in the 1600s, wrote "How blessed is he, who leads a country life, unvex'd with anxious cares, and void of strife!"[7]

Despite the fact that anxiety is part of the human condition, many people feel that suffering from one of these disorders is a sign of weakness. Yet anxiety disorders have nothing to do with weakness. They are illnesses, arising from biological, psychological, and/or environmental causes.

One response to anxiety may lie in early intervention. Findings from Stanford Medical Center, suggest the desirability of identifying and helping teenagers who are beginning to have panic attacks. The researchers say that the roots of panic disorder are sometimes found in occasional panic attacks in teenage years, an assertion that corresponds to reports from adults with panic disorder who recall having their first panic episodes as teenagers. For teens who are timid or frightened of new situations, learning to manage general anxiety would be most helpful, researchers say.[8]

Other evidence suggests that patients need to make sure their primary-care physicians are asking questions that could lead to the diagnosis of an emotional illness. Patients with emotional problems often feel physically ill, so they emphasize physical symptoms during office visits. When doctors neglect to inquire about a patient's life, the stresses the patient faces, and any recent changes or traumas, they frequently miss disorders like depression, anxiety, and panic disorder. If you have physical symptoms with no known physical cause, and your doctor hasn't asked about what is going on in your life, it may be time to look for a new doctor.

The Isolated Woman

Women who have panic disorder with agoraphobia are isolated. Their fear of having a panic attack someplace where escape might be difficult or embarrassing binds them to a limited territory; they are unable to enjoy the freedom and mobility that most people take for granted.

Agoraphobia can range from mild to severe. Some agoraphobics become housebound, living like prisoners in their own homes. In extreme situations, they end up confined to just one room of their home or even to one "safe" chair or their bed. Sometimes they are unable to go to the bathroom without the help of a trusted person.

Whether they are merely inconvenienced or completely powerless, people with agoraphobia typically feel demoralized and depressed. Their time and energy become focused on which places are "safe" and which are "unsafe." Work, family, and friendships suffer. Of all the people who have panic attacks, it's most often those with agoraphobia who seek psychiatric treatment.

In this chapter we'll meet Monica, a woman who endured intense fear and sustained isolation. Although she sought help, she soon became frustrated with the medical profession's failure to understand her illness.

But Monica fought back. Even though her illness restricted her mobility, she engaged in activities that challenged her quick mind. Even in times of deepest despair, part of her clung to the hope of a better life. With the development of new treatments, she was eventually able to function, even returning to college to receive her degree. Today she is married with a family. She drives a car and travels.

Monica's Story

$\mathcal{L}$ ooking back, I can see that my anxiety is rooted in my dependency on my parents. I was very attached to my mother; she latched onto me while I was growing up. (She had been very close to her own mother who died six months before I was born.) I was an only child until I was seven years old, and my mother gave me a lot of attention, even after the birth of my two brothers. I was always more comfortable with adults than with other children.

When it was time to start kindergarten, I would throw up every morning. Mother would keep me home, and I was happy to be there with her. There was always this discomfort, this apprehension at being away from home.

Just after I turned 18, stresses started to build up; too many changes were happening at once. I graduated from high school in June and, soon afterward, my family moved from Queens, New York, where I had lived since I was eight years old, to a small town in Connecticut. It was so different—there were woods and no home mail delivery. I left behind friends and relatives. I felt uprooted.

Another change followed when I began college on a scholarship in the fall. I felt anxious after leaving home. The stress grew and grew. To make matters worse, I found that I couldn't rely on my good grades anymore. Everyone there was bright.

The first panic attack occurred about a month and a half after school started. I was sitting in a classroom. I remember it was a history class taught by a navy lieutenant. He was a stern young guy who warned us of all kinds of consequences if we didn't submit a paper the next day. We were studying the Weimar Constitution and I couldn't understand what he was saying. I was so nervous. The door seemed very far away. I felt trapped.

The anxiety increased until it hit a level that, on a scale of 1 to 10, I would describe as a 7 or 8. I experienced this anxiety viscerally. I could sense my face flushing and feel a lurch in my gut, much like having butterflies in the stomach or being in an elevator when it drops quickly. I was sweating and my heart was pounding. There was this terrible stab of fear, like being hit by a hot flash or a lightning bolt. The anxiety level kept climbing until it reached a point where I felt that I couldn't hold it down, that it would boil over.

I was also afraid that I couldn't hide it inside me. It seemed as if it would run away with me. Because I felt that I couldn't contain it any more, I was afraid it was going to show. I worried that if I went out of control, others would notice. I worried that I might run across the room, that I would cry, or do something foolish or embarrassing. I was afraid of the way I felt and where it would take me.

The attack lasted only about three minutes. The anxiety level came down, and when the class was over I left. But the worry of "Will it happen again?" haunted me. After that incident, I had constant anxiety, although the level went up and down.

Pretty soon I was afraid to go into the dining hall. Breakfast and lunch were OK, because they were served buffet-syle, but dinnertime was a horror. The arrangement at dinner was extremely formal and stiff. There was something in the structure that made me feel trapped. We were served at a long table.

Everyone chatted and socialized. I knew I would be conspicuous if I left. So, I skipped dinners. I just didn't go. I began getting weaker and thinner and had to go to the infirmary more and more often because I was feeling weak and my stomach was queasy.

I told the infirmary doctor about my problem, and he gave me phenobarbital. I also told the housemother; she was nurturing and gave me some tea. When I talked to her, I felt that I was understood and I didn't want to leave. I didn't have to appear perfect with her; she allowed me to be nervous.

At Thanksgiving I went home. But it didn't feel like home; it felt like a strange environment. At the same time, the thought of going back to college was horrible. But I did go back, and, soon afterward, I caught pneumonia. My father came for me and when I got home I knew I couldn't go back. I had to give up the scholarship.

Christmas came and went. In the house I felt a sense of isolation, but if I went out, my anxiety level soared. My parents tried to help but they couldn't. I know now that what I was experiencing was agoraphobia.

About that time, an old friend from Queens, someone I had grown up with, called and asked me to join her and some other friends in New York. They were going to see the show *Kiss Me Kate*. To get there, I needed to take the train, but my first concern was my stomach. Would I get diarrhea? Would there be a bathroom on the train? I went only one stop on the train when I had to get off. The fear was overwhelming. It came over me like a tremendous wave. I had a sense of totally losing it. I called my father to drive me home. He had to page my friends to tell them I wasn't coming. My parents were disappointed and felt sorry for me. I felt like a failure.

After that, I went to the local doctor, but he didn't take me seriously. He felt that whatever I had was insignificant and dismissed it.

The worst attack occurred the year I was 21. That winter my dog died. I had gotten Mitzi as a puppy and she was my last link with my home in Queens. My parents wouldn't let me watch while they buried her. They said something was wrong with me, that I was high-strung and oversensitive.

The next day my mother took me to see a psychiatrist a few towns away. While she drove, I got a panic attack at the level of 7 or 8. We were going up a hill and the bright, winter sun was glaring. I could feel my anxiety level rising. It was like a hot wave that seared over my whole body. I felt a sense of weakness, of being completely overwhelmed, of the fear pressing down and the world caving in. The panic at that moment was uncontrollable. There was no way to stop it. I was afraid that it would go on forever. I felt trapped, in danger, and in a frenzy. I thought that I would be annihilated if I didn't get out of the car.

It was always the same. I was anxious in the car, but I felt safe when I got to the doctor's. His office was safe and home was safe, but the time in between wasn't. When I would finally arrive home, I would have to lie flat on my back and close my eyes.

I was afraid of being afraid, apprehensive ahead of time.

I stopped seeing the psychiatrist because the trip was too frightening, and I began to go to a doctor in town. He didn't know what was wrong with me, but he prescribed Seconal for anxiety. He kept increasing the dose and before long I was totally addicted.

I stayed in or around the house. It was the only way I could cope. Because of the large doses of Seconal, I lay in bed for long hours in the morning feeling lethargic. But I took a sunrise semester TV course on Russian and taught myself shorthand. I read Carl Sandburg's five-volume biography of Lincoln. I wrote a letter to Sandburg and we began corresponding. I made oil paintings and fabric crafts—neckties and scarves—which I sold. I worked hard in the garden.

There were no more psychiatrists, but a country doctor prescribed Librium instead of the Seconal, and that let me function well enough to keep a job caring for puppies and to take a cruise where I met my husband.

But after I had my daughter, the panic closed in again. I tried to push away the feelings of anxiety, but that didn't work. I was alone all day in a garden apartment. My parents were far away and involved with each other. My friends and my brothers were working. So was my husband. I leaned on tranquilizers and alcohol to cope with the fears and isolation.

I was afraid that if I got panicky, there would be no one to help me. What would I do if the baby got sick? I was even afraid to use the phone. I got a lump in my throat if I had to make or receive a call. What if I choked up? I thought. What if I couldn't stop choking? Would I lie there the rest of the day? Who would take care of my daughter? If I called a neighbor for help, would she call the police? Would they throw a net over me or lock me up, thinking I was crazy? The anxiety level kept increasing.

From instinct I avoided certain people, places, things, and situations and tried not to dwell on thoughts, because full-scale panic can arise just from thoughts associated with a situation. I could be sitting in my "safe" place and a thought would come to me that would arouse fear. I was scared that there would be nowhere to retreat to and no one to turn to. The thoughts would intensify. The very thought that I would get panicky would send me escalating toward a full-scale panic attack. The only thing that calmed me were tranquilizers.

I coped while my daughter was growing up and even took a part-time job as a secretary. The routine of work and the socialization there made me feel more comfortable. But having to cope with the stresses of shopping and where to leave the baby while I worked increased my anxiety. I had stopped taking Librium but I was relying increasingly on alcohol.

One day, I had a massive attack in Shop-Rite. I had to sit down on the floor. My vision was blurring, I had difficulty breathing, and I felt my heart pounding. I was terrified that someone would come along and say, "What's wrong with you?" and do something that would inevitably be the wrong thing. Maybe she would say "Come on, get in the car with me and I'll take you to the hospital." I couldn't do that. I was terrified of hospitals and doctors. The doctors didn't know what to do for me anyway.

The attack subsided after four or five minutes. I took the baby and went home, but I was traumatized. After that, when I went shopping, I would have a drink first. Or my husband would go to the store after work. I called my internist and told him I had nothing to rely on, so he gave me another prescription for Librium.

When my daughter was about eight years old, I again stopped taking Librium and just drank. Alcohol seemed like an innocent way to cope with fears. I drank for two weeks straight and wound up in the hospital. I was very ill.

I had to leave the job and I felt terribly defeated. I attended an AA group and a phobia support group, but neither could zero in on what I had. I was losing confidence that I would ever get out of this thing.

Understanding Monica

An Unhealthy Closeness

$\mathcal{I}$t is common for panic disorder to begin in early adulthood, but the signs are usually present long before. Looking back, one will usually find the antecedents early in life when the patient separated from an important person, usually her mother. In fact, a study of more than one thousand pairs of female twins showed an association between panic disorder and maternal separation.[1]

This link is significant. Women are often overly attached to their mothers, as we certainly saw in Monica's story. The dependence may emanate from the mother's need to grasp on to her child, in an effort to quiet her own anxiety and to satisfy her own need for closeness. In some cases, it is the parent who experiences the greater anxiety when a child in whom she is overly invested leaves home. The parent's anxiety increases her child's fear, and a dependency develops.

The child may desire autonomy, but the conflict between that need and the need to remain close, as the mother demands, causes her a great deal of anxiety.

When she leaves home for the first time, goes to college, or gets married, she may have a full-blown panic attack. Even before the big event, the anxiety may start to escalate in anticipation of the separation.

The dry throat, shakiness, fast breathing, and, possibly, depression that these women experience when they try to strike out on their own may echo the symptoms they felt when, as overly dependent children, they were separated from their mothers. While growing up, they might have felt anxious any time they were away from home.

College Creates Anxiety

Major life changes, such as divorce or a death in the family make anxiety problems worse. The more changes one experiences, the greater the risk for anxiety or a full-blown panic attack. Monica's anxiety intensified because she moved shortly before leaving for college.

At college, the first real break from her mother and her home, there was initially no one with whom Monica could feel safe and calm on a regular basis. Although the housemother was nurturing and supportive, allowing and encouraging Monica to be herself, it wasn't enough; Monica was already spiraling downward. Had the housemother entered the picture earlier, Monica might have been able to stay at college.

An accomplished student, Monica fit the profile of the panic disorder patient, who is usually a high-functioning person with above average intelligence. Data shows that people who are high achievers or have high aspirations put pressure on themselves to succeed. Monica did just that, depending on her success in school to feel good about herself. When she found that competition for grades in college was more rigorous than it had been in high school, her self-esteem slipped, and she had trouble concentrating.

Because their self-esteem is typically low, panic disorder patients care too much about what others think of them and about how they appear to the public. The possibility of someone witnessing a panic attack, with its overwhelming symptoms, is catastrophic to them.

Monica was afraid that her terror would show. She worried that if she went out of control, others would notice. To panic disorder patients, it's very important to appear in control. They worry about embarrassing themselves and are afraid of appearing abnormal.

Feeling Trapped

Fueling her anxiety was the concern about being trapped and unable to escape. Monica talks about being trapped several times—in the classroom, in the college dining room, and in the car. Feelings of fear usually recede when there is more mobility. Had Monica been in places where she could have left easily, she might have felt more relaxed.

During dinner, she couldn't leave without someone noticing. In a more casual setting, she would have been less easily noticed. The more casual the setting, the easier it is to contend with some panic.

The attack that occurred in the supermarket wasn't unusual for someone with panic disorder. Many people with this disorder feel trapped in stores or amidst crowds in a mall. Standing in line, which can seem interminable, is problematic for them. They want to finish shopping, but worry that the attack will get so bad that they will have to drop their purchases and leave. They become anxious, brood about the impression they are making on others, and start having symptoms.

Monica displayed common symptoms of panic disorder—sweating, stomach distress, palpitations, and fear of losing control. Because the physical symptoms are so intense, many patients feel that the next step must be death.

Withdrawing from Life

As we have mentioned in earlier case studies, Monica's anticipatory anxiety was typical of people with panic disorder. Trying to prevent attacks, they withdraw, avoiding more and more
places and situations. They increasingly stay home and may
develop agoraphobia. Since one-third of all patients with panic
disorder develop agoraphobia, it was not surprising that Monica displayed symptoms of that disorder.[2]

It is usual for agoraphobics to rely more and more on other
people for everyday tasks. Monica's parents, and later her husband, helped with driving, shopping, and other chores she was
unable to perform.

Monica avoided certain people, places, things, and situations, and even tried to block some thoughts. People with panic
disorder have an emergency response to various situations and
become intensely and quickly alarmed, with strong physical
reactions. They immediately begin to think that something
outrageous will happen, that the fear will be unbearable. Their
thinking is so extreme that they feel, not just some fear, but an
intense terror. Mere thoughts related to a fearful situation,
such as driving over a bridge, for example, can send them into
a panic attack.

Instead of reasoning "It might not happen" or "So what if
it happens," people with panic disorder are convinced they will
experience a worst-case scenario. Whereas most people realize
that a little anxiety is just a normal reaction to stress, panic disorder sufferers immediately catastrophize a situation, fearing it
will develop into a full-fledged panic attack.

Looking for Help—in Vain

Desperate for relief, Monica sought help from a psychiatrist
and family doctors. None of the doctors knew what to do for
her. The lack of help on the part of the medical profession
made her anxiety even greater.

Again and again, women have told us about doctors who were unfamiliar with panic disorder, often misdiagnosing it as a physical problem or an illness that wasn't of real concern. Fortunately, this is changing. Doctors are becoming more familiar with panic disorder and are gaining a better understanding of how to treat it.

When Monica first became ill, doctors prescribed phenobarbital and, later, Seconal. Both are drugs that were commonly prescribed to calm people who were anxious and fearful. But Monica needed more and more of the Seconal to feel relaxed and she eventually became addicted.

Today, tranquilizers such as Valium and Xanax are often the drugs of choice for treating panic disorder. When used as needed, sometimes in conjunction with an antidepressant, which is taken regularly, they seem to help. (See Chapter 19.)

Alcohol is commonly used by panic disorder patients to make their fears more manageable. After her attack in Shop-Rite, Monica would take a drink before going shopping. People with panic disorder sometimes start their drinking this way, anesthetizing themselves to stay calm. Monica eventually lost both her sense of control and the ability to care for herself, drinking until she was ill enough to require hospitalization.

Women like Monica have such intense anxiety that they think they need drugs, including alcohol, in order to function; it is the only way they know to become calm. Certainly, not every woman with panic disorder resorts to these substances. Still, alcohol and drug abuse is high in patients with panic disorder.[3]

Motherhood Brings More Change

Anything that gives stability to the lives of panic disorder patients has a calming effect. Patients' minds are occupied when they have jobs; they have less time for obsessive thinking about the possibility of another panic attack. In addition, a work situation can elevate self-esteem, and supportive colleagues can induce calm. The routine of work, and the socializing that went on there, made Monica feel more comfortable.

But soon her problems worsened because of the responsibilities of motherhood. Having another human being suddenly dependent on her caused tremendous anxiety. Also, because she was away from her parents, Monica felt isolated and, once again, unsafe. Even in her "safe place," her home, she felt anxious.

Again, there was the fear of what others might think. She was afraid to use the phone—lest she were to get choked up and be unable to talk—and afraid that the neighbors would call the police. People who have higher self-esteem, who don't care so much what others think, wouldn't be as paralyzed.

Driving the panic was the worry that someone watching an attack would take her to the hospital—a place that felt unsafe to her. She feared that doctors would make light of her illness, diagnose her incorrectly, or find something terribly wrong. She was terrified that they would take her baby away. Because of her intense fear of doctors and hospitals, she had no way to make herself feel better.

Just as she had to leave school, Monica also had to leave her job. Her illness was interfering with her ability to have any kind of normal life—to finish school, hold down a job, care for her daughter, socialize, or travel.

Many panic disorder patients get discouraged because of their inability to function, to have careers and family lives, to maintain relationships, and to enjoy mobility. They feel that their lives have been ruined.

But Monica's resiliency and intelligence helped see her through. After years of despair, she was finally able to find a doctor who could help.

Monica's Recovery

Treating Panic Disorder with Exposure Therapy

*T*he best way to conquer a fear is to face it. That's what exposure therapy, or simply exposure, helps patients to do.

Because exposure therapy works so well with regard to locations, it can target the fear of specific places that agoraphobics often have. Exposure therapy has made normal existence possible for many women whose lives were once severely limited. It is considered the treatment of choice for panic disorder with agoraphobia.

Experts believe that exposure therapy is useful in treating the anticipatory anxiety that often leads to agoraphobia. Exposure therapy helps patients understand that the fantasy is worse than the reality, that there is no basis for fearing the worst.

Dr. David Barlow says that exposure therapy can help patients change the way they respond to panic attack symptoms. According to him, panic attacks are false alarms issued by the body in response to signals, such as palpitations, that spell danger. While the danger is false, the fear is real. Since false alarms are learned phenomena, the treatment involves corrective learning. Exposure therapy helps patients learn that the signals don't correspond to actual danger, and they begin to respond with less anxiety to these signals.[1]

How Exposure Therapy Works

Exposure therapy works similarly to imagery desensitization, the behavioral technique in which the patient draws up a list of fears, ranging from the least to the most frightening, about a particular phobia and then visualizes herself in each scene on the list. (See Chapter 17.)

The difference between the two techniques is that, while imagery desensitization involves the imagination, exposure therapy goes a step further by taking place in real life. In fact, exposure therapy is sometimes called real-life, or in vivo, desensitization.

Treatment for agoraphobia usually begins with imagery desensitization because it is a good preparation for exposure therapy. Some therapists also use in-office exposure therapy as an interim experience before patients go into the real world; unlike real life, the setting is controlled.

Using exposure therapy in the real world entails a list of about 15 steps and a therapist or surrogate who will offer support and encouragement. In the following pages, you'll see how Monica and another patient, Barbara, used two different forms of exposure therapy. In Part II, we describe exposure therapy in detail and explain the many ways it can help patients.

How Exposure Therapy Helped Monica Recover

Monica had been to so many doctors. She was confused, skeptical, and, as a middle-aged woman, no better off than she had been at the beginning of her quest for relief. Yet despite her fears, she was determined to live a close-to-normal life.

With that goal in mind, she flew to Ireland with her husband, holding onto the thought that, when she got to her destination, she would be safe. Once there, she tried to find ways to calm herself down. Venturing onto buses and into crowded buildings, she hung onto her husband, reasoning that he would know what to do if she had a panic attack.

"It was a terrible way to live," she says. "But I was convinced that this was the way it was going to be, that this was how I'd have to live for the rest of my life."

Shortly after she came home, however, Monica heard about a clinic where phobic people were being successfuly treated with a form of exposure therapy called contextual therapy (which is just one of several variations of exposure therapy).

Contextual therapy is a highly individualized treatment in which the patient confronts the dreaded situation in an orderly, planned manner, using graded, manageable steps. The patient and therapist meticulously agree on the hierarchy before the patient takes any action. This form of exposure therapy helps the patient shift her attention from imagined dangers and the frightening responses they arouse to familiar and reassuring realities in the present.

Proponents of contextual therapy believe that patients who avoid the phobic situation won't get better. Running away from the feared situation just enhances the fear, they assert.

To contend with the fear and stay with the situation, it's important to understand the six points that are the cornerstone of contextual therapy. Here is a summary of them:

- POINT ONE. Expect, allow, and accept that fear will arise. You can't control your reaction to something you fear; your reaction is automatic. But when you learn to expect the fear, you won't be quite so unnerved by it. Expecting the fear diminishes its impact.

- POINT TWO. When fear comes, wait. Let it be. Don't fight the fear. Accept it. Go with it.

- POINT THREE. Focus on and do manageable things in the present. Concentrating on things in the present keeps your mind from focusing on imaginary, frightening things that could happen.

- POINT FOUR. Label your fear from 0 to 10 and watch it go up and down. This activity lets you see that your fear levels change dramatically from moment to moment and that you can control your fear by shifting your attention. Acting as an observer takes some of the fright out of the experience.

- POINT FIVE. Function with a level of fear. Appreciate the achievement. You can function in a phobic situation, even though you are afraid. As you progress with contextual therapy, you will be able to remain in the situation for increasingly longer periods of time, with the fear diminishing as you practice the techniques for controlling it.

- POINT SIX. Expect, allow, and accept that fear will reappear. The recurrence of your fear, after a period of improvement, doesn't signify a relapse. This is a relearning process and learning (or relearning) doesn't happen in a straight, uninterrupted line.[2]

Using contextual therapy, Monica was able to function in ways that she'd never thought possible. Drawing up hierarchies and using the six points, she learned how to respond to phobic situations such as going to the supermarket. With her husband as her "safe person," Monica started up the hierarchy. As she tackled each step of the ladder—from parking in the supermarket lot, to approaching the supermarket, to purchasing one item, all the way to buying several days' worth of food—she remembered the six points.

She expected to be afraid and accepted the fear as part of the treatment. "Before, no one ever said to go with your feelings," she recalls. "I would do everything I could not to feel afraid. But the harder I tried the worse it got."

Treatment with contextual therapy offered a new approach. "I let those feelings happen. I let them sweep over me, " she says. "I didn't try to stop them or drive them away."

She got involved in the present by concentrating on manageable tasks—her shopping list and her purchases—and not on what might happen. "Reality is the safest place to be," she says.

As Monica learned to observe her fears objectively, she thought about whether they were coming from real or imagined threats. She realized that imagined fears could be as intense as real ones. At times she still worried that she would faint or throw up. She feared embarrassing herself if she couldn't go from the supermarket to the car and then drive home. But the relearning process helped her understand that the possibilities she feared were less likely if she got back to reality.

When fear did come, she observed it, labeling it numerically. She studied what was going on, watching to see what made it go up and down, realizing that the fluctuation in her fear was a process affected by her thoughts. She described one panic attack that she had as a passenger in the car as a 5 or 6. She noticed that bright sunlight intensified her fear; so did thoughts of being trapped while riding across a bridge. But concentrating on the directions to her destination decreased the fear.

She knew that she could function despite her fear, and she did. By concentrating on reality, she accomplished, step by step, over a period of time, the challenge of shopping in the supermarket. With each step—driving to the supermarket, walking through the doors, choosing items, standing in line at the checkout counter, paying for the items, and walking out the door and back to her car—Monica came closer to living a normal life. As time went on the fear lessened and the length of time she could shop for groceries grew. No longer did she have to run out of the store without her purchases.

Setbacks occurred but she was prepared for them. She knew that any learning process takes time, that there would be periods when she made good progress and periods when she seemed to take a step backward. One setback occurred during a trip to Florida with her husband, when Monica had a panic attack in her hotel room. The strange area contributed to her anxiety. So did the bright sunshine; once again a factor, it enhanced the sense of unreality.

But the setback was temporary and Monica was soon back on track, confronting other feared situations, such as driving. During a blizzard in 1987, she faced a real challenge. After dropping her husband off at his subway stop, she continued on to her job. "It took three hours to go four miles, but I was all right," she says. "I was coping with the traffic and stalled cars. I was involved with a real problem—getting where I had to go."

She coped with another crisis when her husband suddenly needed emergency surgery. Her neighbor went with her to see him. "I couldn't tell my neighbor how scared I was to drive home," she remembers. "I staggered to the car and thought 'I will die right now. If not, I will go home and die all alone there. I can't go home and I can't go back in the building.'" But, again, she got involved with something practical—driving home.

Today Monica is 90 percent recovered. She still has some anxiety, but she can't remember the last time she had a panic attack.

Years after her illness forced her to drop out of college, she returned to get her degree. She now teaches school. She can fly across the country by herself, take a train to a nearby city, and ride a bus once she gets there. She can drive almost anywhere in her county and neighboring counties, drive over a bridge, and sit in the front row of her church. And, of course, she has no problem going to the supermarket.

Barbara: Another Example of How Exposure Therapy Can Help

Barbara was going through a series of stresses: abandonment by her husband, her sister's death from a sudden heart attack, and the death of her sister's husband shortly afterward. Her sick, demanding mother and pressure on the job didn't help.

Then came the first panic attack. It happened in the elevator of her apartment building, where she lived on the 20th floor. She recalls the incident vividly. "As the elevator went down, I felt as if my body was going up," she says. "When I got off at the lobby, it seemed that my body was still moving. I was afraid that I couldn't get off safely, that I would fall. My whole equilibrium was off."

Her legs were shaky and she thought she was "going wacky." She couldn't catch her breath and thought that her throat was closing. Struck by what she describes as a temporary paralysis, Barbara had to talk to her legs to get them moving. It was only through sheer will, she says, that she forced herself to walk.

After the first attack, Barbara began having panic attacks daily, sometimes more than once a day. Often they happened at work, but sometimes elsewhere. The feeling of being trapped while waiting in line for her car to be inspected precipitated an attack. And, like many other women with panic disorder, she had a problem in large stores. After five minutes in the supermarket (with a friend acting as her safe person), she would drop her basket and run outside. She felt that she would pass out if she didn't leave.

Barbara was terrified that she would have other attacks like the ones in her office and in the elevator. Because of her anticipatory fear she began to develop agoraphobia. At first she could drive if it was necessary, although she wasn't able to cross the town line. As her fear of leaving home escalated, she started to spend more and more time in the house, going out only when she absolutely had to. Even then, someone else had to accompany her and drive. The parameters of her life became extremely limited; she had to stop working, traveling, and socializing. For a woman who had a responsible job and had led an active, independent life, this was a terrible way to live.

Eventually, Barbara stopped venturing outside at all. Depressed, she stayed in bed and slept much of the day. This was her way of escaping from the horror she encountered in the outside world. Getting up and dressing or cooking became an enormous effort. Often, she locked herself in her bedroom, where she felt safe and comfortable. After a month in bed, she moved to the living room sofa.

Meanwhile, Barbara was dealing with more stress: her daughter went through a divorce and her mother entered a nursing home. Barbara had to sell her mother's house, which was two towns away. Her daughter took care of the details, but Barbara decided that she had to see the house one last time. Her daughter drove. Barbara remembers opening the front door, intending to walk through and say good-bye to her childhood home. But she felt shaky and thought she would faint. "I wanted to scream. I wanted someone to hug me and hold me. I had such mixed emotions," she recalls. "I went to the cellar to read the meter, left, and never went back."

Home on disability, Barbara made it her goal to return to work. But she knew that returning to work entailed commuting 10 miles on a busy highway and then riding up on an elevator.

One day, when Barbara had been in the house for six months, she turned on the TV to a morning talk show and there on the screen were women like herself—women who had been trapped in their homes because of fear. One woman had locked herself in her room for 15 years. The program both scared Barbara and inspired her to seek help. "I'm used to being an active person," she thought. "I'm not going to allow myself to get trapped like that."

At that time, Barbara's home and her beloved country cottage, two and a half hours away, were her "safe" places. But she could get to her cottage only when her daughter drove her there, and even then she would often become shaky. Exposure therapy, in a form that was different from Monica's treatment, helped Barbara regain her freedom.

Together with the therapist she consulted, Barbara developed this hierarchy to overcome fear of driving:

1. With her daughter driving, ride around the block.

2. With her daughter driving, ride around town.

3. With her daughter driving, ride through heavy traffic.

4. With her daughter driving, ride on the highway.

5. With her daughter driving, ride to her country cottage.

6. Drive around the block with her daughter in the passenger seat.

7. Drive around town with her daughter next to her.

8. Drive through heavy traffic with her daughter next to her.

9. Drive on the highway with her daughter next to her.

10. Drive to her country cottage with her daughter next to her.

11. Do the last five steps alone.

Barbara remembers shaking the first time she drove alone. She was afraid that she would pass out, but she managed to accomplish that step. Each step was a new challenge that she met, even though she was scared.

To overcome her fear of the elevator, Barbara chose a trusted friend to be her safe person. Her friend coached her and encouraged her, saying, "This won't hurt you. Maybe you're overworked and tired." Barbara remembers feeling dizzy, so dizzy that she thought she would faint. But her friend reassured her and talked to her as they rode in the elevator of Barbara's apartment building. Here's the hierarchy, developed by Barbara and her therapist, that Barbara used.

1. With her friend, stand in front of the elevator, but don't go in.

2. With her friend, go into the elevator, and come out immediately.

3. With her friend, go into the elevator, check out the alarm button and the telephone.

4. With her friend, ride one floor in the elevator and walk back.

5. With her friend, ride one floor down and up.

6. With her friend, ride 10 floors down and up.

7. With her friend, ride the 20 floors to the lobby and back to her apartment.

8. With her friend, ride in a crowded department store elevator up and down.

9. With her friend, ride the elevator in her office building up to the fifth floor and back down.

10. With her friend, ride the elevator in her office building up to her 15th floor office and back down.

11. Do the last five steps alone.

As you can see, there were no great leaps between steps in either hierarchy. Barbara didn't try to ride to the lobby, for instance, before she had tackled some easier steps first. The feeling of accomplishment that she experienced in achieving each step gave her the confidence to progress to the next step.

The Connection Between Panic Disorder and Agoraphobia

*A*goraphobia can exist with or without panic disorder but, interestingly, two-thirds of patients with agoraphobia also have panic disorder.[1] Many experts believe that panic disorder is the cause of most cases of agoraphobia.[2]

What is the link between the two disorders? The anticipatory anxiety that so many panic disorder patients experience can often lead to agoraphobia. The person associates an attack she experienced with the situation or place where it occurred and then avoids that setting. Agoraphobia is most likely to follow panic attacks when the first attack occurs in a car or a public place.

Cindy exemplifies the way agoraphobia develops in someone with panic disorder. On her way to a job interview, Cindy had to ride in a closetlike, two-person elevator that got stuck between floors. Anyone who has ever been stuck on an elevator can relate to the fear that she felt. But for someone with panic disorder, the fear is much more intense. Cindy had a full-blown panic attack in the elevator. The experience was so horrible, she said, that she can't recall whether she was trapped for 15 seconds or 24 hours. That was the beginning of her agoraphobia. Although the trauma occurred a long time ago, it was many years before Cindy could ride on elevators again.

Just as elevators were unsafe for Cindy and Barbara, so cars, buses, trains, stores, bridges, escalators, tunnels, ships, airplanes, classrooms, theaters, restaurants, and other places are unsafe for other women with agoraphobia. While there's a tremendous variability in places that they deem unsafe, agoraphobics are especially sensitive to either small or expansive places.

Some agoraphobics are afraid of being trapped in closed or defined spaces. These people have a greater need for mobility and are more sensitive to being restrained or controlled than other people.[3] They fear being unable to get out of a closed space; sometimes they become so alarmed and befuddled that they can't find a door that will provide a means of escape. Others fear open spaces where they might not have access to their safe place.

Many patients in the suburbs can't travel to a nearby city. Some don't want to go beyond a five-block radius.

When agoraphobics are in an unsafe place, they feel alarmed. They worry that they won't be able to get help if they have a panic attack. In these situations, some people feel an intense dread.

Because women with panic disorder are very sensitive to what others think of them and their behavior, they don't want to face the possibility, however remote, of having a panic attack in a place where people might see them or where they might be publicly humiliated.

They avoid these unsafe places entirely, endure them with terror, or rely on a trusted friend or family member to accompany them. If they become paralyzed with fear, they may stay at home as Monica and Barbara did; home is usually a safe place.

Panic disorder with agoraphobia can arise from other causes besides anticipatory anxiety. As we've noted, women with panic disorder (and this holds true when the disorder is accompanied by agoraphobia) are more anxious than most people. They are likely to have grown up with anxious parents. Children whose mothers are overprotective, and always warning them of dangers, are particularly anxious about separation. They receive a message that says the world is a dangerous place. The situation can worsen if parents are divorced or if a parent dies or leaves because of divorce. These children fear being abandoned and left alone.

This early anxiety sets the stage for future problems. Later in life, when they are apart from a safe person (a mother or husband) or their safe environment, they feel anxious and fear being abandoned once again. That's why women with agoraphobia feel better being with that safe person when they leave home.

In some cases, agoraphobia is picked up from a parent who has panic disorder with agoraphobia. The child sees that the parent is frightened and automatically believes that there is something to be scared of.

Major changes such as engagement, marriage, going away to college, or anything that entails removal from the safe person or place can contribute to the development of panic disorder with agoraphobia.

In the case of one patient, it was a change of location that caused agoraphobia: Fran moved with her husband from a New Jersey suburb, where she lived 10 minutes from her mother, to Manhattan. Even before the move, the knowledge that she would no longer be near her mother caused Fran anxiety. This anxiety put her at risk for a panic attack, and, indeed, she had an overwhelming one in her car just before the move. After the attack, she gradually became afraid to drive, despite the loss of seeing her mother. The situation seems paradoxical because Fran was desperate for her mother's company. Yet the intense dread of driving interfered with her need and desire to visit her mother. Fran eventually developed agoraphobia, becoming more and more afraid to drive or even to leave the house.

Agoraphobia sometimes develops quickly. Some women are unable to leave their homes shortly after the precipitating incident. In other cases, agoraphobia develops gradually; over a period of time, the sufferer feels more and more frightened and becomes increasingly more confined.

Panic attack with agoraphobia is characterized by unpredictability. The intensity of the fear may vary from time to time. Patients may feel calmer at some times, less calm at others. The fear can come and go; sometimes it may disappear completely. Because the parameters of the phobia are not definitive, sufferers may be willing to take a chance and venture out.

Some Facts About Agoraphobia

- One-third of people who have panic disorder also have agoraphobia.[4]

- Agoraphobia is diagnosed three times as frequently in women as in men.[5]

- From 20 to 40 percent of people with agoraphobia have a close relative with the disorder.[6,7]

- The age of onset of agoraphobia is usually from the mid- to late 20s.[8]

- In many cases the onset of agoraphobia follows a traumatic event.[9]

- Rates of depression and suicide are much higher among agoraphobics than among the general population.[10]

- Heavy drinking and sedative abuse are common among agoraphobics who try to self-medicate.[11]

- With adequate treatment, 80 to 90 percent of agoraphobics can have a lasting recovery.[12]

Profile of a Woman Who Has Panic Disorder with Agoraphobia

- highly imaginative

- perfectionist

- needs to please others

- cares intensely about what others think of her

- has low self-esteem

- believes she will fail

- is not assertive

- doesn't like confrontation

- fears criticism

- fears rejection

- is somewhat secretive[13, 14]

$\mathcal{P}$art II

The Path
to Healing

Behavioral Techniques

*W*hen anxiety becomes intense it can interfere markedly with one's ability to function. In fact, a team of experts who surveyed one thousand adults suffering from anxiety and other emotional disorders reported in the *Journal of the American Medical Association* that these disorders impaired physical and social functoning and overall quality of life much more than did common medical disorders such as arthritis, diabetes, heart disease, and cancer.[1]

That's because anxiety produces physiological sensations such as palpitations, sweating, shaking knees, rapid heartbeat, rapid breathing, dizziness, tingling, and difficulty swallowing. It also causes feelings of apprehension and fear. These symptoms can can be quite distressing.

Moreover, anxiety creates confusion and affects thinking and learning. It can interfere with relationships and performance at school and work.

When you are anxious, your autonomic nervous system reacts in ways that affect your heart, respiration, digestion, and glands. Some people with anxiety, especially those with panic disorder, have autonomic nervous systems that respond excessively to the smallest threat or change. Whereas others might ignore these changes, anxious people are immediately filled with dread.

Behavioral techniques can help you deal with the physical responses to anxiety. You will learn to modify your reactions so that you respond to anxiety in ways that are healthy. Behavioral therapy is particularly useful in dealing with both anticipatory anxiety and agoraphobia, because it starts you on a process of helping yourself before you've become paralyzed with fear. The techniques should be part of a comprehensive program that includes other panic-management strategies, such as cognitive therapy.

Many behavioral techniques are relaxation techniques. Since you can't feel both anxious and relaxed at the same time, then it follows that if you are feeling relaxed, you can't feel anxious. By slowing down the body, relaxation techniques such as progressive relaxation and deep breathing, reduce the intensity of the changes you feel when you are anxious. Because relaxation techniques make symptoms more manageable, anxiety sufferers feel a sense of mastery and confidence.

Different techniques work better for different people. It doesn't matter which technique you use; all of them are calming. Read on to see which ones you think would be most comfortable for you.

Deep Breathing

When you are anxious, your breathing is fast and shallow. It feels out of control. Deep breathing reduces tension and produces a state of calmness and tranquility. Your emotions can't be aroused when you are relaxed and subdued.

Stop reading for a moment and take a deep breath.

You had to breathe slowly to do it, didn't you? When you slow down your respiration through deep breathing, you feel a sense of control over your anxiety. And, because you are concentrating on your breathing, you are distracted from mulling over anxious thoughts.

Many experts believe that panic attacks begin with fast breathing. People with panic disorder seem to have slightly higher than average breathing rates[2] and are prone to chest breathing, which is shallow. Interestingly, chest breathing is usual for shy and anxious people; those who are more relaxed and extroverted tend to breathe more slowly and deeply, and from their abdomens.[3]

When chest breathing becomes rapid, it can lead to hyperventilation, sometimes called overbreathing. Hyperventilation causes symptoms almost identical to the symptoms of panic attack. These include dizziness, numbness, light-headedness, tingling, confusion, and heart palpitations. Because these physical changes are alarming to someone with panic disorder, they can precipitate an attack.

Some researchers theorize that the neck, throat, and chest muscles clench in some people who feel stressed. This tightening restricts the lungs, resulting in a sensation of needing to breathe faster—and thus, hyperventilating—to get more air.[4]

When you hyperventilate you may feel as if you are suffocating. You begin to panic. Your body is aroused in a fight-or-flight response, adding to the panic. Thoughts become irrational and include fear of dying. One study found that 80 percent of people with panic disorder became anxious after hyperventilation.[5]

If you use deep breathing at the first sign of hyperventilation or rapid breathing, or when you notice a change in bodily sensations, there's a good chance that you'll be able to abort a panic attack.

Deep breathing is a simple, quick way to relax. Unlike some of the other techniques that we'll be talking about, deep breathing can take just a few minutes. You can use it anywhere at any time. You can practice deep breathing while you are stuck in traffic, in a supermarket line, at a meeting, flying in a plane, or waiting to make a speech. You can do deep breathing in a crowd of people without anyone knowing what you are doing.

Deep breathing is the essence of relaxation and provides the basis for other relaxation techniques including meditation and visualization.

Practicing Deep Breathing

For this technique and the ones that follow, you'll need a quiet room where you're sure that you won't be disturbed. This should be a place where you feel safe and comfortable. Close the door, dim the lights, and turn off the phone.

Practice deep breathing while lying on your back on a mat for the first week. Later on, when you've become familiar with the technique, you can sit in a comfortable chair or recliner. When you are sitting, keep your legs uncrossed and your hands relaxed on your lap or on the arms of the chair. Wear comfortable, unrestricted clothing.

You'll be breathing in and out through your nose (the smaller opening will give you more control than if you breathe through your mouth). And you'll be breathing from your abdomen, using your diaphragm (a muscle that separates your lungs from your abdominal cavity) rather than from your chest as you normally would. Diaphragmatic breathing is a more efficient way of breathing; it allows you to breathe more deeply, take in more oxygen, and feel more relaxed than when you breathe with your chest.

When you lie on the mat, your organs aren't as crunched together as they are when you sit, so there's more room for your diaphragm to move up and down as you breathe. Also, when you're lying down, you'll be able to observe and feel your diaphragm rising and falling. If you put a book or sheet of paper on your abdomen (just below your rib cage), this rise-and-fall motion will become more obvious.

After a few days, when you feel you have gotten the knack

of diaphragmatic breathing while lying down, sit up and breathe. Put your hand lightly on your abdomen. If it swells outward, you know you are breathing correctly.

The number 5 will help you remember how to practice: Inhale deeply to the count of five and exhale to the count of five. Do this five times a day, for approximately five minutes each session. Pause after each exhalation. Breathe as slowly as you are comfortable doing, feeling your lungs filling with each inhalation.

After the first week, instead of repeating the numbers *1* to *5* to yourself, substitute a short phrase. You might say "I feel relaxed" as you inhale, for example, and "I feel calm" as you exhale.

After some practice, you should be able to use deep breathing outside your home. Take a deep breathing break at work when the pressure builds up. Try practicing it when you are driving. Once you become accustomed to using deep breathing, you'll find it's an invaluable tool.

Progressive Relaxation

This technique, which Dr. Edmund Jacobson developed more than 50 years ago, continues to be a well-regarded method for inducing relaxation.

To understand how progressive relaxation works, think of your body as divided into six muscle groups:

1. hands and arms

2. feet and legs

3. lower trunk

4. upper trunk

5. neck and throat

6. face and head

As you focus attention on each of these groups, you will get a sense of how your muscles feel when they are tense and how they feel when they are relaxed.

People experience tension in different parts of their bodies. Some feel it in their shoulders; others get a stiff neck, an aching lower back, or a tight scalp. These exercises will help you recognize which muscle groups get tense in your body. After a while, you may want to isolate the area or areas that affect you and practice tensing and relaxing those particular muscle groups.

While you tense and relax your muscles, you will repeat certain key phrases to yourself. Ultimately, you will be able to eliminate the tensing part of the exercises and relax simply by repeating the calming words or phrases. At that point—in what is a good example of the mind-body connection—you will have associated mental thoughts with a resulting physical action. Of course, this ability to relax on cue will take a lot of practice, but once you become proficient, relaxation should be automatic.

In time you will become adept at recognizing the physical signs of anxiety when they first begin. If you learn to use progressive relaxation as soon as you notice your muscles tensing, your anxiety won't get out of hand. As this technique becomes part of your life, you will become a more relaxed person.

Practicing Progressive Relaxation

You'll need the same quiet environment and unrestricted clothing that you used for deep breathing. You can either sit in a comfortable chair or recliner or lie on a mat. If you are lying on a mat, keep your arms at your sides and your palms turned upward.

Practice twice a day, 20 minutes each time. One session should be in the morning and one in the evening, but avoid practicing right before bedtime (you don't want to fall asleep during your relaxation exercise) or within two hours after mealtime (the body is busy digesting food at that time and you won't get the same benefit). Don't set an alarm—after a while you'll be able to tell when 20 minutes have passed.

Close your eyes and take a couple of deep, calming breaths. Then, tense your hands and arms, making a tight fist. Hold the tension for 10 to 15 seconds while you repeat over and over "Hold it. Hold it. Feel the tension." You might feel your fingers trembling from the tension at this point.

Gradually relax the tension as you say "Relax, relax, let it go, let it go." You'll feel the tension leaving your hands and arms. Now say, "My hands and arms are becoming more relaxed." Go through the same procedure, tensing and then relaxing the muscles in your feet and legs; your abdomen, buttocks, and lower back; your upper trunk including your shoulders; your neck and throat; and your face and scalp. Remember to repeat the appropriate phrases as you tense and relax each muscle group.

End by tightening the muscles in your whole body, saying, "Tighten, tighten everything. Hold it. Hold it." Now slowly release the tension as you say "Relax, relax, let it go, let it go." When the tension has left your body say "My body feels relaxed."

As you practice progressive relaxation, you'll feel a sensation of warmth as well as relaxation. When you've finished, lie quietly for a few minutes.

You'll probably practice this technique for at least three weeks before you see any noticeable benefit, although you may certainly see some benefits earlier. The longer you practice, the more proficient you will become. After several months you will be ready to achieve relaxation using only the relaxing phrases. Your body will remember the tensing exercises that you have eliminated.

Visualization

During visualization you'll replace distressing thoughts with calming ones by conjuring up pleasant scenes and images. Like the other relaxation techniques, visualization results in reduced stress. The less stress you experience, the lower your risk for a panic attack.

To use visualization effectively, you first need to get into a relaxed state by doing deep breathing for five minutes. Then picture a peaceful scene, a place associated with pleasant memories, someplace where you can detach from the stress of life, let go of anything bothering you, and feel refreshed and rejuvenated. Many people choose a beach scene because of the calming effect it has on them. Walking in the woods runs a close second, while a country scene comes in third. When concentrating on one of these tranquil scenes, it's hard to think about whatever is causing anxiety.

Practice visualization twice a day. Some people enjoy a routine in which they use deep breathing, progressive relaxation, and visualization in one session. For 20 minutes twice a day they practice a set that begins with 5 minutes of deep breathing, followed by 10 minutes of progressive relaxation, and finishing with 5 minutes of visualization.

Whichever way you practice visualization, be sure to make it part of your routine; don't just use it when you are stressed. Incorporating visualization into your life will eventually help you feel calmer. You'll be able to add it to your repertoire of tools and use it to relax whenever you feel an attack coming on.

Practicing Visualization

Use the same room in which you practice deep breathing and progressive relaxation. After you have relaxed with deep breathing, choose a scene that you find extremely calming, one that you can recall in great detail. The more detail you can put into it, the more realistic and useful your scene will be.

These questions will help you remember details that may be hazy:

- What time of year is it in your scene?

- What time of day?

- What is the weather?

- What does the sky look like? (Are there puffy white clouds, for example, or is it cloudless?)

- Is your scene predominantly dark or light? What colors does it contain? Are they vivid or subdued?

- What are the prominent features of your scene (sand, sky, water, for instance)?

- What are some of the less noticeable features (a sailboat, a surfer, a baby with a pail, perhaps)?

Describe your scene using all your senses, so that you'll visualize not only what you see, but also what you hear, feel, smell, and taste. For example, a beach scene might include the sounds of seagulls flying above and waves hitting the shore; the salty taste of the air and water; the distinctive smell of ocean air; and the feel of ocean spray, warm sun, and sand crunching beneath your feet.

The more you practice, the more expert you will become in using visualization.

Systematic Desensitization

Systemic densensitization (somethimes called imagery desensitization) uses visualization to help you to diminish anxiety about a particular situation by gradually replacing that anxiety with feelings of relaxation. This is done in three steps:

1. Make a hierarchical list of different scenes of a feared situation.

2. Visualize yourself in each scene.

3. Use relaxation techniques to reduce the fear.

One of the main features of desensitization is the hierarchy you create by imagining the least dreaded scenes first. When you can feel relaxed while imagining one scene, it is time to move on to a scene you fear slightly more. The list generally comprises 10 to 12 scenes. After each scene, you will use relaxation techniques such as deep breathing. Eventually you should be able to tackle your fear in real life.

Like many people with panic disorder, you may also have a public-speaking phobia. What could be worse, you reason, than the possibility of having a panic attack with so many people looking at you? Using desensitization, you could start by picturing yourself practicing the speech. After you feel relaxed about that picture, you might visualize visiting the empty auditorium in which you will be speaking, and so on. Here's how the complete hierarchy might look:

- Practice the speech in front of a mirror.

- Check out the room in which you'll be speaking. You might stand on the podium and test the microphone.

- Practice your speech in front of a family member or a close friend.

- Practice the speech before a small group of people you know well.

- Enter the auditorium.

- Hear your name called to speak.

- Walk up to the podium.

- Stand in front of the microphone.

- Look out at a small audience.

- Give the speech to a small audience.

- Look out at a larger group.

- Give the speech to this larger group.

You may find that it takes some discipline to practice desensitization; the situations you will be visualizing are ones that make you anxious, ones that you would rather run from. But persistence is important. If you keep your goal in mind—freedom from what you fear—then it will be easier for you to keep going.

Practicing desensitization eases the stress of actually facing the dreaded situation, since the relaxation you will begin to feel while imagining your scenes will eventually transfer over to real life.

Like the other behavioral techniques, desensitization is extremely useful in dealing with anticipatory anxiety because it keeps the anxiety from becoming overwhelming. As we've noted, patients with anticipatory anxiety expect that they will continue to experience anxiety about whatever caused them anxiety in the past. Both Jane and Monica had panic attacks in the supermarket and were conditioned to feel fear in (and consequently to avoid) those situations.

But behaviorists believe that what has been conditioned can be reconditioned. In reconditioning, you unlearn the connection between your anxiety and a particular situation. It doesn't matter how you learned this connection, you can unlearn it.

Practicing Systematic Desensitization

Think of something that you fear and make a hierarchy of 10 or 12 scenes relating to this fear. Your list should begin with the least feared scene and progress, step by step, to the most feared scene.

If you have trouble deciding on which step a scene belongs, think of your reaction to it. You should have the least fear of the least dreaded scene, with your reactions increasing in intensity as you progress through the hierarchy. The most dreaded scene should produce the strongest reaction.

Let's use anxiety about going to the mall as an illustration since many people with panic disorder fear crowds and large spaces. They frequently worry about what they would do if they had a panic attack in such a situation. Some say they have had panic attacks while walking through a mall and believe they will have another attack if they try again. They are afraid that they will be unable to find their way out and become trapped while having a panic attack.

First you need to create a hierarchy. The following is an example:

- See the mall from the outside.

- Enter the mall with a friend.

- Walk around near the exit with your friend.

- Look at a map of the mall with your friend.

- Walk past a few stores with your friend.

- Walk half the length of the mall and back with your friend.

- Walk the length of the mall and back with your friend.

- Walk through the mall, and stop in stores, with your friend.

- Spend half a day in the mall with your friend.

- Go to the mall alone and practice the last few steps.

Begin practicing desensitization by getting into a relaxed state, using either deep breathing or progressive relaxation. Next, envision a peaceful scene, similar to the way you did when you practiced visualization. By now you should feel quite relaxed.

Envision the first scene of your dreaded situation. In this case, it will be the least frightening aspect of going to the mall: picturing it from outside. Now switch to the peaceful scene that you envisioned earlier and spend some time enjoying the tranquility while you talk to yourself, saying "I am calm and relaxed."

After a few minutes, when you feel calm and relaxed, you can move up the hierarchy. Now picture yourself entering the mall with a friend. To combat the anxiety that you will inevitably feel, switch back to the peaceful scene and the self-talk.

Wait until you feel relaxed. Then picture yourself walking near the exit of the mall with your friend; follow this with the peaceful scene and self-talk.

When you feel relaxed, envision looking at a map of the mall with your friend. Then flick on the peaceful scene and your self-talk again.

After you feel relaxed, move up to the next scene in which you and your friend walk past a few stores. Follow this, again, with the peaceful scene and self-talk.

When you are relaxed, you're going to picture yourself walking half the length of the mall and back with your friend. Now, picture your peaceful scene and use your self-talk. You should feel yourself becoming calm.

As you climb the hierarchy, you'll visualize both of you walking through the mall, then stopping in stores as you walk through, and, finally, spending half a day in the mall. Each scene will be followed by your peaceful scene and self-talk. Finally, you will visualize going to the mall alone.

Using your own dreaded situation, follow these same steps. Remember, you can expect to feel some tension when you picture a scene you fear. Before you move to the next step up the ladder, always make sure that your anxiety has diminished and that you feel relaxed.

When you have gone through your entire list of scenes (which will take some time), try the first step of the feared situation in real life and see how you feel. If you feel calm, go on to the next step in real life. If you feel anxious, then visualize the feared scene, followed by your relaxation techniques before trying it in real life again. We'll talk more about this later on in Chapter 20.

Meditation

The ancient Hindu discipline of yoga helps control the body and the mind through postures, breathing, and meditation. Yoga is an excellent relaxation technique, but it requires formal instruction to ensure safety and proper form. For our purposes, then, we will focus only on meditation.

Yoga and Zen Buddhist meditation techniques have been quieting minds and protecting against stress for thousands of years. In recent times these Eastern forms of meditation have become increasingly popular here. Transcendental meditation, or TM, a simple yogic technique, gained many adherents in the 1960s. It involves a secret word or phrase, called a mantra, chosen by the meditator or provided by an instructor. Meditators repeat the mantra over and over in their minds. The purpose is to prevent distracting and worrisome thoughts.

Herbert Benson, M.D., a Harvard cardiologist, studied many different Hindu and Buddhist meditation techniques before deciding on TM as a meditation-yoga model. He developed what he calls the Relaxation Response. Today this technique is virtually synonymous with meditation. It is the one you'll be learning in this section. However, the term *relaxation response* is also used to describe other relaxation techniques such as deep breathing and progressive relaxation.

As you know by now, when you get anxious you experience the fight-or-flight reaction, the inborn response to danger. Your blood pressure increases, your heart rate and breathing speed up, and blood flows to your muscles as your body prepares for battle or escape. People who live with a lot of stress are often in this heightened state of arousal. Not only is this constant arousal emotionally unhealthy, it also poses physical risks such as high blood pressure, heart attack, and stroke.

The Relaxation Response helps counter the effects of the fight-or-flight response by bringing about bodily changes that decrease heart rate, lower blood pressure, and decrease rate of breathing.[6] By using the Relaxation Response, you can control or block the tension, anxiety, or fear that is causing these increased bodily functions.

The Relaxation Response also offers additional benefits. Some people say that it makes them feel mentally sharper. Others report that their senses are more acute, that they have an increased sense of awareness, feel more rested, and have an enhanced feeling of well-being.

Practicing Meditation

The four elements of meditation are:

1. A quiet environment with no distractions. Sound, even background noise, may prevent the elicitation of the Relaxation Response.

2. A word or phrase (mantra), repeated silently, on which you will concentrate. Some people use the word *one* or *love*. Repeat your mantra every time you exhale.

3. Maintaining a passive attitude. If distracting thoughts enter your mind, don't get upset. Just return to your mantra.

4. A comfortable position. A comfortable chair and restful position will help reduce muscular effort, making you better able to relax. You can remove your shoes and prop up your feet, if you like. Clothing should be comfortable.[7]

Close your eyes, relax your muscles, breathe slowly through your nose, and repeat your mantra.

Make sure to maintain a passive attitude. Trying too hard will just make you tense. If that speech you have to give comes into your mind, just go back to your mantra. Don't try to judge your performance or force your response.

Practice 10 to 20 minutes once or twice daily but not within two hours after a meal, since the digestive process seems to interfere with the elicitation of the Relaxation Response. Also, don't practice right before bedtime because you might fall asleep; sleeping is not the same as meditating.

You can open your eyes to check the time but don't use an alarm. Sit quietly for a few minutes after you finish, first with eyes closed, and then with eyes open.[8]

As you practice the Relaxation Response, you will be turning your attention inward and away from the events and problems to which you usually attend. When you are concentrating on your mantra, you can't think about what is making you anxious.

Biofeedback

Biofeedback allows patients with stress-related ailments to see the physical results of their efforts to achieve relaxation. We include biofeedback in this section because it is a valuable self-help tool. But, unlike the other relaxation techniques, which you can learn on your own, this technique requires instruction from someone trained in biofeedback before you can use it yourself. At the end of this section we'll tell you how to find a biofeedback therapist.

The concept of biofeedback will perhaps be clearer if you think about the uses of feedback in other areas of your life. If you've ever been on a diet, you have no doubt stepped on the scale to see how much weight you lost. When you have the flu, you take your temperature; the thermometer tells you if you have a fever. When you drive, you look at the speedometer to see how fast you are going. In each of these situations, you take certain steps depending on the feedback you receive. You may cut back on calories to lose more weight, see a doctor for the fever, or ease up on the accelerator.

Biofeedback works in a similar way. The root *bio* refers to any living organism; hence, the word *biofeedback* refers to the feedback of biological information. Experts believe that we can exert a certain amount of control over our autonomic nervous system; you already know this if you have begun practicing any of the relaxation exercises. When you use these tools, you can feel your muscles relaxing, your breathing and heart rate slowing down, and the tension draining from your body. Biofeedback can give you tangible evidence that you have relaxed.

Experts believe that some patients, whose bodies are repeatedly aroused, have forgotten how to relax. Biofeedback is aimed at changing these habitual reactions to stress. The information you receive from the monitor helps you recognize a relaxed state. It also acts as a reward for reduced tension. Biofeedback is particularly useful for patients with panic disorder, since they typically have an elevated baseline level of anxiety. Regularly practicing relaxation techniques increases a person's resistance to anxiety; biofeedback confirms the results. You can be confident that progressive relaxation, for example, is producing a state of relaxation if you do biofeedback with it.

In addition, biofeedback can be individually suited to each patient. People experience anxiety in different ways; these include sweating, cold hands and feet, tension around the jaw, rapid heartbeat, and rapid breathing. After testing and observation, biofeedback therapists can match relaxation techniques and biofeedback training to the individual. For instance, a patient who experiences a rapid heartbeat when she has a panic attack can learn abdominal breathing. Biofeedback lets her observe the way her heart rate increases when she breathes with her chest and how it slows down when she breathes abdominally.

Biofeedback not only validates the patient's complaint by providing feedback about tension, it also monitors progress and creates performance goals. Because panic disorder patients are typically goal-oriented type A personalities, they enjoy trying to improve their performance. If their hands are warmed to 91 degrees (extremities warm up during relaxation), they feel motivated to try to reach 92 degrees during the next session.

Practicing Biofeedback

In a biofeedback session electrodes are attached painlessly to fingers, neck, or forehead. A wire carries information about stress indicators like skin temperature, perspiration, heart rate, or muscle tension from the electrodes to a computer monitor. There are a variety of ways to see the results. You may watch the readings on a graph, see a flashing light bulb, or hear clicks as the therapist guides you through relaxation exercises, such as deep breathing, progressive relaxation, or visualization. When you see the flashing or clicking, you know how well you are relaxing.

The feedback increases your ability to know your own body and to voluntarily control certain body processes so that eventually you will be able to lower your heart rate, slow your breathing, or warm your hands and feet without the equipment. After completing biofeedback training, you may want to monitor your progress at home with a portable unit such as a commercially available temperature-measuring strip that is placed in your open palm.

To begin learning biofeedback, you need to find a psychotherapist or doctor who has been trained to use the technique. You will probably need eight to ten sessions of training. Speak to your family doctor for a referral or send a self-addressed stamped envelope to the Biofeedback Society of America, 10200 West 44th Ave., Suite 304, Wheat Ridge, Colorado 80033.

Cognitive Therapy

*Y*our beliefs are formed when you are young. Some of these beliefs are negative and destructive; they imply that the world is unsafe and that there is much to fear. As we've noted, it's often a mother or main caregiver who inadvertently instills these perceptions. The distorted beliefs produce fears that can contribute to panic attacks. To recover from panic disorder, it's essential to correct faulty thinking.

You might consider your thinking—or cognitions—as the way you talk to yourself. Cognition also involves pictures you form in your mind of your thoughts. The self-talk and pictures, when faulty, can cause you to act inappropriately.[1]

Cognitive therapy will help you change your distorted thinking so that it becomes more positive and realistic. The purpose of the therapy is to help you talk to yourself more accurately and form more realistic pictures in your mind. Your mood and behavior will improve as a result, and you will be able to prevent panic attacks or reduce their incidence.

According to Dr. Herbert Benson, cognitive therapy changes beliefs and attitudes, as well as thoughts. That makes sense since cognition refers to what a person knows and perceives. Taken in this broader sense, cognitive therapy, ideally, results in more positive attitudes and a better outlook on life.[2]

Cognitive therapy was developed by Dr. Aaron T. Beck more than 30 years ago at the Beck Institute for Cognitive Therapy and Research in suburban Philadelphia. It is a short-term treatment, typically requiring three months. As we've noted, it is usually combined with behavioral therapy in a treatment referred to as cognitive-behavioral therapy or CBT.

Treatment with this therapy produces noticeable gains for most patients.[3] And the results are long-lasting. One study found that 85 percent of patients had experienced no panic attacks at a 15-month follow-up;[4] in another study, more than 86 percent of patients were panic-free after two years.[5] Other data show relatively low rates of relapse among panic disorder patients who are treated with cognitive-behavioral therapy.[6] According to many studies, CBT is as effective for calming anxieties as other therapies and/or medication.

One advantage of cognitive therapy is that patients treated with it may not require medication. That's a benefit since non-drug approaches are generally safer. One study showed that the use of psychotropic medication (antidepressants and tranquilizers) during CBT for panic disorder actually produced a poorer outcome than treatment without medication. That's probably because certain medications prevent the evocation of anxiety necessary for cognitive-behavioral therapy to work.[7]

Cognitive therapy involves direct intervention and dialogue with the therapist, who teaches strategies for coping with anxiety. If you decide to use cognitive therapy, make sure to choose a therapist who is specially trained in the discipline.

Your therapist will teach you how to deal with the automatic, fear-provoking thoughts that flash through your mind. These thoughts are specific to a situation and you accept them without question. While giving a speech, for instance, you might get dizzy and think that you will fall off the podium. Thinking you will faint is the distortion in this case. In another situation, palpitations might cause the distorted thought that you are having a heart attack.

Sometimes multiple negative thoughts flash through your mind. The thoughts cause your heart to race, and your racing heart makes you feel anxious. The anxiety then triggers more physical symptoms. The entire incident may take just three seconds.

In panic disorder it's typical to lose perspective. Everything seems alarming, and you overreact to what others would consider minor situations. Cognitive therapy helps you to recognize why you are so scared and prevents you from becoming overwhelmed. (Of course, sometimes negative thoughts are appropriate; it's when they are the result of faulty logic that they need to be corrected.)

A significant example of an inappropriate thought stemming from faulty logic is the idea that you are out of control during a panic attack. Actually, you don't lose control when you panic; you just function in a different way, a way that gives you a form of emergency control.

The therapist will ask you to observe the thoughts that come into your mind when you are anxious and to make note of them. Then the two of you will work on each one to try to correct it. Together you will examine statements like "The pounding in my heart comes from a bad heart." You will start to become skeptical about negative thoughts instead of accepting them as pure facts. Once you learn to recognize that physical symptoms like palpitations or dizziness will not cause you to die, faint, or have a heart attack, these symptoms will lose their power over you.

To help you identify distorted thoughts, your therapist will ask you questions. If you fear that your pounding heart will result in a heart attack, the therapist might ask, "Do you have a history of heart disease? Have you ever had a heart attack? Has your heart ever slowed down or stopped beating?" If you fear fainting while giving a speech, the therapist's questions might include "What's the evidence that you'll faint while standing on the podium? Have you ever fainted? Do you faint regularly?" Questions like these will help you to see that your dire thoughts are exaggerated and illogical.

Dr. Claire Weekes, the eminent authority and pioneer in the field of panic disorder, pointed out that, although people whom she called "nervously ill" may *feel* faint, few actually faint. To truly collapse, she said, one's blood pressure must fall dramatically. But in panic, blood pressure usually goes up, not down.

As for going crazy, she said, no crisis is so great that the sufferer can "go berserk." Any movement or diversion will thwart a crisis. Besides, one thing a self-conscious person does not do is cry out and act in a bizarre manner.[8]

By now you've probably had a physical checkup to eliminate any possibility of a medical cause for your symptoms. In case you haven't, call for an appointment as soon as possible. To relieve your concerns, you can ask your doctor to talk to you about the medical causes of problems that worry you. If you fear having a heart attack, the doctor will explain how heart attacks occur, by discussing clogged arteries, cholesterol, genetics, and other factors. You'll probably find this information reassuring and soothing.

Assuming that there are no medical causes for your symptoms, you will learn to look for alternative explanations for them. (You'll find that it's helpful to write down your distortions and the alternative explanations.) Your pounding heart, for example, could be caused by caffeine, excitement, exercise, or anxiety. As we've seen, bright sunlight and feelings of being trapped can bring on symptoms. Whatever the cause, the symptoms are usually not significant. You get anxious because you attribute your symptoms to something unrealistic. You are most likely more sensitive to bodily changes than other people and are consequently more aware of when your heart beats faster. Cognitive therapy will help you understand that there is no cause for alarm.

The earlier you catch distorted thoughts, the better. That way they won't get out of control. Instead of thinking that the twinge in your chest is a heart attack, you could abort a panic attack by remembering, for instance, that you ate too quickly.

Correcting distorted thoughts takes time, patience, and practice. Practice outside of the therapist's office is essential. In fact, that's where most of the learning takes place.

Some of the techniques that can help you change the way you think include these, suggested by Dr. David Barlow:

1. Decatastrophizing. After examining the faulty logic in your thinking, go a step further and ask yourself "What if the worst thing I fear actually happened?" If you fainted, for example, someone would come to your aid. If you made a mistake while giving your speech, probably no one would notice. And, if they did, so what? Does it really matter what they think?

2. Rescue. This technique helps you become aware of factors such as nearby doctors and hospitals that can help and makes you feel less incapacitated should the improbable happen.

3. Hypothesis testing. With this technique, you write out catastrophic predictions, such as "I won't be able to talk during the speech," and then examine the evidence that either supports or refutes them. You'll then see for yourself that few, if any, of your dire predictions actually happen. Even if you do have a panic attack during your speech, for instance, you'll still be able to function.

4. Reattribution. Like many anxious people, you commonly blame yourself for a particular event instead of considering other causes. This technique will help you reattribute responsibility and understand that some things are out of your control. For example, you may think that people aren't listening to your speech because the panic attack you had in the middle of it caused you to stumble over some words. The

reality may be that their minds were wandering and that they were thinking about something else. [9]

Principles of Cognitive Therapy

These 10 principles developed by Aaron Beck comprise the basis for cognitive therapy.

1. Cognitive therapy is based on a cognitive model.

2. Cognitive therapy is brief and time-limited.

3. A good therapeutic relationship is necessary for effective cognitive therapy.

4. Therapy is a collaborative effort between therapist and patient.

5. Cognitive therapy primarily uses the Socratic method.

6. Cognitive therapy is structured and directive.

7. Cognitive therapy is problem-oriented.

8. Cognitive therapy is based on an educational model.

9. Cognitive therapy relies on the inductive method.

10. Homework is a central feature of cognitive therapy.

Principle 1

In cognitive therapy, the therapist explains to the patient that her anxiety is based on an unrealistic view of the situation: because the patient incorrectly interprets what she is experiencing—her pounding heart, for example—she becomes quite alarmed. Her exaggerated, distorted, automatic thinking might lead her to fear that she is having a heart attack. Cognitive therapy helps to correct the patient's distorted thinking and calm her down.

Principle 2

Cognitive therapy generally requires 5 to 20 sessions over a period of several months. When patients hear that treatment is time-limited, they get the message that their problem is curable. This enhances their motivation and their feelings of hope. Brief therapy also encourages patients' self-sufficiency; when the sessions are over, they have the tools to solve some problems on their own.

Principle 3

For cognitive therapy to work, it's important for the patient to choose a therapist with whom she feels comfortable, someone with whom she can be open, someone she can trust and rely on. She should find the therapist empathetic and supportive.

Principle 4

Cognitive therapy entails collaboration. Therapist and patient work as a team in problem solving. The patient brings the information and the therapist provides the expertise. The patient is encouraged to be an active participant.

Principle 5

Cognitive therapy uses the Socratic method: through questioning, the therapist gains an understanding of the patient's thoughts and distortions, so he or she can help correct them.

This method is more powerful than offering direct suggestions and explanations to the patient.

Principle 6

The cognitive therapist provides structure and direction. When a patient is anxious, she feels out of control. A sense of structure helps her feel more in control; as she regains control, she feels calmer. The therapist, with the patient, sets an agenda for each session and provides a treatment plan that focuses on specific targets: symptom relief, teaching the patient to recognize distorted automatic thoughts, training her to respond logically to these thoughts, and helping her to identify and change long-held incorrect assumptions.

Principle 7

Cognitive therapy helps treat a patient's current problems by identifying and correcting distorted thinking that is causing problematic behavior. (When thinking is distorted, behavior is distorted, too.) The cognitive therapist uses a variety of strategies and tactics; the choices depend on the patient's specific problem. Therapist and patient will assess the treatment's effectiveness.

Principle 8

The cognitive therapist is like a teacher. He or she explains the problem, suggests alternative ways of thinking, assigns homework, and may suggest additional resources such as tapes and lectures. The therapist also helps patients "learn how to learn," that is, how to profit from their experiences and not repeat their mistakes.

Principle 9

The therapist uses a scientific way of thinking about the problem. Therapist and patient look at actual facts and evidence that will negate incorrect thinking.

Principle 10

One of the central features of cognitive therapy is homework. The patient corrects her distorted thinking in the office with the therapist and then practices what she has learned in the real world. Back in the therapist's office, she discusses her recent successes and failures.[10]

Cognitive Distortions

A relationship exists between the way you think and the way you feel. Dr. David Burns asserts that your emotions are a result of the way you look at things. If your understanding of a situation is accurate, your emotions will be normal; but if your perception is distorted, your emotional response will be abnormal.[11]

Although the emotional response Dr. Burns refers to is depression, the same premise holds true for anxiety—the emotion that leads to panic attacks. Cognitive therapists believe that panic disorder sufferers' fear arises from imagined thoughts rather than from real events. To put it another way, the patient's inaccurate perception of what is occurring causes her or him to be afraid. Yet the patient clings to these distorted perceptions because they have become an integral part of her or his life.

For a list of cognitive distortions that Dr. Burns developed, refer to his book *Feeling Good: The New Mood Therapy*. Study these distortions and compare them with your experiences. You will become aware of how unrealistic your thoughts are. You'll also find Dr. Barlow's four techniques (decatastrophizing, rescue, hypothesis testing, and reattribution) helpful in correcting your distortions.

Coping Strategies

To help correct your distorted thinking, you need to change the way you talk to yourself—or what some cognitive therapists call self-talk.

What exactly is self-talk? It's what you tell yourself about what you experience. Self-talk comprises automatic thoughts, but these thoughts are not necessarily the truth. For instance, the inner voice saying, "I'm about to faint" comes from the automatic thought that the dizziness you experience will cause you to faint.

Self-talk is fast and can consist of a number of messages such as "My head is spinning," "I can't keep my balance," "I'm going to fall over," "I'm losing control," or "I'm going to faint." You use self-talk until it eventually becomes a pattern.

Like many people with panic disorder, you probably engage in a lot of negative self-talk, which only serves to worsen your symptoms and to cause you to avoid certain situations. You feel an ever-present sense of danger when you walk around with all those negative thoughts in your head.

Begin changing negative self-talk by recognizing your distorted thinking. Write down thoughts you have before and during a panic attack. You'll notice that you tend to repeat the same anxiety-provoking thoughts and that you say the same things over and over to yourself.[12]

Think about where your thoughts are coming from and why you are having them. Are they the result of negative thoughts that your parents held? What triggers the thoughts? A room with a closed door? A moving vehicle? Understanding the source of your negative thoughts can help lessen their impact.

While you can't change your experiences, you can change the way you think about them. If you get stuck in an elevator, for example, instead of thinking "I will be trapped, have a panic attack, and suffocate," you could say "The phone works; I'll be rescued in just a short time."

Realize that negative thoughts are not facts. Look for evidence that will refute them. When you find this evidence, you'll see that what you fear is unrealistic and improbable. If you think that you'll faint while riding on a department store escalator, try it out. When you see that you made it to the second floor still standing on your feet, you'll understand the distortion and you'll start to think positively and talk to yourself differently. Before getting on an escalator again, your statement can change from "I'm going to faint" to "I know that I can do this."

Negative statements often arise from worrying about what could happen. So in place of the what-ifs that are so common to self-talk—for example, "What if I have a panic attack while I'm in the supermarket?"—try saying "So what?" as in "So what if I have a panic attack in the supermarket? I can handle it."

Whenever you can, phrase your statements in a positive way, so that they say "I'm calm" rather than "I'm not nervous," for example. For this strategy to work, you need to really believe the statements. But once you check out your negative thoughts so that you know they are unrealistic, you should have no problem believing your positive self-talk.[13]

To recover from panic disorder, you need to get into the habit of changing negative self-talk into positive self-talk. Here are some typical negative statements and the ways that you can turn them around:

"I'll have a terrible time at this party. I don't know anyone."

"This is a chance to meet new people. It might be fun."

"The supermarket is so big. I'm going to panic when I shop."	"I know exactly what I need. I can do the job."
"There's a line at the car wash. I'll feel trapped."	"The line will move quickly. It will be nice to have a clean car."
"What if I have a panic attack during the meeting? Everyone will notice."	"So what if I have a panic attack during the meeting? I can function anyway. And no one will notice."

To use this strategy in various situations, choose positive statements that have meaning to you, write them down, put them on tape if you like, learn them, and practice them. You can carry them around with you on index cards and use them before you are about to do something that is apt to cause you anxiety. Start using them in the early stages of anxiety, before it becomes overwhelming. It's a good idea to elicit the help of a coach—your husband or a close friend—who will remind you to use your coping statements.

You can repeat general statements like the following until they become almost like slogans:

I can do it.

I can handle it.

I can cope.

Easy does it.

Talking to yourself in a calming way will make you feel more in control.

Along with positive self-talk, you can use relaxation techniques. If going to the supermarket makes you anxious, do deep breathing when you enter the store. You can also try to distract yourself by thinking of the task at hand; you might think about the items you are buying and what aisle they are in. Or you might try to distract yourself by thinking of something entirely different. While waiting in line to check out your purchases, pick up a magazine that's on display and thumb through it. If anxiety-provoking thoughts enter your mind, you can picture a stop sign to deter them. Stay in the present and don't focus on a panic attack you had in the past or on what could happen in the next hour or so.

You may feel some anxiety but that's OK. As you recover, you'll learn that anxiety is just anxiety, nothing more. Symptoms like dizziness or a pounding heart are unpleasant but they aren't harmful. In fact, you may work with a therapist who will purposely evoke frightening symptoms by having you hyperventilate or run up and down stairs, for instance. Experiences like these could cause physical symptoms that might make you anxious, but you'll see that the symptoms aren't dangerous. In fact, you need to experience anxiety in order to learn to control it. You may feel that you can't cope with your symptoms, but you can. Don't underestimate your abilities.

Here are 10 rules for coping with panic that were developed by Dr. Andrew Mathews. Following them will make it easier for you to stay with the fear and make progress toward recovery.

1. The feelings are normal bodily reactions.

2. They are not harmful.

3. Do not add frightening thoughts.

4. Notice what is happening, not what might happen.

5. Wait for the fear to pass.

6. Notice when it fades.

7. It is an opportunity for progress.

8. Think of what you have done.

9. Plan what to do next.

10. Start off slowly.[14]

To help you adhere to Dr. Mathews's rules and to change your pattern of negative self-talk, try these coping statements.

1. The feelings are normal bodily reactions.

My heartbeat speeds up when I'm stressed.

I'm a little tense today; it will pass.

I'm breathing a little faster because I'm nervous.

The tightness in my chest is the way I react to anxiety.

My stomach acts up when I'm under pressure.

2. They are not harmful.

These symptoms aren't dangerous.

I'm going to live.

I don't have a serious illness.

Anxiety doesn't kill anyone.

It's uncomfortable but not serious.

3. Do not add frightening thoughts.

I can distract myself.

I have control over what I think.

I'll think positively.

I'll think of something pleasant.

I'll think of health and wellness.

4. Notice what is happening, not what might happen.

I'm going to focus on how I feel now.

I have some symptoms but that's OK.

I can cope with these symptoms.

I'm relaxing my muscles.

I'm slowing down my breathing.

5. **Wait for the fear to pass.**

   I'm frightened, but so what?

   I know the fear will stay awhile.

   I've gone through this before and survived it.

   I can manage even though I'm anxious.

   I know these symptoms will pass.

6. **Notice when it fades.**

   My heart has stopped pounding.

   I'll watch the fear rise and then fall.

   It's already getting better.

   I feel myself becoming more relaxed.

   I'm gaining control.

7. **It is an opportunity for progress.**

   I need to feel this anxiety in order to get better.

   It's time to face my fear.

   Each time I face my fear, I feel stronger.

   I'm making progress day by day.

   I become less frightened each time that I feel the anxiety.

8. **Think of what you have done.**

   It really worked.

   I'm so proud of myself.

   I did better than I thought I would.

   I'm more relaxed.

   I'm looking forward to trying again.

9. **Plan what to do next.**

   I'm going to continue to work on my distorted thinking.

   I'm going to use my coping statements.

   I'll use deep breathing.

I'm going to use visualization.

I'll continue to fight my fear.

10. Start off slowly.

I won't take on too much at one time.

I have to remember to take it slow.

I know that at times I'll feel anxious.

I'll take it step by step.

I realize that recovery will take time.

Medication

*M*edical treatment for panic disorder has come a long way since the time when doctors could offer little except sedatives to "calm the nerves." Today there are a variety of drugs from which to choose. In this chapter we'll discuss the ones most often prescribed and examine the pros and cons of taking medication for panic disorder.

Medications for panic disorder fall into four categories: tricyclic antidepressants, monoamine oxidase inhibitor antidepressants, selective serotonin reuptake inhibitor antidepressants, and benzodiazepine tranquilizers. Let's look at the advantages and disadvantages of each group.

- Tricyclic antidepressants (TCAS). These drugs block panic attacks but have little effect on anticipatory anxiety and agoraphobia. They lessen the depression that panic disorder patients often suffer, and they don't lead to physical dependence. The best-known drug in this group is Tofranil (imipramine). Others are Anafranil (clomipramine) and Desyrel (trazodone). Possible side effects include jitteriness, difficulty sleeping, nausea, dizziness, headache, dry mouth, constipation, and weight gain. Most of these side effects disappear or lessen after a few weeks. To minimize side effects, patients start taking TCAS in small amounts and work their way up to therapeutic doses. The medication must be taken every day and may take up to four weeks to work.

- Monoamine oxidase inhibitor antidepressants (MAOIS). This class of antidepressants also blocks panic attacks without physical dependence. The MAOI most studied is Nardil (phenelzine). Research suggests that it may be even more effective than imipramine, especially for severe cases of agoraphobia and panic disorder.[1] But because of the serious side effects that can result when MAOIS interact with foods and medications that contain a substance called tyramine, they are prescribed mainly for patients who don't respond to other medications.

- Selective serotonin reuptake inhibitor antidepressants (SSRIS). This newest group of drugs currently is prescribed more often than any of the other groups. SSRIS have won acclaim for treatment of panic disorder because they are as effective as TCAS but have fewer side effects. And they don't lead to dependency or withdrawal symptoms. Drugs in this group include Prozac (fluoxetine); Zoloft (sertraline); Paxil (paroxetene), which was recently approved by the Food and Drug Administration (FDA) for treatment of panic disorder; and Luvox (fluvoxamine).

- Benzodiazepine tranquilizers (BZs). Used to prevent panic attacks and treat anticipatory anxiety, these drugs reduce anxiety quickly and can be taken as needed rather than on a set schedule. The most well-known of the group is Xanax (alprazolam), the first drug approved by the FDA to treat panic disorder. Others BZs are Ativan (lorazepam) and Klonopin (clonazepam). While BZs have fewer side effects than TCAS, patients can become dependent on them, developing anxiety and other serious side effects when they try to get off the medication, especially if they have been taking high doses for long periods of time. To prevent these withdrawal symptoms, patients need to taper off these drugs gradually. It is rare, however, for someone with panic disorder to become truly addicted. After discontinuing BZs, patients may experience a short-term rebound effect of intense panic symptoms.

The Benefits of Medication

If you are in severe distress and unable to function because your panic attacks are so intense and/or so frequent, then medication, rather than cognitive-behavioral therapy (CBT) should be your first line of defense. While both medication and CBT claim a high success rate, medication will relieve your symptoms and, some experts believe, help you take control more quickly.

Medication is also appropriate if your anticipatory anxiety becomes so severe that you begin avoiding certain situations, and are at risk for developing agoraphobia; if you are very depressed; or if you have chronic, severe anxiety.

There's no doubt that medication can provide symptom relief and give you the confidence you need to face the world without fear of having a panic attack. Dr. Mark Gold, a biopsychiatrist and pioneering researcher into the brain mechanisms that produce anxiety disorders, maintains that given proper diagnosis and a treatment plan tailored to the individual (that is, the right drug, proper dosage, and proper duration of therapy), biopsychiatry (a psychiatric subspecialty that treats both body and mind) can approach a success rate of 90 to 95 percent for panic disorder.[2] Some other experts, however, feel that Gold's statistics are exaggerated.

Medication Versus Therapy

Many people with panic disorder resist medication. To them it represents weakness and loss of control. They worry about side effects and are concerned about what will happen when they stop taking their medication. Many are simply opposed to taking drugs.

These are valid concerns. Medications can cause adverse effects. And the relapse rate is high once medication is stopped; patients are likely to have panic attacks again and need another round of medication.[3,4] In addition, BZs can cause physical dependence, with the risk of withdrawal symptoms when the drug is stopped.

Other problems should to be considered, too. Medication can somewhat interfere with exposure therapy and CBT. During these forms of treatment, you need to feel the fear in order to learn to cope with it. But medication will lessen sensations of fear, creating a treatment dilemma. Furthermore, BZs can affect short-term memory, somewhat interfering with cognitive therapy.[5]

If you are pregnant or planning to become pregnant you should opt for therapy instead of medication to prevent risk to your fetus.

The issue of medication versus therapy has sparked much controversy among experts. Those who favor medication contend that many patients may have difficulty managing psychological approaches because they can't tolerate the fear they must endure for CBT and exposure therapy to work. They say that CBT creates a willingness to stoically endure or reframe symptoms rather than eradicate them.[6]

Panic disorder is a chronic condition with a genetic cause and cannot be relieved by therapy, they assert. They say it is best treated with medication over a period of time. While Dr. Gold, for example, concedes that behavior therapy alone relieves anticipatory anxiety and diminishes avoidant behavior, he believes that it leaves the actual cause of panic attack untreated. He says that panic attacks eventually return after behavioral treatment, leaving patients with a sense of failure.[7]

He adds that many people benefit from medication, and maintains that the risk of side effects is minimal when medication is started at low doses. As for the question of control, he says that these medications do not make patients lose control; instead, they give patients control over their actions by preventing panic.[8]

Cognitive therapists believe that while medication relieves symptoms, it doesn't eliminate panic on a permanent basis or teach coping skills. They say patients need to learn to rely on their own efforts to achieve lasting gains.

As for the theory that panic disorder should be treated with medication because it has a genetic basis, therapy advocates argue that psychological treatments can help biologically based problems. Cognitive-behavioral therapist Dr. Michael Otto notes that CBT creates important changes in brain activity.[9]

In response to the argument that panic disorder is a chronic condition needing long-term medication treatment, Otto questions why it appears to be a chronic condition when treated with medication but not when treated by CBT. He speculates that the conclusion is biased by the high rates of relapse that occur when drugs are discontinued.[10]

While both Otto and Gold vehemently argue their case, both do agree that, despite the drawbacks, CBT should be used in conjunction with medication. The relatively new field of biopsychiatry, while emphasizing the biological origins of panic disorder, embraces treatment plans that incorporate the best of both therapy- and medication-based psychiatry.

Research supports anecdotal evidence showing that the combination of medication and therapy works well. When used in concert the two treatments relieve symptoms completely in approximately 30 to 40 percent of patients and reduce them significantly in another 50 percent. Only 10 to 20 percent of patients continue to have symptoms severe enough to interfere with their daily lives, according to one report.[11] Other research found that 80 percent of patients who received 15 weeks of therapy plus a nine-month course of the tricyclic drug Anafranil (clomipramine) were free of panic attacks, compared with 25 percent of those who received only the drug.[12]

When and How to Use Medication

If your illness is severe, your physician will probably prescribe medication—most likely, an SSRI or a TCA. You'll start on a low dose and then gradually increase it, taking the medication daily for at least six months. If you suffer a relapse after stopping the medication, you'll need to resume taking it.

For avoidant behavior and anticipatory anxiety, your doctor may prescribe a BZ tranquilizer. You'll also need CBT and exposure therapy.

If your situation is less severe, it's probably best to start with therapy. You may find that you don't need medication at all. If you do, though, you should try to delay taking it until you've learned some coping skills. (Remember, medication will block some of the fear you need to experience while learning those skills.) When you eventually go off the medication, you'll have the tools you need should panic strike.

Patients sometimes feel that they are not responding to medication. The reasons behind the failure to respond are often easily corrected. If you think that your medication isn't helping, one of the following could be the cause:

You may be neglecting to combine treatment with CBT.

You may be taking too low a dose.

You may need a different drug.

You may not be waiting long enough for the medicine to work.

You may be mistaking anticipatory anxiety for actual panic attacks.

Your doctor must prescribe the right medication in the correct dosage for the right length of time. She or he may need to adjust the dosage or switch medications.

That leads to the question of which doctor to choose. You may be more comfortable talking to your family doctor than to a therapist. If you do, you take the chance of getting a prescription for medication without much therapy. According to one report, only half the people who relied on their family doctors for help were highly satisfied with treatment, compared with 62 percent who were highly satisfied with treatment by someone in the mental-health field.[13]

When it comes to emotional problems, it seems that family doctors may not be the most effective source of help. The patients surveyed said their doctors didn't have the time to discuss emotional issues. Other research found that the family doctors failed to diagnose 50 to 80 percent of psychological problems, and sometimes prescribed psychiatric drugs for too short a time or at doses too low to work.[14]

What's more, if you begin treatment with your family doctor, you may not go on to consult with a specialist. The first report found that family doctors referred their patients to a mental health specialist in only one out of four cases. Sixty percent of patients with panic disorder or phobias were never referred.[15]

You're better off seeking the help of a therapist who can refer you to a psychiatrist if medication is indicated. Make sure you are aware of all your options involving both medication and therapy so you can take part in decisions about your treatment.

Exposure Therapy

*A*fter you've done some imagery desensitization and practiced deep breathing, you're ready to use exposure therapy, a treatment that's an elaboration of a behavioral technique called flooding.

Flooding is sudden exposure to a feared situation, somewhat like being thrown into a pool when you are afraid of water. Unlike exposure therapy, which is gradual, flooding exposes you to the feared situation all at once. In treatment with flooding, someone afraid of elevators wouldn't overcome her fear gradually, the way Barbara did with exposure therapy (see Chapter 15). Instead she would just get on the elevator and ride all the way down.

Gradual exposure, or exposure therapy, is easier on the patient because the feared situation is tackled in small steps. And it's highly effective. It's been proved that prolonged exposure to the feared situation eliminates the fear. Moreover, researchers say that reduction in panic and anxiety during exposure therapy is a good predictor of a successful outcome.[1]

For panic disorder with agoraphobia, exposure therapy is more effective than any other treatment.[2] That's important because agoraphobics don't recover without treatment.[3]

Practicing Exposure Therapy

To achieve success in using exposure therapy you need to play an active part by planning the hierarchy, feeling the anxiety, and practicing the relaxation techniques.

Imagery desensitization has prepared you for exposure therapy; the basic concepts are the same. Perhaps you've also had some in-office exposure therapy, which has helped you build your skills.

When you venture out in the real world to confront your fears, you'll need a therapist or a surrogate (a support person trained to help) to accompany you. Facing fears in the real world can be very alarming. It is reassuring to have this support person nearby, telling you that you are doing a good job, encouraging you to stick with the situation, and assuring you that everything will be fine. This person should be someone whom you respect, trust, like, and feel comfortable with. She or he should be someone to whom you can reveal your fears.

Because it is more frightening to tackle fears in the real world than in the mind, exposure may require a longer hierarchy with more steps than would be used in imagery desensitization. Breaking 10 steps into 15 smaller components entails fewer gradations between the steps. This makes each situation less alarming and ensures a greater chance for success in overcoming the fear. The sense of accomplishment and mastery that you feel in completing each step will encourage you to tolerate the anxiety you are bound to experience and allow you to go on to the next step. When you complete a step or stay with the anxiety longer, reward yourself.

A hierarchy to overcome fear of riding a subway might look like the following.

1. Walk to a nearby subway station with your surrogate.

2. Go down into the station with your surrogate.

3. Go to the token booth with your surrogate and buy some tokens.

4. Go into the station and stand on the platform for three minutes with your surrogate.

5. Watch the trains go by for 10 minutes with your surrogate.

6. Step into a car and go one stop with your surrogate.

7. Get back on and go three stops with your surrogate.

8. Change trains, riding in the second train for two stops.

9. Take a trip to a destination of your choice with your surrogate.

10. Repeat steps 6 through 9 by yourself.

With the help of a therapist, you'll be creating your own hierarchy of goals that can be broken down into small steps, starting with the least feared ones and progressing to the most feared. (At this time avoid tackling goals such as conquering fear of flying, which can't easily be broken down into manageable steps.)

To use exposure therapy successfully, you'll need to do deep breathing before and during each step. Positive self-talk also helps. When you are frightened, you might say calming words or phrases such as "Relax," "Stay calm," "I can stay here till the fear passes," "I can cope with this," "I'm going to get better," "I'm in control," or "I'll be able to manage." Try choosing a favorite slogan, such as "Face the fear" or "This will pass."

Staying with the Situation

As you progress through the hierarchy, you are going to encounter anxiety-provoking situations that you previously avoided. Initially, your fear will increase because you are forcing yourself into these feared situations, and you'll find your-self tempted to run away. Exposure therapy will fight that impulse to escape, to avoid facing the fear.

Of course, it may not always be easy to stay with the situation. To succeed, you'll have to make a real commitment to the treatment. The knowledge that exposure therapy can help you conquer your fear should provide the motivation you need and make enduring the anxiety worthwhile.

Still, there may be situations that you just can't stand. Planning ahead for those difficult times can be helpful. You'll be more relaxed if you think about how you can leave some-place that is overwhelming. Plan an escape route by noticing where the exits are. Being aware of the exit signs will make you feel less trapped in a movie theater, for instance. If you must leave a situation, decide also how you will calm down, where you will go, and how you will return.

It is helpful to know what you can and can't tolerate. When a situation becomes unbearable, leave and use deep breathing and self-talk. Once you are calm, come back to that step or try it another day. Or if that step is insurmountable, go back a step or two to a point where you were successful. Doing so will make you feel less overwhelmed and renew your confidence. Sometimes a step is too large and needs to be broken down into more manageable, less anxiety-provoking steps. If steps are too difficult, the anxiety you feel might overwhelm you and cause you to feel defeated.

A relaxed attitude will help prevent discouragement. Progress is not steady; some days you'll do better than other days. Getting too anxious about lack of progress will only add to the anxiety level. Try not to be negative or worry about how well you will do in the future. Instead, stay in the present.

Even when you're not successful in accomplishing a step, the experience can be useful if you use the opportunity to gather data by observing yourself. You'll notice that at some times you experience more anxiety than at other times. Think about what triggers your anxiety, what it does to you, and how you react to it. Some people react strongly to darkness, bright lights, or strange odors. Others feel anxious in rooms that have few people, or many people, or are very hot or have little air. Looking more objectively at yourself helps you to learn about yourself. As you gain insight, you'll feel more in control and your anxiety will diminish.

It should help to remember that anxiety, like a panic attack, is self-limiting. Eventually it will dissipate. By using exposure therapy, you'll see that frightening feelings do pass and that they are not dangerous. You'll understand that nothing horrendous is going to happen. You won't faint or die; you will survive. With that knowledge, you should feel more comfortable about feeling the anxiety.

Remember, if you don't experience anxiety, you won't get better. You must feel the fear. It is part of the cure. Dr. David Barlow says that it is important to accept, and even exaggerate, the physical problems that arise when you practice. For example, if you enter a situation looking for—and wanting to experience—dizziness, you have already changed your attitude.[4] You no longer have a feeling of dread and a desire to flee. You realize that as you experience and cope with anxiety you are making progress.

To see results, however, you'll need some patience. While exposure therapy has a good track record for treatment of panic disorder with agoraphobia, it takes some time to work. According to Dr. Barlow, "Exposure treatment should be prolonged, repeated, graduated, and planned." In other words, it should incrementally tackle fears, from low stress to high stress, until the anxiety is eliminated.[5]

To help you adhere to treatment with exposure therapy, Elke Zuercher-White, Ph.D., suggests the following:

- Practice often, from three to five days a week. If you experience fear in between sessions, practice at that time, too.

- Plan practice times carefully. Don't say that you'll practice just when you feel like doing it; you may never feel like doing it.

- Even though you may feel anxious, try to stay a few more minutes in a situation. Try not to run away.

- If you work with a coach or therapist, ask that person to tell you how you look when you are anxious. Although you may think everyone notices your anxiety, the reality is that you probably look calmer than you think.[6]

Psychotherapy

*Y*our panic disorder is intricately bound to your emotional life. If you can improve your emotional life, your illness should improve, too. Psychotherapy alleviates emotional problems that can contribute to panic disorder and may be used as an adjunct to other treatments after panic attacks have been lessened.

While cognitive-behavioral therapy is the first line of defense against panic disorder, research suggests that psychotherapy can be an extremely useful weapon in fighting the illness. In a survey of four thousand people with emotional illnesses including panic disorder, almost all of the respondents said that psychotherapy brought some relief and made life more manageable. They made gains in three ways: the problems for which they sought treatment eased; they improved in the way they functioned, worked, related to others, and handled stress; and they experienced increased self-esteem, confidence, self-understanding, and enjoyment of life.[1]

Other studies show that about 50 percent of patients improve after eight sessions of psychotherapy and about 75 percent improve if they stay in psychotherapy for 26 sessions; patients with anxiety tend to respond by the 20th session.[2]

Additional reports indicate that brief psychotherapy may be helpful in treating panic disorder. Post-treatment studies show that patients experience significant improvement with this treatment.[3]

Using psychotherapy as another option for treating panic disorder makes sense. Since the factors that contribute to panic disorder are so diverse, the treatment plan should be multidimensional as well. This allows for the consideration of many contributing causes, including emotional ones.

Psychotherapy doesn't directly relieve the symptoms of panic disorder, but it does help to relieve the anxiety and stress that can lead to panic attacks. In therapy you talk with someone who is professionally trained to help you to deal with your problems in a healthier way. Your therapist's objectivity and expertise can help you identify your self-destructive patterns such as drinking or staying in a bad relationship. A good therapist can help you to understand these problems and correct them. The two of you will decide on your goals and work together to achieve them.

Your therapist may also help you recognize, express, and deal with feelings that you have suppressed, both during sessions and in the outside world. When you can't identify and express feelings, you may cry or act out without knowing why. You just know that something is weighing you down and making you unhappy.

Many women with panic disorder grew up in families where they were discouraged from discussing feelings. If your parents adhered to the old adage "Children should be seen and not heard," then you probably suppressed your feelings. As an adult, you sometimes don't know what you are feeling and that might make you anxious. Some therapists believe that suppressed feelings can contribute to panic attacks; they maintain that panic occurs when these feelings threaten to break through. If you can identify and release some feelings, you can lower your level of anxiety considerably.

Emotional problems frequently have their roots in childhood. Your fear today may stem from the anxiety you felt as a child when you separated from a person who made you feel safe. Maybe you've felt anxious, insecure, and scared ever since your parents' divorce or the death of someone close. Childhood traumas such as physical, mental, or sexual abuse can, of course, cause severe problems later on.

Because panic disorder doesn't occur in a vacuum, just about any severe problem or conflict can put one at risk for developing it. It's also possible for some earlier emotional problem to contribute to one's panic disorder. For example, a young girl's pattern of dependency on her mother might conflict with her need to be assertive. This conflict could lead to much anxiety and guilt, causing a possible susceptibility to panic attacks as an adult. Feeling safe with her therapist, she can gain insight into this conflict and relieve her anxiety.

You might be not be aware of what a toxic environment you grew up in until you start exploring some life issues. Once you begin, you'll see that you may have to make significant changes in order to recover from panic disorder.[4]

Psychotherapy can help you resolve your problems, relieve anxiety, and make those changes. Specifically, psychotherapy can help you to:

increase assertiveness

elevate self-esteem

reduce stress

improve your relationships

get in touch with your feelings

reduce perfectionism

reduce the need to control

feel more hopeful

set priorities

reduce shame and guilt

deal with anger

relieve depression

We'll now discuss the first three items on this list since lack of assertiveness, lack of self-esteem, and overwhelming stress are so common in women with panic disorder.

Assertiveness

Like many women with panic disorder, you are probably too passive. This passivity exhibits itself in ways that may fall into one of the two categories we are about to discuss: difficulty asking for what you need and problems saying no.

You have difficulty standing up for yourself, and you don't ask for what you need because you're afraid that you'll be rejected or refused. You might speak too low, look down, and appear timid.

You give in too easily to the demands of others; you don't say no to anything anyone asks you to do even if you're already overwhelmed. People take advantage of you, and, as a result, you become overburdened and stressed out. You become angry and resentful toward others (without showing it, of course) and also toward yourself for being so passive. Your anger at yourself may lead to depression. These feelings add considerably to your anxiety level, and the increased anxiety puts you at risk for panic attacks.

A psychotherapist can help you change all that. The assertiveness skills you learn will enable you to ask for what you need and to say no when it is appropriate. As you become more assertive, you'll gain self-esteem and a feeling of mastery over your own situation. You won't repress as much anger and resentment; consequently, you'll feel less anxious.

What is it like to be an assertive woman? The assertive

woman expresses herself directly and honestly. She is able to say what she means in an open, forthright, and respectful manner. When she doesn't want to do something, she can refuse. She isn't intimidated or overwhelmed by guilt, anger, or hostility. People who deal with an assertive woman know exactly where they stand.

Assertiveness is often confused with aggressiveness, but there's a big difference. Aggressive people are overly demanding and often express themselves in a hostile and demeaning way. They won't engage other people in an open manner and can easily become angry and ready to fight. Others are put off by aggressive people and withdraw from them.

In learning to become more assertive, it's helpful to recognize the body language, mannerisms, and demeanor that belong to each of the three personality types that we have mentioned. Here are some general profiles.

The Aggressive Woman	The Assertive Woman	The Passive Woman
is overbearing	has a calm manner	shakes
points her finger	has a modulated voice	looks down
is critical		has low voice
touches and pushes	listens carefully	pleads
is demanding	has straight posture	hesitates
is angry	makes eye contact stands her ground	apologizes
is blaming		has poor posture
is bossy	encourages conversation	grimaces
	expresses herself clearly	

To become more assertive, you need to learn how to ask for what you need or want. Here are some suggestions:

I need . . .

I'd like . . .

Could you . . .?

Do you have . . .?

Can you help . . .?

I want . . .

I'd appreciate . . .

Please . . .

Check the areas below that are particular problems for you and practice working on them. You may want to add some of your own problem areas.

changing an appointment

making a date

dealing with criticism

approaching someone new at a party

returning something to the store

asking for a raise or a promotion

initiating a conversation

asking a doctor a question

talking in a group

speaking up when being treated unfairly

When you begin to take a stand on your own behalf, insist on your rights, and deal with others confidently, you will develop a sense of control, assurance, and empowerment. Here are some tips that will help you.

1. Repeat yourself. If you don't get what you need, repeat your request.

2. Accept criticism. Instead of arguing or accepting blame when someone criticizes you, say you'll think

about the matter. Using this technique, you'll avoid anger and defensive retorts and be able to get on with being assertive.

3. Promote conversation. You will feel less shy with other people if you can develop the ability to understand what is interesting or important to them.

4. Compromise. If you've been assertive, but the other person isn't budging, suggest a compromise instead of dropping the matter altogether.[5]

Because passive women have a lot of trouble saying no, you'll find it helpful to practice skills related to this problem. First examine the following list and put a check mark next to the people whom you have difficulty refusing.

mother	mother-in-law
father	father-in-law
sister	sister-in-law
brother	brother-in-law
husband	friends
children	boss
neighbors	colleagues at work

Look at the names you have checked. Try to analyze why you can't refuse these people. Are you afraid of displeasing them? Are you worried that they won't like you? Unassertive people are people pleasers. They don't want anyone to dislike them or to be angry with them.

After you have identified the people whom you are having the most difficulty refusing, take small risks with them. Eventually, you should feel more comfortable about saying no. Give some thought beforehand to what you are planning to say and, once you've said it, don't feel guilty or apologize over and over. Use body language to be assertive and look directly at the person. Be specific about what you are refusing. Go over anything you already agreed to do and don't do anything extra. Here are some suggestions for ways to say no:

I'm sorry but I can't.   I won't have the time.

I'm afraid I'm busy.   I'm overly committed.

I have previous plans.   I don't want to.

Keep your rights in mind as you learn to assert yourself. You might want to copy the following list on an index card and look at it any time you feel you are being too passive.

A Woman's Rights

You have a right:
to speak your mind
to get what you need
to be treated with respect
to be treated fairly
to be heard
to make a mistake
to disagree
to spend time the way you want

Self-Esteem

Your self-esteem depends on how you feel about yourself. If you essentially like yourself and think that you are a competent and worthwhile person, then your self-esteem is high. But if feelings of disapproval, shame, and unworthiness predominate, your self-esteem is probably low.

Women with high self-esteem can understand and express their feelings. They do well in social situations, enjoy satisfying relationships, and are usually successful in their career choices. They are assertive and capable of asking for—and accepting—what they want or need from others. They are also able to give to others.

Women with low self-esteem usually don't relate well to others; their problems cause their relationships to suffer. Because they think others will reject them, they are oversensitive and defensive, feel angry at anyone who doesn't treat them perfectly, and are generally disappointed and hurt. Many times, they turn their anger inward, blaming themselves for the way others treat them. They end up feeling unloved and unwanted, perpetuating the feelings of low self-esteem and causing anxiety, anger, guilt, and depression.

Frustrated and angry at their inability to get along with others, women with low self-esteem can be hostile, overly aggressive, and difficult. This makes people withdraw from them, causing their self-esteem to plummet even further. Or they may be withdrawn, incapable of communicating well, and unable to express their feelings. They have trouble asking for the things they need or taking what is offered because they don't feel deserving. And they can't give much to anyone else since they feel so depleted themselves.

Edmund Bourne, Ph.D., describes two traits that cause anxiety in women with low self-esteem: needing approval and trying to be perfect.

A woman who needs approval feels that she's not good enough. Therefore, she acts, to her detriment, in ways that get people to like her more. Trying so hard to get approval exhausts and frustrates her. She ends up angry and anxious, and thus more at risk for panic. If she has a panic attack with others watching, the situation will worsen—she'll assume that they like her less and will never approve of her. That makes her more anxious.

A woman who tends to be a perfectionist doesn't like herself and attempts to make herself feel better by trying to be perfect. She overcompensates, reaching for unattainable goals rather than being satisfied by just doing well. Nothing is good enough, including herself. She winds up frustrated and unhappy because she can never measure up to her own standards. Striving for perfection is exhausting and contributes to chronic stress.[6]

Self-esteem isn't something you're born with; it's not genetic. Rather, it is learned and comes from your early interactions with the people around you. If, as a youngster, you didn't get the nurturing you needed, you may have thought it was your fault that your mother wasn't loving. Perhaps you believed that you weren't a lovable person. The messages you receive from your parents about their opinions of you persist through life and have a tremendous impact on your self-esteem.

The following are some examples of how early childhood experiences cause you to devalue yourself:

1. Critical parents, who never accept anything you do and never hesitate to tell you so, make you feel that you never measure up.

2. Childhood loss of a parent, because of death or divorce, can lead to the belief that you caused the loss by not being good enough.

3. Physical, verbal, emotional, or sexual abuse can have enormous and far-reaching consequences. The feelings of rage, guilt, and lack of trust that abuse causes stay with you throughout life, making it hard to have a close or trusting relationship.

4. Alcoholism or drug abuse causes chaos in the family. When you grow up in a family with substance abuse, you feel angry, depressed, insecure, and unable to trust others.

5. Neglect by parents causes you to grow up feeling that you weren't worthy of their attention.

6. Rejection by parents, either overtly or subtly, sends a message that you aren't wanted, or that you aren't good enough or smart enough. You may feel that your parents are sorry they had you. You lose confidence and don't like yourself.[7]

The good news is that self-esteem is a learned trait; therefore it can be improved. To raise your self-esteem, you need to value yourself more. Psychotherapy will help you do that. With the help of your therapist, you'll begin to understand the impact of the past on your feelings about yourself. As you gain insight, you'll start to view yourself more clearly—and like yourself better. Once you like yourself better, you'll treat yourself better.

How can you be good to yourself? Making sure that you get what you need is one way. To identify your needs, think about what you consider essential to your emotional health. Here are some typical needs, but you may want to add others:

a close relationship	a sense of accomplishment
a network of friends	feeling worthwhile
spirituality	being creative
humor	meaningful activities
nurturing	productive work
time for yourself	learning new things

Think of ways that you can nurture yourself. It will give you something to look forward to and remind you that you're worthy.

Choose some items from this list daily.

Take time out for a walk.	Listen to some favorite music.
Read a book.	Buy yourself a small present.
Call a friend.	Make a lunch or dinner date.

See a movie.   Buy a bouquet of flowers.

Take a day trip.   Prepare a special meal.

Here are some other suggestions for raising self-esteem:

1. Try to achieve goals within your reach. First recall
   your past achievements; most people with low self-
   esteem don't give themselves enough credit for what
   they have done. Think not just of tangible
   achievements like a good job, but also of less tangible
   ones like helping out a family member at a time of
   need. Then begin to formulate new goals. List them
   and pick an easy one to start with. Success in the
   beginning will increase your confidence. Later on, you
   can tackle more challenging goals. Perhaps you'd like
   to run a marathon or take piano lessons. Or maybe
   you've always wanted to return to college or start a
   new career. You'll see your self-esteem improve as you
   accomplish your goals.[8]

2. Use the skills of self-talk that you learned in Chapter
   18 to counter negative feelings and thoughts that you
   have about yourself. Remember how important it is to
   talk to yourself in a realistic, positive manner.[9]

3. Build a support network. Call people; try to get
   together more often with those you like. Share
   intimate thoughts and ideas to encourage others to
   open up. Doing so will lead to closeness and deeper
   relationships.[10]

4. Forgive yourself for what you consider past mistakes.
   Constant negative evaluation erodes self-esteem, so
   move on and let go of the past.

5. Try to lessen your feelings of guilt and shame. Don't
   take everything so personally; attribute negative events
   to other causes. Realizing that people see things in
   different ways will help you to feel less rejected when
   others don't agree with you.

6. Don't call yourself names and don't allow others to do so either. Instead talk about the behavior and actions that may have caused problems.

Stress

You feel stressed when you perceive a situation as too hard to handle. It's well known that stress contributes to the development of physical ailments like high blood pressure and migraine headaches. Stress can also lead to psychological disorders such as depression and anxiety, a link that in recent years has become increasingly acknowledged.

Once you become anxious, you may not calm down quickly; that anxious feeling may stay with you for a while. The more anxious you are, the higher your risk of a panic attack.

Stress arises from a variety of sources. Losses such as the death of a loved one, divorce, or giving up a home are very stressful. So are illness; financial problems; troubles with an employer; and life changes—even if they are happy ones like marriage, a promotion at work, a move to a bigger house, or the birth of a child.

But the most deadly form of stress is the kind that persists and escalates over a period of time. Constant stress is debilitating and draining. It can come from trying to balance work with home and family life, continual money problems, or chronic dissatisfaction with a job.

Unresolved conflicts are another cause of chronic stress. Here's an example that has been mirrored by numerous women. As an only daughter, Alice felt she should provide care for her elderly, ailing mother. But she never got along with the emotionally abusive, rigid, domineering woman who always tried to control her by imposing rules that were unfair and demanding standards that were unreasonable. When Alice was a child, her mother had been very intrusive and had allowed her little privacy; she was also opinionated, leaving no room for compromise or negotiation. As the years went by, the situation became worse. Even after Alice married and had her own family, her mother attempted to control her. Their relationship deteriorated and, as her mother aged, she demanded more of Alice's time and attention and tried even harder to maintain control of Alice's life. The conflict between wanting to be a decent person who fulfilled her obligation to her mother and her anger and resentment toward this cruel, destructive parent caused Alice so much stress that she began to have panic attacks.

Stress usually produces problems in areas that are weakened or vulnerable. When you experience stress, whatever you're susceptible to becomes more pronounced. For instance, if you normally get headaches, you may develop a migraine when you're stressed. If you are usually an anxious person, stress will cause more intense anxiety. Sometimes women who are worriers become incessant worriers after a panic attack, because the loss of control they experience makes them feel more fragile and vulnerable.

Like many people, you may tend to ignore the warning signs of excessive stress. You may walk around feeling very anxious without taking the time to think about what is going on in your life. Remember Carol, the Sad Woman? She was caring for a new baby, working 10-hour days, and going to school. She kept trying to do more and more without being fully aware of her anxiety, exhaustion, and depression. Some women don't know when to stop. They ignore their limitations, overtax themselves, and accumulate stresses.

If you think that's what you are doing, you need to pay more attention to stress alerts—signals that tell you to reduce the stress in your life. You might view a panic attack as a call to action, a signal that you need to do things differently. It causes you to stop, examine your lifestyle, recognize what is causing your anxiety, and change something.

As you get to know yourself, you'll become more adept at recognizing the signs of emotional stress. Which of the following apply to you?

tearfulness   frustration

crying   defensiveness

screaming   anger

arguing   nervousness

short temper   irritability

mood swings   excessive worrying

The following Life Events Survey should help you determine the amount of stress in your life.[11]

Life Events Survey	
Life Event	*Average Stress Score*
Death of spouse	100
Divorce	73
Martial separation	65
Jail term	63
Death of close family member	63
Personal injury or illness	53
Marriage	50
Being fired from work	47
Marital problems	45
Retirement	45
Change in health of family member	44
Pregnancy	40

Sexual difficulties	39
Gain of new family member	39
Business readjustment	39
Change in finances	38
Death of close friend	37
Change to different line of work	36
Change in number of arguments with spouse	35
Mortgage or loan for major purchase (such as a home)	31
Foreclosure of mortgage or loan	30
Change in responsibilities at work	29
Son or daughter leaving home	29
Trouble with in-laws	29
Outstanding personal achievement	28
Spouse begins or stops work	26
Beginning or finishing school	26
Change in living conditions	25
Revision of personal habits	24
Trouble with boss	23
Change in work hours or conditions	20
Change in residence	20
Change in school	20
Change in recreation	19

Change in church activities	19
Change in social activities	18
Mortgage or loan for lesser purchase (such as a car or TV)	17
Change in sleeping habits	16
Change in number of family get-togethers	15
Change in eating habits	15
Vacation	13
Christmas	12
Minor violations of the law	11

Determine which life events have occurred in your life over the past two years and add up your total stress score. For example, if you got married, changed to a different line of work, changed residence, and took two vacations, your total stress score would be 50 + 36 + 20 + 13 + 13 = 132. If your total stress score is under 150, you are less likely to be suffering the effects of cumulative stress. If it is between 150 and 300, you *may* be suffering from chronic stress, depending on how you perceived and coped with the particular life events that occurred. If your score is over 300, it is likely you are experiencing some detrimental effects of cumulative stress. Please note that the stress scores on the above survey are averaged over many people. The degree to which any particular event is stressful to you will depend on how you perceive it.

Keep in mind that some stress is inevitable. That's because change—a major source of stress—is part of life. If you're looking for a life without change, loss, conflicts, or problems, you won't find it. Believing that you can have a stress-free life is merely chasing something illusory and will add to your unhappiness and anxiety.

Everyone experiences stress now and then. And, certainly, some stressors are infinitely more overwhelming than others. Yet some people are resilient, while others fall apart. What matters is how you *manage* your stress. The poorer your coping skills, the more stressed out you will be. Coping mechanisms prevent the buildup of anxiety and help you deal with stressors. If you have an array of coping mechanisms, you learn what works in different situations.

How you perceive stress is important. When some women have to deal with a major change, like a move to another state, they feel overwhelmed. Calmer people view the event as a challenge, an opportunity, or an improvement in their lives. They find stress energizing. You may not be able to change the situation, but you can change your perception of it.

Here are some other suggestions for dealing with stress:

1. Try thought-stopping. Whenever you find yourself worrying excessively, picture a stop sign and make an effort to think of something else.

2. Practice deep breathing. When you feel stressed, stop and use this technique for a few minutes.

3. Choose a relaxation technique like meditation or progressive relaxation and practice it every day.

4. Exercise regularly. Workouts are great stress busters.

5. Pause, breathe deeply, think, and then act.

6. Prioritize. Choose the most important tasks to take care of and leave the rest for later.

7. Don't procrastinate. Once you've decided what you will do today, go ahead and do it.

8. Share your feelings; talk to a trusted friend about a problem.

9. Try to add to your network of support people.

10. Do something for others, perhaps volunteer work.

11. Get enough sleep.

12. Try not to deal with too many changes at once if you can help it.

13. Avoid caffeine, alcohol, and cigarettes.

14. Don't skip meals.

15. If nothing helps, talk to a therapist.

If you deal with your stress, your overall anxiety and your potential for panic attacks will decrease.

Next you'll read about Sharon, a woman whose story illustrates the way the three problems we have discussed—lack of assertiveness, lack of self-esteem, and stress—contribute to anxiety and panic attacks. And you'll see how psychotherapy helped her get back on track.

Sharon's Story

Sharon, a divorced mother of two daughters aged 8 and 12, was at the top of her career as a high-powered lawyer in a prestigious New York law firm. She had a long commute to work from her suburban New Jersey home and a hectic, fast-paced life. Still, she thought she had things under control.

Then the nanny whom her children adored returned home to Ireland. For the next two years, Sharon went through a succession of nannies. One quit to go back to college. Another left the children alone one afternoon while she went to the store. Still another brought her boyfriend over almost every day. A fourth one watched soaps on TV instead of paying attention to the children.

While trying to find a solution to the nanny problem, Sharon experienced another stressor: the sudden death of her mother to whom she had been very close. The two were more than mother and daughter; they were best friends who spoke on the phone daily and saw each other at least once a week. It was her mother who gave Sharon support and encouragement during the divorce, and it was her mother who was there for her during the difficult days afterward. Sharon missed her mother acutely; the loss was a terrible blow.

Sharon was also trying to help her grief-stricken father, who felt terribly lonely and isolated since his wife's death. His recent retirement made things worse; he didn't know how to spend his time. Then Sharon had a brainstorm. Since the nannies weren't working out, she decided to ask her father to take care of the girls. At this point in their lives, they just needed someone who could supervise them and drive them to their activities. To Sharon's delight, her father liked the idea.

Unfortunately, the arrangement didn't work out. The girls started to become withdrawn and teary. When Sharon questioned her daughters, she found that her father was denigrating them and intruding on their lives. He belittled their clothes, their schoolwork, and their friends. He demanded to know what they talked about on the phone. One child caught him opening a letter from one of her friends; the other daughter found him reading her diary.

Meanwhile, Sharon was facing problems at work. Colleagues had been let go because of downsizing. With the staff reduced, Sharon's workload increased and she was now putting in long hours of overtime. Even though she knew that she was being treated unfairly, she didn't dare complain because she felt that she, too, would be fired. She worried constantly that she would lose her job.

She also worried about her daughters who, still under the care of her father, were being shuttled between after-school activities and friends' homes, grabbing whatever they could for dinner. The older girl began to hang out with a fast crowd and

Sharon suspected that she was drinking. Upset by what was going on, Sharon's ex-husband, who lived nearby and had visitation rights, sued for custody. Sharon was devastated at the thought that she might lose her children.

It was at this point that Sharon had her first panic attack. She was at work, overwhelmed by the three cases she was already laboring over, when a partner dumped a fourth case on her desk. Her head swam, her heart palpitated, and she felt as if she couldn't breathe—as if she couldn't take in enough air and was going to suffocate.

More attacks followed that one. Sharon was anxious, unhappy, and terribly distraught much of the time; she felt as if her life had been turned upside down. But she realized that her symptoms had to be the result of the stress that was piling up, and she knew that she needed help. At the recommendation of her family doctor, she began seeing a psychotherapist.

Working with the psychotherapist, Sharon addressed her untenable job pressures and the terrible conflict between wanting to spend more time with her children and trying to achieve success in the workplace. Reevaluating her job with its long commute and overtime, she decided to look for a position closer to home. She found one with shorter hours and fewer demands, just 15 minutes from where she lived. Since she was away from home fewer hours, she could spend more time parenting. Her husband realized he had no case and withdrew his claim for custody of the children. Sharon was enormously relieved.

Meanwhile, Sharon acknowledged the overwhelming sense of loss she had felt since her mother's death. She began to explore the relationship she and her mother had, to understand why she missed her so much, and to grieve appropriately.

The psychotherapist also helped Sharon understand how angry she was toward her father. Sharon realized that this anger didn't emanate from just the current situation. As she began to think about her own childhood, she recalled that her father had treated her in exactly the same way that he treated her children. The verbal abuse and intrusiveness had taken its toll, terribly damaging Sharon's self-esteem.

She became less passive with her family, learning to take more control of her children, particularly with the daughter who was getting into trouble. She also worked on asserting herself with her father.

Sharon's psychotherapist helped her realize that she was bright and capable. As her self-esteem grew, she began to consider her health and appearance. Because of stress, Sharon had been overeating. Feeling anxious and deprived, she had snacked on candy bars. As her tension and anger eased, she was able to stick to a diet. Her trimmer body and the positive feeling that accompanied it made her feel better about herself and further increased her self-esteem.

Because of psychotherapy, Sharon's life was coming together. She was more relaxed and even took up a former hobby—watercolor painting. She began to develop a network of friends she met in her painting class and on the job. As she made changes and improvements, her panic attacks subsided.

Contextual Therapy

*I*n the early 1970s—about the same time that therapists began using exposure techniques to treat phobias— Manuel Zane, M.D., developed a form of graded exposure that he called contextual therapy. The difference between the two treatments is that contextual therapy focuses on the phobic reaction itself. The patient learns to observe how she reacts to her fear in its context, that is, in the actual place where it is occurring. By doing so, she is able to lessen its intensity to a point where it causes little or no discomfort.

Dr. Zane asserts that contextual therapy, while not a panacea, can be the beginning of a cure. It provides some tools, some hope, some techniques, and some understanding to start patients on the road to recovery. The goal is to stay longer in the phobic situation, tolerate the fear, and not run away.

At the White Plains Hospital Phobia Clinic and other clinics where contextual therapy is used, thousands of patients have been helped. A six-month follow-up study showed that 90 percent of patients had improved significantly. A four-year follow-up found that 9 out of 10 patients maintained the gains they had made.[1]

The key to recovery using contextual therapy involves facing and dealing with your phobia in individualized, manageable steps, rather than running from fearful situations. As you confront the phobic situation (it might be a car, bridge, tunnel, crowded store, open field, or whatever you find terrifying), you'll think about the way you respond to your fear. Through your observations you'll learn to identify what makes your reactions better and what makes them worse. You'll ask yourself questions such as:

What am I thinking when I am terrified?

What is happening to my body?

What do I predict will happen?

What are others thinking?

What is happening around me?

How bad is my fear?

You'll start to notice that your fear fluctuates, and you'll think about how and why this happens. You'll reflect on what you are seeing and thinking when you are afraid. Eventually you'll understand the relationship between the fluctuations in your fear and what is going on both outside of you (the environment) and inside of you (your imagination). By examining the fear in its context, you'll learn that how you react is very much affected by your mind, your imagination, your body, and the environment. If you understand the impact of these factors on your fear, you will ultimately be able to control your reaction to the panic.

Contextual therapy will help you understand that your intense terror is a by-product of your active imagination. According to Dr. Zane, patients who develop phobias have the ability to feel and experience what they imagine more strongly than the average person.

Think about the way you overreact to perceived dangers. Do you imagine that your pounding heart signifies a heart attack? Do you react to a slightly increased rate of breathing and think that you can't catch your breath, get enough air, or swallow properly? Do you then feel that you will choke, faint, or instantly die? These feelings are most intense when you go into the phobic situation.

Consider how difficult it is to deal with just one reaction to fear, such as palpitations. During a panic attack, a host of over-powering thoughts, imaginings, feelings, and physical sensations come into play. Think of the impact on your body and mind as you try to fight these reactions.

Women describing the way they feel during a panic attack often use words like *dread*, *horror*, and *terror*, rather than just *fear*. They say they feel a complete loss of control. What they are experiencing is a total emotional disintegration resulting in disorganization and chaos.

Just as your panic attacks started because of incorrect reactions to imagined dangers, so can they end as you correct your misconceptions. With the help of contextual therapy, you'll realize that your frightening feelings, symptoms, and scary thoughts derive from your imagination and do not pose a real threat or danger. You'll understand that the imagined dangers, while fear-provoking, aren't realistic. A realistic explanation for your racing heart or increased respiration, for instance, could be anything from rushing to answer the phone to watching an exciting movie.

Contextual therapy provides new techniques to help you see the reality of a phobic situation. You will

- enter the phobic situation

- focus on the reality of the situation

- perform manageable activities in the phobic situation

- observe and understand the spiraling of frightening thoughts and bodily reactions

- switch away from frightening thoughts and become more realistic

While Dr. Zane advocates using a helper to comfort, reassure, and assist you in achieving your goals, he says it is possible (though more difficult and initially more frightening) to use contextual therapy on your own.

Whether you enter the phobic situation with or without a helper, you'll need to be familiar with the six points mentioned in Chapter 15. Here they are in detail:

- POINT ONE. Expect, allow, and accept that fear will arise. When you go into the situation that you fear, expect to be afraid. Allow for the fear, accept it, and welcome it. Don't pretend that you're not afraid and don't try to fight it; fighting the fear just makes it worse. Realize that your reactions are automatic. You'll experience some physical symptoms, such as a pounding heart, rapid heartbeat, trouble swallowing, or trembling hands; your past experiences trigger these physical reactions. As you experience the fear you've been running from, you'll understand that your fear is a product of your imagination and that your imagination predicts dire events.

- POINT TWO. When fear comes, wait. Let it be. When you experience fear, your impulse is to flee rather than to stay and feel the fear. At first you may be able to stay in the fearful situation for just a short time because you find the fear unbearable. If you desperately need to leave, be proud that you entered the feared situation and stayed in it at all. Try to stay a little longer next time. In taking this important step, you'll learn that the fear does recede.

- POINT THREE. Focus on and do manageable things in the present. Try to stay in the present instead of predicting what might happen. Concentrate on some small manageable tasks so you keep connected to the present. For example, you might count pictures on the wall or people in the room or observe the different colors that the room contains. You could read a magazine article, drink water, or count loose change. If you absorb yourself in some task, your imagination won't run away with itself.

- POINT FOUR. Label your fear from 0 to 10 and watch it go up and down. Notice that your fear level doesn't remain steady; it changes. Label your fear from 0 (no fear at all) to 10 (intolerable fear). Notice how your fear rises when your imagination takes over and how it lowers when you keep connected to the present. Thinking about your fear level will help you stay connected to the present. You'll see that shifting your attention from your imagination gives you some control over your fear.

- POINT FIVE. Function with a level of fear. Appreciate the achievement. Your goal is to stay in the phobic situation even though you are afraid. Continue to talk or to keep on with whatever you were doing. As you stay in the situation for longer periods each time, you'll be making progress, keeping the fear from getting out of control, and continuing to function.

- POINT SIX. Expect, allow, and accept that fear will reappear. Don't be discouraged if the fear reappears after you are doing well. It will recede again, but expect it to come back. When it does, look upon it as an opportunity and a challenge to figure out why you've had a relapse. Ask yourself questions such as "Am I keeping up my practicing? Do I have additional stress?"[2]

You'll use contextual therapy in three stages: confronting the phobic situation, controlling the phobic situation, and understanding the phobic situation.

As you confront the phobic situation you'll remember that

- the anticipation is greater than the reality

- your helper is there

- you're using manageable steps

- you can always retreat

As you control the phobic situation, you'll remember that

- avoidance makes the dread worse
- the six points will help you manage your fear and give you a sense of control

As you understand the phobic situation, you will consolidate your gains and remember that

- instead of responding automatically with fear that spirals out of control, you'll respond automatically with less and less fear
- healthier reactions become automatic
- the control is inside of you[3]

Here are some tips that you should find helpful as you embark on your recovery with contextual therapy.

- Check with a doctor first so you won't worry about physical symptoms.
- Plan to work at contextual therapy at least once a week, possibly more, for at least one hour.
- Communicate with your helper. Be open and honest; express the way you feel.
- Plan all details in advance. Decide how and where you will face the feared situation.
- Be open about your problem. If you don't hide it so much, it won't seem so terrible, and you won't feel so embarrassed. You'll find that people can be very understanding.
- Don't be discouraged if your progress isn't consistent.
- Expect to feel more panic initially because you'll be facing dreaded situations.

- Cope with anticipatory anxiety by telling yourself that you'll deal with situations, not now, but when they happen.

- Keep in mind that progress is highly individualized.

- Expect the parameters of your world to increase as you practice. If you are agoraphobic, you'll start getting out more.

- Avoidance reinforces your panic disorder.

- Carry a card on which are written the six points.

- Remember that you have the power to keep your fear from spiraling.[4]

Support Groups

*W*hile the concept of people helping each other is hardly new, the idea became firmly established in the nation's consciousness when the first support group, Alcoholics Anonymous (AA), was formed in 1935. Since then there's been a proliferation of support groups, with the last decade, in particular, witnessing a rapid growth in their numbers. Today there are about half a million such groups in the United States.[1] It's difficult to say exactly how many people participate in support groups, but the latest figures indicate that the numbers range from 9 to 20 million people.[2]

It seems that a group exists for virtually every illness or problem. There's one for each disease listed by the World Health Organization, and a vast number for mental disorders, addictions, and dysfunctional behaviors.[3] Groups are available for people who share just about any situation or crisis. Crossdressers, single parents, impotent men, and people who are simply lonely on Saturday night find solace in groups. So do infertile couples, widows, well spouses of ill persons, parents of handicapped children, and parents of murdered children.

While all of the groups have leaders, support groups are led by professionals who facilitate the meetings by intervening when necessary and generally keeping discussions on track. Self-help groups are led by a trained member of the group. For our purposes we will refer to both types of groups as support groups.

Overall, people say the groups help them.[4] Supporting their assertions is research showing that groups substantially improve participants' quality of life.[5] Women with panic disorder have the same reaction as other respondents. Many of the women we spoke to belong to support groups and speak enthusiastically about the benefits.

Advantages of the Group

Why do people flock to support groups? Part of the answer lies in the value of social support. Studies have again and again substantiated the salutary effects of relationships with others and of belonging to a group.

Marc Ian Barasch, recounting his experience with life-threating illness, says about his group, "I soon discovered the great relief of sharing humor, anguish, hope, jargon, and gossip with people of your own genus of suffering, or encountering those who were further along the road of healing. And seeing those worse off than I was knocked the props out from my own self-pity."[6]

Support groups offer an excellent opportunity to share experiences, as everyone in the group has the same problem. You feel validated when someone listening to your experience says, "I've been there, too," or when you hear another woman's story and can say, "That happened to me." Before joining a group, you may think you are the only one in the world living through your particular nightmare. It's comforting when you find that you are not alone. One member of a panic disorder support group said, "Most people with panic disorder feel alienated. When they meet others who have exactly the same problem, the same symptoms, they see a mirror image of themselves. They feel someone understands them, someone is there when they need help."

A member of another group said, "You're relieved to find out that you're not alone, that quite a few of us have this disorder. You know that you're not really crazy. It's just your thinking gone haywire. You have to reprogram your thinking."

Being isolated with your fears is a terrible burden. When you're surrounded by others who have similar problems, you feel safe in exposing your fears.

Dr. Dean Ornish, talking about the heart groups (for patients with heart disease) he established, said, "The support groups are probably the most powerful therapeutic intervention of all. We create a place where people feel safe enough to show who they are beneath these masks they wear. Even in our own families, with our own spouses, we have trouble letting ourselves be seen."[7]

When you suffer from panic disorder, feeling comfortable about discussing fears is particularly relevant. Your illness seems more real and you feel more normal when people aren't judging you or dismissing your fears as insignificant or crazy. A benefit of the group is that you become less self-conscious. One woman said, "Members of our group try to find out if other people's fear is similar to theirs. When other people are afraid, do their hearts and legs feel like theirs, they ask. Are the others also afraid to drive, to shop? We can empathize with each other."

Support groups are calming, too, because of the way that they help with reality testing. When you tell the group that you think you're going to faint each time you get dizzy, for instance, you'll probably get reassurance that you'll be OK from others who have gone through the same experience.

The support group also serves as a source for suggestions that can help you cope. Comments from other members provide ideas for making changes and giving up unwanted behavior. As you start to use what you learn, you gain a sense of control. One group leader said, "We see people making progress through behavioral techniques and coping mechanisms. Suggestions from others are the whole idea. They share their experiences and tell what's helpful—like taking along a bottle of water to ease their fear of being unable to swallow or breathe. It calms them and relieves the anticipatory anxiety. Coping skills help people stay with the phobic situation. Then they have the confidence to try again."

The leader of another group said, "We give advice and talk about positive things you can do to help yourself. The principles [of cognitive therapy] are taught easily, but you need discipline to keep on track and get away from negative thought patterns. We concentrate on the upbeat, the positive, and don't dwell on the negative. We do much with thought and behavior and put together body, mind, and soul so we can function as human beings. It's like pieces of a puzzle that fit together."

You benefit, not just from the suggestions of other members, but also from sharing what you know about recovery from panic disorder. This phenomenon, known as helper's high, is the experience of euphoria that people feel when they are helping others. Knowing that you have made a difference in someone else's life increases your feelings of self-worth and makes you feel healthier.[8,9]

Irvin D. Yalom, a leading authority on groups, cites the following as the curative factors of groups. His ideas are applicable to all groups, including support groups.

- Instillation of hope. Because the group consists of members who are at different points in their recovery, you have continual contact with others who have improved. Some of these people have had problems very similar to yours and have dealt with them effectively. This gives you hope, and when you have hope you are more likely to recover.

- Universality. The belief that no one else has the same problem that you do can cause much misery. Dr. Yalom says there is no human deed or thought that is fully outside the experience of others. Knowing that others have the same concerns is a tremendous source of relief.

• Imparting of information. In some support groups, leaders provide instruction and guidance. In every group, however, members give advice to each other. Dr. Yalom claims that it's the process of advice giving, more than the content of the advice, that may be beneficial, since it implies interest and caring.

• Altruism. At first you may not appreciate the concept of helping yourself by giving to others; you may feel you have nothing to offer anyone else. But patients will often listen to observations from other members more readily than they will from the group leader. They credit other members, not only for their support and advice, but for helping them learn about themselves. The group also has the subtle benefit of letting someone become absorbed in something outside herself.

• The corrective recapitulation of the primary family group. In many ways the group resembles a family. You'll interact with leaders and with each other the way you once interacted with parents and siblings, and early familial conflicts may be corrected. There are many patterns, such as helpless dependence on the leader, defiance toward the leader, competition with other members in attempts to get attention and caring from the leader, or an alliance with other members in an effort to topple the leader. For many patients, working out problems with the leader and other members is also working through unfinished business from long ago.

• Development of socializing techniques. Learning basic social skills takes place in all groups; you learn to recognize and alter social behavior. Those who have been in the group for a while often acquire certain skills—they learn to be responsive to others, they acquire methods of conflict resolution, they are less prone to be judgmental and are more capable of experiencing and expressing empathy.

- Imitative behavior. You may model yourself on aspects of other group members as well as of the leader. Imitation is an effective therapeutic tool. It may also function to help the individual free up by experimenting with new behavior.

- Interpersonal learning. Through feedback and self-observation, you learn to understand your behavior and to appreciate the impact of your behavior on other people. When relationships improve, they become more satisfying, and you can lead a fuller life.

- Group cohesiveness. Members of cohesive groups—that is, ones in which members have a liking for their group and for the other members—are more accepting of one another, more supportive, and more inclined to form meaningful relationships within the group. When members are accepting and understanding, they are more inclined to explore and express themselves, and to relate more deeply to others. Group cohesiveness is a necessary factor for effective group therapy and a positive outcome.

- Catharsis. Because there's no benefit from ventilating feelings in an empty closet, it's important to express feelings to someone else. The group provides that opportunity. Furthermore, the strong expression of emotion enhances the cohesiveness of the group.

- Existential factors. Although you are part of the group, you are still separate. No matter how much guidance and support you get from others, you will learn that you must take ultimate responsibility for the way you live your life.[10]

A Closer Look at the Group

Sometimes a woman with panic disorder starts a group because she wants to share with others the techniques that helped her recover; she wants to let others know that there is hope. Other groups are formed by a therapist or affiliated with a mental health center. Still others are part of organizations that may include a network of several hundred groups.

The groups don't seem to advertise much in newspapers. People find out about them through their therapists, word of mouth, posted notices, community calendars, or self-help clearinghouse lists.

Panic disorder support groups generally meet anywhere from once a week to once a month, in sessions that last from one and a half to two hours. Such groups usually comprise from five to twelve members who stay in the group for an average of eight months to two years. Some women stay longer because they like the support and inspiration. People who are agoraphobic or are afraid to drive usually come to meetings with a support person.

There is no pressure to speak up at meetings, but everyone is encouraged to contribute to discussions. Members usually exchange phone numbers and call each other when a problem arises. Sometimes members who have left return to talk about their recovery, providing hope and incentive for newer members.

Experts are often invited to talk about ways that nutrition, massage therapy, holistic medicine, hypnotherapy, yoga, or cognitive therapy can help women with panic disorder. "We try to find as many new ways as we can to cope with our situation," said one group leader.

Meetings generally begin with each member talking about what happened during her week. Here's how one member described a typical meeting: "Everyone explains how she feels, what is especially worrisome, or how the week went. A new person might talk about what makes her anxious or what causes a panic attack. Anyone can ask questions or give a suggestion. We might discuss an article from the paper or a new book.

Everyone sets a goal every week. If a member walked one block last week, then her goal could be to walk two blocks this week. If she went to the store for five minutes this week, she'll try to go to the store for ten minutes next week. At the next meeting she'll tell if she accomplished the goal, and how well she did. If they don't work at it, they don't get better."

A member of another group described a typical meeting this way: "Each member talks about her goals and where she is stuck. The others discuss what worked for them in a similar situation. We learn to change ourselves by switching our thought processes from negative to positive. One woman was agoraphobic and couldn't go out in public. The others told what helped them get out of the house. They helped her turn something that was fearful into something that was fun. You don't have to stay stuck in a negative thought process.

Each member has homework that's appropriate for her situation. It might be to drive with someone else in the car or to drive alone. They have to take some action and come back the next week and tell how it went."

Some participants emphasize that support groups alone aren't enough to achieve recovery. They are most helpful, they say, when they are used as an adjunct to treatment like therapy and/or medication. One group leader reported that 90 percent of her group is in therapy and that 75 percent of them came to the group at the suggestion of their therapist. She noted that some members take medication.

Another leader said that while some of the members of her support group do take medication, many were able to cut down their dosage after joining the group. The women in some groups say they were able to get off medication completely after they'd spent some time in a group.

Many women with panic disorder would rather not be on medication if they can avoid it. They prefer to take some action to help themselves—and that, of course, is the focus of the support groups. One group member, who was able to go on a Caribbean cruise after being housebound for 10 years recovered by changing her thinking and practicing new behavior. "I don't really believe in medication," she says. "Pills are like a cast on a broken leg; eventually you have to do the work yourself." Hers is one success story out of many that are shared in groups.

Some Caveats

While support groups are certainly beneficial, they can have some drawbacks that you should be aware of. For the most part, these drawbacks result from interpersonal problems with certain members. A group member talks about two problem types: "Some people with panic disorder are filled with self-pity. When they join a support group, they are only looking for sympathy and don't try hard enough. They waste time and complain, 'Life is no good, life isn't fair, if only things were different.' They cry, 'Why me?' We all could say 'Why?' and dwell on the negative rather than focus on the positive. Some people like the sympathy and attention. If they got better, life would have to change, they would have to go to the supermarket. Sometimes two self-pitying types exchange phone numbers and talk about their symptoms all day long, rather than doing what they have to do to get better.

Others might be arrogant or hostile. If someone else doesn't do well, they say, 'Give me a break, you're in denial, you didn't try, you never carry through.' They focus on other people's problems rather than trying to help themselves. They love the negative attention put on the other person. It takes away from what they themselves have to do to recover."

Dr. Irvin Yalom describes other types who can adversely affect the group.

- the help-rejecting complainer or the "yes . . . but" member who continuously pulls advice from others only to reject their suggestions and frustrate them

- the member who seeks attention and nurturance by asking for suggestions about a problem that is either insoluble or that has already been solved

- the member who soaks up advice but never reciprocates

- the member so intent on seeking high status or on looking self-sufficient that she never directly asks for help[11]

Dealing with a troublesome member or members requires a leader who is well trained and able to guide discussions. Leaders should screen potential members who might be destructive to the group or who are unable to participate in the group process.

One group member put it this way: "A good leader really sees the dynamics of the group and talks to people who are manipulative or not working hard enough. Without a good leader, people will just say, 'What a terrible week I had.'"

A member of another group added this thought: "If meetings are run in a negative way, people complain and swap symptoms without anyone guiding them. Other members who are susceptible and highly suggestible can hear a bad story and become afraid to come to the group. They're afraid they will develop those symptoms. That's why it's important to focus on the positive, on healing, rather than on symptoms."

The lesson to be learned here is that you must choose a group carefully. Try it out to make sure it has a competent leader and that it is well run. (See the appendix for more information on finding a group.)

The right group will be another tool you can use in your recovery from panic disorder. You'll glean ideas you hadn't thought of, change your thinking and your behavior, and participate more in life. Your self-esteem will increase, and you'll function a lot better.

Humor

*H*umor is an effective way to counter the stress and anxiety that often contribute to panic attacks. When you find something funny and burst out laughing, you experience a release of tension and a freedom from fear. As comedian Bill Cosby said, "If you can laugh at it, you can survive it."[1]

It may seem odd to think of humor as a therapeutic tool; in fact, until recently, many psychotherapists and the medical profession considered humor inappropriate and regarded it with disdain. But research has shown that laughter actually does have salutary effects, underscoring once again the mind-body connection. As a result, humor is now considered a respectable and important coping skill. Using it can be a most enjoyable part of your recovery.

The Effects of Humor

In 1979 Norman Cousins wrote his pioneering book *Anatomy of an Illness*, in which he recounted the way he had used humor and laughter to recover from ankylosing spondylitis, a severe inflammation of the spine and joints. The disease is crippling, painful, and supposedly irreversible. Knowing that negative emotions could adversely affect body chemistry, Cousins speculated that positive emotions might produce positive changes in body chemistry. He found that watching old Marx Brothers films and reruns of *Candid Camera* produced 10 minutes of laughter that was like an anesthetic, allowing him to sleep without pain for two hours. Lab tests taken before and after the laughter episodes showed a reduced sedimentation rate (a measure of inflammation)—evidence that laughter does indeed have a healthy effect on body chemistry.[2]

Cousins's experience gave rise to a new specialty—humor therapy. During the past 20 years research focusing on humor has flourished. Here are some of the findings.

- Laughter helps fight off disease by boosting the body's production of white blood cells, which attack infectious agents in the body, and by producing an increase in salivary immunoglobin (IgA), a virus fighter found in saliva.[3]

- Shortly after laughing, blood pressure decreases, heart rate and respiration slow down, and muscles relax.[4]

- Laughter may cause the brain to release endorphins, the same stress reducers that are triggered by exercise.[5]

- Laughter stimulates the brain into greater alertness, enhancing memory and sociability.[6]

- People are better able to solve problems, think more clearly, and see consequences of their decisions after watching or experiencing comedy.[7]

- People who use humor have fewer symptoms of fatigue, tension, anger, depression, and confusion when they do experience stress.[8]

- It's not just engaging in humor but also the *anticipation* of humor that has stress-reducing benefits.[9]

- People who are encouraged and taught to use humor can gain a sense of control in their lives.[10]

• Humor reduces anxiety better than other kinds of distraction.[11]

Humor can help you fight panic disorder by relieving fear as well as anxiety. You already know that panic disorder causes you to perceive certain places and events as threatening. You react to these stimuli with fear, a negative emotion that paralyzes you emotionally, mentally, and physically. But humor can diminish or eliminate these negative emotions.[12]

While you may not be able to control your environment, you can control your emotional response to fear-provoking events. If you can step outside yourself and recognize the humor in situations that ordinarily cause negative emotions, you can prevent these negative emotions from taking over. You'll feel calmer, more upbeat, and more in control.

Think of a situation that caused you great anxiety. Now that it's over, can you look back and see the humor in the predicament? As you gain experience in using humor, you'll learn to laugh at yourself without putting yourself down. If you take yourself less seriously, you will be less anxious and less at risk for panic attacks.

Sometimes it takes a while before you can acknowledge the humor in a situation. At the time the situation occurs, you may be too caught up in dealing with your anxiety. But with some practice, you'll learn to laugh at the situation while it's happening. Erma Bombeck was a master at pointing up the humor in everyday events. For inspiration and a good chuckle, read Bombeck's *At Wit's End* or *If Life Is a Bowl of Cherries, What Am I Doing in the Pits?* or any of her other books.

Why Humor Works

Just as you can't feel relaxed and tense at the same time, neither can you laugh and feel bad at the same time. As the French writer Victor Hugo said, "Laughter is the sun that drives winter from the human face."[13]

In our discussion of cognitive therapy, we explained the way thoughts affect feelings. If you think about something funny, your feelings will become more positive.

Humor helps you cope by distracting you, releasing tension, diminishing fear, and providing a sense of perspective— that is, by helping you see things in a new way, a way that demonstrates that things aren't all that bad. It gives you a break from ongoing stress and allows you to replenish your depleted emotional resources so that you can keep coping.[14]

What's So Funny?

Where do you find humor? How do you use it? Humor is a tool that you can learn to use; as with other coping tools, you'll find that your skill with humor improves with practice. Here are some ideas that will help you develop or enhance your sense of humor.

1. Imagine that you are a standup comedian relating the humorous side of an incident that made you anxious.

2. Collect funny bumper stickers, buttons, T-shirts, cartoons, and signs.

3. Watch funny movies and TV shows.

4. Write down jokes you find funny.

5. Go to a comedy club.

6. Read collections of cartoons by Gary Larson and humor books by Erma Bombeck, Jean Kerr, Andy Rooney, Art Buchwald, Dave Barry, and Woody Allen, among others.

7. Recall what amused you as a child. Recapture some of what used to be fun.

8. Smile. A smile will alter your mood, trigger happy
   thoughts, and endear you to others.

Not everyone reacts to the same kinds of humor. A humor
survey in *Psychology Today* magazine found that different people laughed at all sorts of different things. What some people
found very funny, others found not at all funny.[15] Find out
what makes you laugh and use it as a resource. You'll agree
with the experts that humor is one of the best coping devices.

Spirituality

*W*hen you think of spirituality, you probably conjure up images relating to religion. But spirituality can refer to a belief in any kind of higher power or eternal force, not just in God. Accordingly, we refer here to spirituality in the broader sense, that is, a feeling of oneness with the universe or of belonging to the natural world. Seen in that context, spirituality is not just something experienced in a church, synagogue, or mosque. You can experience spirituality anyplace that gives you a feeling of serenity, inspiration, or connection to something larger than yourself. Some people find their spiritual side amidst the beauty of nature. For others, works of music or art evoke feelings of spirituality. Still others need only to sit quietly in a special corner of their own homes. Through contemplation, reflection, meditation, or prayer, you can achieve the inner peace with which spirituality is associated— no matter which path you take to reach it.

Spirituality Soothes

Spirituality, like humor, helps you put your problems in perspective. The anxiety that these problems cause diminishes when you think of the larger picture. Looking up at the stars and contemplating the universe can make fear of going to the store seem insignificant. Sitting on a beach and considering the vastness of the ocean or gazing at a panoramic view from atop a mountain can produce similar results.

When you believe in a higher power or in a connection with the rest of the universe, you feel less alone; you know you are not carrying your burden by yourself. This feeling of trust makes it easier to cope with fear.

Indeed, faith is the antidote to fear. When fear of the unknown makes you anxious, faith in something outside yourself can give you the confidence to face the fear. Faith also helps to reduce the anxiety that results from problems such as fear of abandonment, humiliation, loss of control, confinement, injury, or death. Because love is stronger than fear, the love that arises from the feeling of unity with someone or something other than yourself, can overcome fear.[1] As your fears and anxiety lessen, you will experience greater peace of mind.

Spirituality Works

The history of spirituality as a therapeutic technique mirrors that of humor therapy. Until recently both were looked on by most medical practitioners with skepticism and disdain.

Today doctors, therapists, and researchers are taking seriously the use of spirituality as a healing tool, and an increasing number of medical schools are adding courses that focus on spirituality. Evidence showing that spirituality actually works is accumulating rapidly.

- A study of 232 heart-surgery patients found that those who drew strength and comfort from religion were three times as likely to be alive six months after surgery as those who found no solace in faith.[2]

- Churchgoers have lower blood pressure and half the risk of dying from coronary-artery disease, compared with those who rarely go to church.[3]

- A study of four thousand nursing-home residents found that those who attend religious services are less depressed and physically healthier than those who don't attend or who worship at home.[4]

- A study of 30 female patients recovering from hip fractures showed that those who found a source of strength and comfort in their religion and who attended religious services were able to walk further after they were discharged from the hospital and had lower rates of depression than those who had little religious faith.[5]

- Many studies found lower rates of depression and anxiety-related illness among those committed to religion. Nonchurchgoers were found to have a suicide rate four times higher than church regulars.[6]

- Patients practicing meditation techniques at a Massachusetts clinic reported significant reductions in the frequency and severity of panic or anxiety attacks.[7]

- A five-year study of patients using meditation to fight chronic illness suggested that those who felt the presence of a higher power had better health and more rapid recoveries.[8]

Prayer and the Relaxation Response

As we noted in Chapter 17, the type of meditation known as the Relaxation Response counteracts the fight-or-flight response, by calming you. Your heart rate, respiration, and brain waves slow down, your muscles relax, and the effects of stressful hormones diminish. Since anywhere from 60 to 90 percent of visits to doctors are stress-related, it's easy to appreciate the benefits of this calming technique.[9]

Although any word or phrase can be used to elicit the Relaxation Response, prayer seems to be favored: Dr. Herbert Benson, who developed the technique, reported that 80 percent of his patients chose a prayer as their method of achieving the response.[10] (Interestingly, prayer operates along the same biochemical pathways as the Relaxation Response, leading to lower blood pressure and slower heart rate and respiration, according to Dr. Benson.)[11]

But what's important is the patient's own belief system, whether it includes religion or not. Dr. Benson found that a person's religious convictions or life philosophy enhanced the average effects of the Relaxation Response by increasing adherence to the elicitation routine, as well as enjoyment of it, and by bringing forth what he calls "remembered wellness."[12]

What Is Prayer?

The ways in which we pray depend on our culture and religion. In this country, we're most familiar with prayers from the Bible and, indeed, many people take comfort from prayers with which they have grown up. Many of these prayers praise God or offer thanks to God, but prayers can also take the form of requests for guidance, fulfillment of a wish, or relief from pain and suffering. The way that you pray isn't important. Any form of prayer will make you feel less anxious and less fearful.

Anthony J. Rippo, M.D., cofounder of the Santa Fe Institute of Medicine and Prayer, teaches people what he calls prayerful meditation. He has them repeat a mantra with words related to a perceived problem, such as lack of trust or lack of faith. They might say "I trust you" over and over, for example. Dr. Rippo found that if people learn to trust and have faith, they relax and consequently enjoy a consistently lower stress level.[13]

You don't have to be religious to pray. In his book *When Therapy Isn't Enough*, Dr. Sam Menahem discusses ways that prayer can be used as an adjunct to psychological treatment. He says, "Surprisingly, even atheists engage in practices that resemble prayer. They just don't call it prayer." Dr. Menahem asserts that atheists can pray in the form of affirmations or positive statements relating to a goal. (The coping statements we suggested in Chapter 18, for example, would work well.) A concept of God is not necessary for affirmative prayer to be used. As long as you are aware that something—perhaps natural law—guides your life, then you can successfully use affirmations.[14]

How Paula Uses Spirituality

Paula, a woman suffering from panic disorder with agoraphobia, recalls how spirituality has helped in her recovery. Here is her account:

> Before I began using spirituality I was preoccupied with my inner self. I thought constantly about what was going on inside my body. Then I began practicing spirituality on a daily basis. Spirituality isn't religion and it doesn't make you religious. It doesn't take place just on Sundays and Christmas. Spirituality is a feeling that there is a higher power. It's a technique that's readily available; you don't have to go to church to use it.
>
> However, spirituality isn't something that you just acquire. You have to work on it before it can become a tool that you can use when you need it. I practiced saying over and over, in a calming way, phrases like "Grant me serenity" or "Higher power be with me" until they became tools I could use in my recovery.

When I feel a panic attack coming on, I concentrate on these phrases. They slow my pace, calm me down, and they often prevent the attack. Sometimes I'll just repeat the word *peace*.

But sometimes an attack can't be prevented. It can come on just from a thought or because I'm stressed. Then holding onto a card with these phrases helps lessen the intensity of the attack.

I can remember the first time I used spirituality to prevent a panic attack. After being housebound for months, I left the house to walk around the block. My support person was with me. As I walked I kept saying "Peace be with me." The phrase got me to where I wanted to go.

One day I decided to try driving again. I hadn't driven in quite a while. As I drove, I focused on a higher power guiding me and protecting me. I knew that I was OK. An inner voice said to me, "Be calm. Nothing will happen. I'm with you." I could feel that connection, that spirit within telling me, "You can do it." Now I can drive everywhere. I know that a higher power is with me and I feel less alone and less afraid.

Spirituality has given me a feeling of serenity and made me more aware of my surroundings. Where before I looked mostly inward, now I can take a walk outside and really see the beauty of a tree or a bird.

Choosing a Therapist

$\mathcal{I}$f you had a heart problem you'd go to a cardiologist. If your knee hurt you'd visit an orthopedist. Yet there's a reluctance to seek help for mental illness, even though it's just as real as physical illness. Statistics show that 80 percent of those who suffer from psychological illnesses don't get treatment.[1] Because of the stigma still attached to mental illness, many people, afraid of discovering that they have something terrible wrong with them, wait until their suffering becomes unbearable before getting help. Others just don't know how to go about finding help.

Among panic disorder sufferers, only 25 percent seek treatment in the form of therapy.[2] That's unfortunate because therapy is an important part of the treatment for panic disorder. A survey of people who had therapy for emotional illnesses that included panic disorder showed that therapy can have a substantial effect. Almost everyone who sought help experienced some relief, and the people who started out feeling the worst reported the most progress.[3]

Taking the initiative to seek professional help is a sign of strength. It shows that you have the motivation to help yourself and the courage to try something new.

In this chapter we'll give you some basic information on

therapists and types of treatment, and explain how to go about selecting a therapist. You'll find more information in the appendix.

Types of Therapists

- *Psychiatrists (M.D.)* have completed medical school plus a one-year internship and a three-year residency in psychiatry. They are trained to detect medical problems that can affect one's mental state and are qualified to make psychiatric diagnoses and prescribe medication. Psychiatrists usually treat people with more severe mental disturbances, such as schizophrenia, in or out of the hospital. They may combine talk therapy with medication.

- *Psychologists (Ph.D. or Psy.D.)* hold doctorates in psychology, having completed a training and research program that takes four to five years. The program comprises a one-year clinical internship that involves practicing psychotherapy, under supervision, in a treatment facility. Psychologists have expertise in human behavior and treatment. Sometimes they are involved in research and teaching.

- *Social workers (M.S.W.)* have completed a master's degree in social work comprising course work and a two-year clinical internship. They are trained to practice psychotherapy with individuals, couples, and families, and are familiar with community resources.

- *Marriage and family therapists* should have a master's degree in a mental health field such as counseling. They have had supervision doing some clinical work. These therapists are, as their name suggests, trained to help with marriage and family problems.

- *Psychiatric nurses (RN)* are registered nurses, sometimes with master's degrees, who have experience in a mental health field. They look for biological aspects of problems while they do counseling.

People seem to be just as satisfied, and report similar progress, whether they see a psychiatrist, psychologist, or social worker. Statistically, however, those who consult a marriage counselor are less likely to feel that they have been helped.[4]

Whichever type of therapist you choose, it's important that she or he meets certain professional standards. To make sure, ask the following questions on your first visit.

1. *Are you licensed or certified?* Most of these professionals are licensed or certified by governing boards in most of the states. Licensing or certification ensures that the therapist has the required years of education and experience, has passed the necessary exams, and has done clinical work under supervision. Periodic renewal of licensing ensures that your therapist continues to meet high standards, professionally and ethically, and that she or he participates in continuing education.

2. *Are you a member of professional organizations in your field?* Professionals can join these organizations only if they have fulfilled certain criteria, such as having graduated from an accredited university. Membership in these organizations indicates that the therapist adheres to high professional and ethical standards.

3. *What is your training?* Each specialty has its own training requirements. A psychiatrist's training includes study in the prescribing of medication, for example, while a social worker is trained to have a knowledge of community resources, such as support groups or facilities to treat substance abuse problems. Professionals often have extra training in certain areas.

4. *Do you have a particular orientation?* Therapists may specialize in behavioral therapy, cognitive therapy, psychodynamic psychotherapy, or any of several other kinds of therapy. (See the section entitled "Types of Treatments" later in this chapter.)

5. *Do you have an area of expertise or specialization?* Therapists often have different areas of interest and expertise. You'll want to choose a therapist who treats anxiety disorders and who has a lot of experience with panic disorder.

6. *How long have you been practicing?* It makes sense to choose someone who has been practicing for a while and has accumulated some experience.

7. *What are your fees?* Fees vary greatly depending on the therapist's training. A psychiatrist will charge more than a psychiatric nurse and anyone with extra training will set higher fees. What you pay will also depend on where you live. Therapists in the New York metropolitan area, for instance, will generally charge more than those in the Midwest.

8. *Will the treatment be covered by my insurance?* Most outpatient psychotherapy is covered, in some part, by insurance. HMOs usually cover treatment by psychiatrists, psychologists, and social workers, and require a small copayment from patients.

9. *What is your policy regarding cancellations?* Some therapists consider it fair to charge for missed appointments since they have set aside 45 to 50 minutes for the patient. Some offer a makeup session when possible. Others have a more flexible cancellation policy—they don't charge for the visit if the patient has canceled within 48 hours. And some therapists don't charge at all for cancellations. Be clear on the therapist's policy so you can avoid misunderstandings.

Types of Therapy

You'll need to think about the type of therapy you require. Here are a few of your options.

- *Individual therapy* is the traditional way to get help for panic disorder. But if your panic attacks are not alleviated after some time, you might want to add one of the other therapies discussed below.

- *Couples therapy* can be helpful if marital problems are contributing to your stress level. Your therapist may ask your husband to accompany you to some therapy sessions.

- *Family therapy* is used if stress is coming from other family members. In *family therapy* sessions, you, your husband, and children focus on particularly difficult areas, such as sibling rivalry. In both *couples therapy* and *family therapy*, the therapist will provide vital education about panic disorder to your spouse and/or your family.

- *Group therapy* is helpful in reducing your anxiety. In this form of therapy, people with a wide range of problems participate. They work on enhancing social and communication skills and getting in touch with feelings. As part of a group, you'll benefit from social support and feel less alone.

- *Support groups*, a variant of group therapy, focus on a particular problem, such as panic disorder, and are led by a therapist or trained group member. You'll find more information about these groups in Chapter 23.

Types of Treatments

There are many types of treatments. These are some of the more popular ones.

- *Psychoanalysis,* which was developed by Sigmund Freud in the early 1900s, focuses on uncovering unconscious conflicts that influence behavior, as well as helping the patient understand the impact of early childhood experiences on personality. Patients in psychoanalysis lie on a couch facing away from the therapist and free-associate (say whatever comes to their mind). Patients see the therapist at least three times a week, over a period of years. Practitioners may be M.D.s, Ph.D.s, or M.S.W.s who have received special training at a psychoanalytic institute.

- *Psychodynamic psychotherapy* is based on the same principles that underlie psychoanalysis. It also focuses on uncovering unconscious conflicts that interfere with healthy functioning, as well as exploring early relationships and their impact on emotions and behavior. But patients in this therapy usually sit up facing the therapist. Sessions are generally once a week and therapy can be short- or long-term. More patients are opting for this therapy because of the realities of time and expense.

- *Interpersonal therapy* emphasizes understanding and enhancing the communication and social skills that go into relationships. The focus is on evaluating one's interactions with others realistically. This therapy is helpful in relieving anxiety and depression.

- *Behavioral therapy* focuses on symptoms rather than on unconscious conflicts and is based on principles that systematically change behavior. One technique used is desensitization. The aim is to replace harmful behaviors with healthier ones.

- *Cognitive therapy,* which is based on the work of Aaron Beck, M.D., aims to identify and change distorted thinking that leads to worrisome emotions and behavior. The cognitive therapist plays an active role in the therapy and assigns homework.

Each of these treatments has a distinct orientation. But rather than adhering to any one of them, therapists today seem to take a more flexible approach that depends on the individual patient's problem. Surveys show that at least 50 percent of all therapists define themselves as eclectic, employing various approaches.[5] In one survey, a panel of 75 experts predicted that a hybrid approach would be the wave of the future.[6]

Signs of a Good Psychotherapist

A good psychotherapist

- is warm, human, interested, and caring rather than cold and arrogant

- makes you feel comfortable and safe

- has proper affiliations, credentials, and licenses

- is well trained in psychotherapy—can make a diagnosis, understand and use therapeutic techniques, choose the right treatment plan for you, and refer you to a psychiatrist for medication, if necessary

- acts professionally—never touches you, or makes sexual advances toward you, never suggests meetings outside the office, or does anything that you might consider improper

- doesn't interrupt a session by taking phone calls, reading notes or files, writing letters, or eating lunch

- doesn't do anything illegal regarding insurance

- makes sure that both of you are clear about goals and assesses whether these goals are being achieved

- gives you feedback and insight

- tries to understand any criticism or complaint that you have about the therapy

- treats you with respect at all times

After the First Session

An essential factor in your recovery is the bond formed between you and your therapist. It shouldn't take too long to decide if the therapist you have chosen is really the right one for you. Studies suggest that in most cases, the signs of a promising relationship between therapist and patient are present during the first few sessions.[7]

As you reflect on your first session, ask yourself if the therapist was empathetic, insightful, and supportive. Did she really listen? Did she inspire a feeling of trust? Was her office setting comfortable? If the answer to any of these questions is no, then you need to move on to the next person on your list.

The therapist you choose to help you recover from panic disorder should be someone with whom you have rapport and good chemistry. Remember, you'll be talking about the most intimate, personal, and sensitive subjects, so you need to pick someone who puts you at ease, someone you feel good being with.

While experience and training are important, therapists are born and not made. Jerome Frank, Professor Emeritus of Psychiatry at Johns Hopkins Medical School says: "It's analogous to musical talent. Some people are just tone deaf. Those therapists who can carry a tune seem to share certain qualities. Empathy, warmth, and genuineness pop up repeatedly."[8]

If you can, try to set up appointments for consultation with more than one person. This way you can compare therapists, get your questions answered, and decide with whom you have a good fit.

Choosing a therapist is an important decision and a big commitment. If you choose wisely, it can be one of the best decisions you'll ever make.

Sources for Referral

1. You might start with your doctor since she or he will be experienced in making referrals. Feedback from other patients confirms good sources.

2. If you know that a family member or friend is in therapy, ask if that person can recommend the therapist. You might ask for a referral from someone who appears to be making positive changes and seems happier and healthier than before.

3. Call local associations and societies, such as the Society for Clinical Social Work, for a referral in your geographic area.

4. Call community mental health centers or family counseling agencies in your neighborhood for a referral.

5. Ask another health professional, such as a nurse, for a referral.

6. Ask your priest, minister, or rabbi for information.

New Findings

$\mathcal{R}$esearchers and mental health professionals are making gradual progress as they attempt to solve the mystery of panic disorder. Through their ongoing efforts we are discovering more about causes, diagnosis, anxiety in children and adolescents, effects of pregnancy, links to other conditions, and new treatments. What follows are some of the more interesting and more important findings.

Diagnosis

Test Predicts Who Will Panic

Individuals with high anxiety sensitivity, or a tendency to over-react to harmless body sensations, are more likely to panic because of their fear that a racing heart, shortness of breath, and other unpleasant symptoms of anxiety will lead to a heart attack or other life-threatening situations.

A study at the United States Air Force Academy suggests that a test measuring anxiety sensitivity may help predict who will develop panic attacks. Researchers administered a simple questionnaire to 1,172 recruits, who noted how strongly they agreed with 16 statements such as, "It scares me when my heart beats rapidly."

The higher the score on the test, the more likely the cadet was to experience a panic attack during the five-week training. Cadets with the highest scores (upper 25 percent) were more than six times as likely to develop a panic attack as those with the lowest scores (bottom 25 percent).

This test should be useful in identifying people at risk of developing panic disorder. It might also be of use to people in—or planning to enter—a high-stress situation, such as a job or graduate school, so they can get cognitive-behavioral treatment before panic attacks become a problem.[1,2]

Diagnostic Tool Evaluates Mental Disorders

Studies show that one patient in five who seeks help from a family doctor suffers from a mental disorder. Yet doctors fail to diagnose or treat the problem up to 75 percent of the time. A new questionnaire, Prime-MD, which has been taught to six thousand primary-care doctors, should help remedy the problem.

The simple one-page diagnostic test was designed by a team of psychiatrists and other physicians to help primary-care doctors detect problems like depression and anxiety, even when the symptoms aren't readily apparent. Questions include "During the past month have you often been bothered by feeling nervous, anxious, or on edge?" and "Have you had an anxiety attack?"

Patients themselves might not recognize their own depression; they might think their doctors aren't interested in their problem, or that there is a stigma attached to mental disorders.

A study of one thousand patients in four medical clinics

showed that Prime-MD significantly improved doctors' ability to recognize mental disorders in primary-care settings. Of the 1,000 patients, 287 were identified as having a psychiatric diagnosis. In about half the cases, doctors had failed to recognize the problem during earlier visits.

The study reported that it took doctors an average of only eight minutes to follow up Prime-MD with a psychiatric diagnosis. These extra few minutes are well worth the time, as patients' conditions can worsen if they don't receive the treatment they need. The extra time could also help reduce the cost of health care for mental illness, since undiagnosed and untreated mental illness cause patients to return to family physicians again and again.[3,4]

Causes

Suffocation Alarm Theory
May Explain Panic

The suffocation alarm theory, postulated by Dr. Donald Klein, seems to explain spontaneous panic attacks, such as those that frequently occur during the night. According to the theory, a monitor called the carotid body, located in the neck, measures the blood levels of both carbon dioxide and oxygen and warns the individual when suffocation is imminent. One of the primary physiologic indicators of suffocation is an increased level of blood carbon dioxide. But because people with panic disorder may be especially sensitive to even a small rise in carbon dioxide, the monitor can send a false alarm.

The theory implies that when people with panic disorder think they are suffocating, they are likely to panic. Paradoxically, they often panic when they try to relax, Dr. Klein notes. He explains that half of these patients are chronic hyperventilators (blowing off carbon dioxide); when they try to relax, they stop hyperventilating and their blood carbon dioxide rises dramatically. The rise in blood levels of carbon dioxide brought about by sleep and relaxation might be interpreted as a physiologic sign of suffocation.

But false alarms can be controlled with medication. Serotonin is extensively involved in respiratory regulation, and antidepressants with serotonin activity seem to control panic disorder by down-regulating the suffocation alarm system, Dr. Klein says. He adds that the SSRIs are among the most effective drugs for panic disorder.[5]

Big-City Stress Can Cause Panic Attacks

A big city can make some people anxious. Its tall buildings, crowded streets, steamy subways, complex transportation system, elevators, taxis, and frantic pace can trigger phobias or panic attacks, according to a recent report that focused on New York City.

One young woman, recently transplanted from out of town, experienced depersonalization (a feeling that she was viewing herself from outside her body). She also felt faint on the subway and had palpitations as she rode the bus. Soon afterward she developed panic disorder with attacks of sweating and an inability to catch her breath. Eventually she became a recluse.

She says that she never had a panic attack while growing up in Florida. Nor does she have any when she leaves New York to visit elsewhere. New York did this to her, she says. Thousands of other people also blame their panic attacks on big cities.

Psychiatrists say many people, who can manage just fine outside the city, have strong anxiety reactions to features of a big city, and sometimes to the city itself. Sometimes they need a friend to help them get around.[6]

Children and Adolescents

Inhibited Youngsters May Become Anxious Adults

Researchers at the Harvard Infant Study Laboratory found that 10 to 15 percent of children have a fearful temperament and that the temperament seems to persist through life. As infants, they are irritable and wary, becoming frightened and withdrawn in unfamiliar situations. They are shy and fearful as toddlers and quiet, cautious introverts by the time they reach school age.[7]

A Harvard Medical School study of 13-year-olds, who were originally assessed at 21 months or 31 months of age, suggests that young children who are very shy and inhibited are at risk for anxiety later on. Almost half of the youngsters studied had been classified as extremely inhibited. When they were introduced to strangers and unfamiliar objects, they clung to their mothers and were unable to relax. The other group of youngsters was outgoing and eager to explore new situations.

At age 13, members of the more inhibited group were more likely than the outgoing group to be very nervous, shy, and uncomfortable with other people. Interestingly, their responses to a psychological test resembled those found in adults with panic attacks, phobias, general anxiety, and other emotional problems.

The researchers note that diagnosing and possibly treating anxiety problems early in life can prevent problems later on.[8]

Other data from Harvard Medical School also suggests that recognition of early warnings is one way to prevent attacks. The researchers studied 30 children with an average age of eight years, whose parents were being treated for panic disorder. They found that 60 percent of the children had a fearful temperament; about a quarter of those children already had two or more anxiety problems, such as extreme reluctance to be separated from parents, fear of speaking up in class, or fear of going outside alone. The researchers note that panic attack patients report a childhood history of shyness in unfamiliar situations, development of phobias in childhood, and then panic attacks in adolescence or early adulthood.

The researchers theorize that the tendency toward panic attacks is inherited in the form of a specific temperament that contributes to shyness. That the shyness shows up so early in life adds to their belief that it is inherited.

Although these children are at an especially high risk for severe anxiety problems, such as panic attacks in adulthood, the researchers say parents can recognize their infants' wariness long before these youngsters develop phobias. They can then learn ways to help ease their children's anxieties. Although such help won't make shy children outgoing, it can help them feel more confident and less susceptible to anxiety disorders.[9]

Panic May Begin at Puberty

Stanford Medical Center researchers believe that the onset of panic attacks is closely linked to puberty. In a study of 754 sixth- and seventh-grade girls, they found that those girls who had few signs of puberty reported no panic attacks while 8 percent of those who had gone through puberty reported symptoms. The new findings corroborate the results of other studies showing that the roots of panic disorder are found in occasional panic attacks in the teenage years.

The attacks usually start out of the blue, with the girls experiencing heart palpitations, shortness of breath, and sometimes the feeling of choking, say the researchers. When the girls start worrying that something terrible will happen to them, with the apprehension growing into fear of the fear, they are on their way to developing regular panic attacks.

While the researchers emphasize that isolated panic attacks

in teenagers don't necessarily pose a problem, they note that teens who have attacks are at the highest risk of developing panic disorder later in life. Indeed, other studies of adults with panic disorder showed that the first panic attacks usually occurred in the teen years.

Learning to manage general anxiety is the most helpful strategy for youngsters who are beginning to have attacks, say the researchers. They believe that a modified form of cognitive-behavioral therapy offers the best preventative approach for teenagers.[10]

When puberty occurs early, the risks for panic can be even greater, according to findings from a Stanford University study. Researchers there found that girls with early puberty were three times as likely to develop panic attack symptoms as those who had average or late sexual maturation. They were also about twice as likely to have symptoms of eating disorders and about 1.5 times as likely to develop symptoms of depression. These effects persisted into high school.[11]

Pregnancy and Panic

The results of the following two studies are consistent with the hypothesis that women with panic almost uniformly experience a lessening of symptoms during pregnancy and that only a very small minority experience an increase in panic.

Researchers at the Medical University of South Carolina investigated changes in panic symptoms during pregnancy in 22 women who had been diagnosed with panic disorder before they became pregnant. A majority of the women reported a decrease in panic symptoms during pregnancy.[12]

In another study, researchers at New York State Psychiatric Institute and Columbia University questioned 20 panic disorder patients about the course of their illness before, during, and after each of their pregnancies. They found that a majority of those with active panic disorder improved during pregnancy. After delivery, the women experienced a worsening of symptoms.

The researchers, led by Donald Klein, M.D., also found that breast-feeding suppressed panic for some women. For women who did not breast-feed, the onset of panic occurred rapidly after delivery.

The researchers theorize that pregnancy, labor and delivery, and postpartum panic data conform to the suffocation false alarm theory of panic mentioned earlier. They say that, during the last two trimesters of pregnancy, high levels of progesterone, a natural respiratory stimulant, lead to lowered levels of carbon dioxide. Therefore, women with active panic disorder should steadily improve during pregnancy. During labor and delivery, panic is unlikely because a period of extreme hyperventilation at that time drops blood carbon dioxide to very low levels.

The results call into question the cognitive theory of panic, say the researchers. The distressing internal sensations experienced during pregnancy, labor, and childbirth, should easily be interpreted as danger signs, especially in those who tend to catastrophize, they say. They add that panic patients should more readily panic as pregnancy proceeds and that panic should sharply increase during the severe hyperventilation of delivery. It is significant, they point out, that instead the opposite is true.[13]

Links to Other Conditions
Winter Depression Linked to Panic Disorder

Patients with winter depression appear to be at high risk for panic disorder, according to findings from Ohio State University. When researchers there studied 38 subjects (10 men and 28 women) who fulfilled the criteria for major depression on a recurrent basis in the wintertime, they found an unusually large incidence of panic disorder. Nine of the subjects (four women and five men), or 23.7 percent, met the criteria for panic disorder. For those patients, panic disorder and depression appeared simultaneously in the fall or winter and remitted spontaneously in the spring. These findings are consistent with results from studies in which panic disorder was linked to depression, without consideration of the season.[14]

Correlation Found Between Chronic Fatigue and Panic Disorder

Researchers at the University of Connecticut studied 405 patients (65 percent women) to determine which medical and psychiatric diagnoses have a role in chronic fatigue. In three-fourths of the patients, psychiatric diagnoses accounted for the chronic fatigue. The psychiatric conditions most frequently found were major depression, diagnosed in 58 percent of patients, and panic disorder, diagnosed in 14 percent of patients.

Thirty percent of patients met the criteria used to define chronic fatigue syndrome (CFS). These patients had a similarly high prevalence of psychiatric disorders.

The researchers concluded that most patients with a chief complaint of chronic fatigue suffer from mood, anxiety, and other psychiatric disorders. More research is needed to determine whether CFS is a separate entity or a variant of these psychiatric illnesses.[15]

Relationship Found Between Eating Disorders and Panic Disorder

To investigate whether binge eating disorder was associated with psychiatric disorders, researchers at the NIMH studied 43 moderately to severely obese subjects (33 women and 10 men) who met the criteria for binge eating disorder. The researchers concluded that moderately and severely obese people with binge eating disorder are significantly more likely than those without the disorder to have a lifetime prevalence of a psychiatric disorder and to have undergone counseling. The lifetime rate of panic disorder was significantly higher in subjects with binge eating disorder.[16]

In another study, researchers at the Medical College of Virginia who interviewed 2,163 female twins to assess the risk factors for bulimia, concluded that bulimia affects about one in 25 women at some point in her life. They found evidence of a significant relationship between bulimia and panic disorder.[17]

PMS Linked to Panic Disorder

Researchers administered sodium lactate, a substance that can cause panic attacks in people with panic disorder, to 35 women who had PMS (premenstrual syndrome) and to 16 control subjects. The patients with PMS also took a structured clinical interview to ascertain whether they suffered from panic disorder; nine of them met the criteria.

The purpose of the study was to determine whether women with PMS were sensitive to sodium lactate or whether only women with panic disorder were sensitive to the substance. The sodium lactate test induced certain cardiovascular symptoms in all the women whether they had panic disorder or not. However, the panic and mood scores were higher in those patients who had panic disorder.

The researchers concluded that the PMS subjects' sensitivity to sodium lactate is not *primarily* accounted for by the presence, also, of panic disorder. The results conform to other findings that suggest a biological similarity between women with PMS and those with panic disorder.[18]

Correlation Found Between
Sexual Abuse and Panic Disorder

In an attempt to assess the long-term effects of childhood sexual abuse, researchers at the University of Washington analyzed data from 100 women who had received physician-administered psychiatric and sexual abuse interviews. They grouped the women according to severity of childhood sexual abuse and then compared the groups with respect to lifetime psychiatric diagnoses and medically unexplained symptom patterns. They found that the risk for lifetime diagnoses of psychiatric problems, including panic disorder, was significantly higher in the severely abused group compared with women with no abuse or less severe abuse.[19]

In another study, researchers at the Washington University School of Medicine attempted to describe the type of psychiatric illness associated with incest during childhood. They interviewed 52 women who had been victims of incest during childhood, as well as 23 comparison subjects. They found that 19 psychiatric disorders were higher in the incest group. Panic disorder was significantly higher in the incest group, compared to the control group.[20]

Women with Mitral Valve Prolapse
Are at Higher Risk for Panic Disorder

Mitral valve prolapse is a common condition, especially among women. It occurs when the mitral valve, through which blood flows from the lungs to the heart, fails to close properly. This makes a characteristic clicking sound.

The condition seems to be linked to panic disorder. Researchers attempting to determine the incidence of mitral valve prolapse disorder in cases of panic disorder studied 65 patients (37 women) with panic disorder and without known cardiac disease. Using echocardiographic study, they diagnosed mitral valve prolapse in 45 percent of the patients. They concluded that mitral valve prolapse occurs in panic cases in greater incidence than in the general population.[21]

A related report from The Mitral Valve Prolapse Center of Alabama states that individuals with mitral valve prolapse seem to be at higher risk to develop panic disorder than the general population. It stresses, however, that not everyone with mitral valve prolapse will develop panic.[22]

Panic Attack Link to Suicide Questioned

A study reported by Dr. Aaron Beck and his colleagues at the University of Pennsylvania disputes the commonly held belief that panic disorder sufferers are much more susceptible to suicide than other people. The researchers say there was only one suicide among 151 people treated for panic attacks at a University of Pennsylvania clinic. They emphasize that suicide is very rare in people whose main problem is panic attacks.

Dr. Beck explains that thoughts of suicide may occur during an attack but usually not after the attack subsides. These thoughts do not translate into actual suicide attempts and, so, do not place people at greater risk of suicide, he adds.

Dr. Beck's report challenges the findings of a well-known 1989 national study of several thousand people, led by Dr. Myrna Weissman at Columbia University Medical School. In a door-to-door survey, the researchers there found that the rate of attempted suicide for people with panic disorder was 20 percent higher than the rate for the general population. Other studies substantiate this conclusion.

But Dr. Beck believes that other problems—such as depression, which sometimes occurs with panic disorder—rather than the panic attacks themselves, put people at risk for suicide. (Many patients can develop other problems when untreated panic disorder persists.) He found that in patients who had panic disorder and depression the suicide rate rose.

He faulted the Columbia study for failing to diagnose panic disorder clearly as well as for failing to consider patients with other problems, such as depression or borderline personality disorder.

Other studies support Dr. Beck's viewpoint. One study found that among patients who have panic attacks, but no other psychiatric problems, the rate of attempted suicide was only 2 percent, which is higher than the 1 percent rate for the general population, but nowhere near as high as the rate found by the Columbia University Medical School researchers.

According to Dr. Beck, the best indicator of suicide risk is how hopeless the panic attack patient feels.[23]

New Treatments

Virtual Reality Helps Conquer Fears

In a study led by an Emory University researcher, virtual reality helped 12 subjects greatly reduce their fear of heights. The researchers took environments they would use in actual therapy with patients and then re-created these worlds in virtual reality. The settings included the 49th-floor glass-walled elevator in the atrium lobby of a hotel, four outdoor railings with balconies from the ground floor to the 20th floor, and three footbridges over a river.

The settings were designed to appear realistic. The balcony setting, for example, was a cartoonlike depiction of the view from a balcony. Patients viewing it stood at a railing in a treatment room. As they moved they felt they were getting closer to or further from the edge of the balcony.

One advantage of virtual reality is the ease and speed with which people can climb to a new level, by using a handheld switch, noted the researchers. In a real situation, such as an elevator, getting used to a trip to higher and higher floors would be a much more gradual experience for most patients.

The therapy comprised seven weekly sessions of up to 45 minutes each. The patients spent as much time in each situation as they needed for their anxiety to diminish, usually taking 20 to 40 minutes at each level. During the treatment, a therapist sat in the room, giving moral support.

For the treatment to work, patients needed to feel that the virtual reality was real; they needed to experience a sense of immersion in the reality rather than just watching a picture on a video screen. The researchers noted that the patients had the same physiological changes that they would have had in the actual situation.

Experiments are under way using virtual reality to treat other phobias like fear of public speaking and agoraphobia.[24]

An Unlikely Treatment
May Relieve Panic Attacks

Eye movement desensitization and reprocessing (EMDR), developed by Dr. Francine Shapiro in 1987, is being used with some success by twenty thousand trained therapists throughout the world to treat post-traumatic stress disorder (PTSD), agoraphobia, and panic attack. Anecdotal evidence suggests that EMDR works well in reasonably healthy adults who have suffered a trauma or have agoraphobia or other phobias.

In this technique, a trained therapist moves her hand back and forth about 20 times, some six inches from the patient's eyes, while the patient follows the movements. Meanwhile, the therapist asks the patient to picture an intensely upsetting scene and the emotions, thoughts, and body sensations that accompany it. Afterward, the patient relaxes and reports what came into her mind. The therapist asks her to note the intensity of her distress and the relief that she receives.

Although we don't yet understand why this technique causes someone to relive and rapidly resolve a trauma, some patients report that their thinking changes and the memory of the trauma loses its power. People suffering from panic attacks become aware of emotions, thoughts, and images without judgment or fear during EMDR and are able to report them without shame.

While some people say the technique is a big advance, others call it a gimmick. They question its putative success, noting mixed results, and saying that some people don't get anything out of it. These critics feel EMDR was marketed before it was properly tested, and so its benefits are as yet unproved. Many believe there is more to resolving trauma than lessened anxiety.

Furthermore, Dr. Shapiro has received complaints about her stance on training: she has trainees sign a waiver promising not to teach the technique to others because she feels it is dangerous in untrained hands.

Still, EMDR remains a theory that has its supporters. More research is needed to prove its effectiveness.[25]

New Therapy Technique
May Help Panic Sufferers

Research has shown that cognitive-behavioral therapy (CBT) is very effective in treating panic; other treatments, however, haven't been as extensively tested. Now researchers at the University of Pittsburgh and Cornell University, questioning whether CBT is the only way to relieve panic attacks, compared CBT with what they call a focused nonprescriptive treatment (NPT) for panic.

The study compared 24 subjects who attended 15 sessions of CBT with 21 subjects who attended 15 sessions of NPT. Both groups began with three sessions of education about panic attacks that included an explication of hyperventilation and its impact on anxiety, misconceptions about panic attacks and their symptoms, and possible triggers.

For the CBT group, the remaining 12 sessions focused on breathing retraining, progressive relaxation, and cognitive help that aimed to correct catastrophic misinterpretations of bodily symptoms.

In the NPT group, subjects were told that panic disorder often begins as a reaction to life stress. The theory was that if they could understand and manage stress better, their overall anxiety would decrease and their vulnerability to panic attacks would lessen. The therapist listened reflectively in order to help patients recognize and cope with hidden feelings.

A six-month follow-up of both groups showed equivalent outcomes in bringing about remissions of panic, thereby bringing into question the sole usefulness of CBT for treating panic disorder. The results were unexpected, as the researchers had predicted a significantly better response to CBT than to a credible psychotherapy. Other studies have also shown that psychotherapy is helpful in treating panic disorder.

While the information about NPT is important to patients who seek an optional treatment approach, further research is needed before its effectiveness can be established.[26]

Words from
the Experts

*W*e asked some leading experts in the fields of anxiety and panic disorder to talk to us about women and panic. We invited them to share their views on the most helpful treatments at this time, new treatments on the horizon, prevention and treatment of anxiety in children and adolescents, and recovery.

You'll notice some areas in which these professionals disagree, underscoring the fact that the study of panic disorder, like the study of illness in general, is not an exact science. On the other hand, it's extremely encouraging to witness the increased amount of thought and research into panic disorder, as well as discussions and debates about theories and findings.

Here are the experts' comments as they were related to us.

David H. Barlow, Ph.D.

Barlow is a professor of psychology, director of clinical training programs, and director of the Center for Anxiety and Related Disorders at Boston University.

On Women and Panic

Those with anxiety disorders in general, and panic disorder in particular, are most often women. The gender imbalance increases as agoraphobia becomes more severe: while 67 percent of panic disorder patients with mild agoraphobia are women, 85 percent of those with severe agoraphobia are women.

Why is panic disorder more common in women? While the prevailing theories are separation anxiety and hormonal imbalance, most evidence, on the basis of a variety of findings, indicates that panic disorder patients experience the same causal factors as some patients with mood disorders. Panic disorder is closely related to major depression. At the heart of anxiety and some forms of depression is a vulnerability related to a lack of perceived control over the environment, a perceived inability to cope with upcoming negative events, or things that go wrong in life.

When we looked back at child-rearing practices, we saw evidence of a parenting style that puts children who have a biological vulnerability (those who are uptight or high-strung), at risk for anxiety disorders. If these children had been subjected to an overcontrolling, overprotective parenting style in which they did not learn to experience failure—where every eventuality was foreseen and headed off—then they didn't learn that they could cope effectively with negative events, that they could pick up and keep going and succeed. When combined with the biological vulnerability and significant stress, this led to a psychological vulnerability to developing anxiety. In our society, girls are basically protected more than boys and seem to be subjected more often to this protective style.

On Treatment

A recently completed clinical trial conducted with the support of the NIMH concluded that there did not seem to be any advantage to combining drugs and CBT for treatment of panic disorder. Psychological treatment alone did as well as combined treatment, although combined treatment worked better than medication alone on some subjects.

The conclusion we drew was that the best treatment strategy, especially for women with concerns about future pregnancies, would be to start with CBT and then if there was a less-than-optimal response, add an SSRI. That would be the same strategy used for hypertension or diabetes: start with the least intrusive treatment. In the case of hypertension, you'd start by controlling diet and exercising, and then add drugs if those didn't work. In the case of panic disorder, the least intrusive treatment is CBT. However, drugs have proved effective and can be very helpful.

On Children and Adolescents

If fears begin to develop beyond normal childhood fears, and the child exhibits persistent phobic reactions, parents can help the child to reality-test. Parents can also teach their children that they can cope with mild threats and challenges. They can help them develop self-confidence and teach them that life is full of ups and downs. It's important for kids to understand that they have to experience the downs and be able to pick themselves up.

On Recovery

Yes, there can be recovery. Effective treatment can eliminate much of the disorder, but patients may be susceptible to occasional temporary relapses when they experience stress.

Judith Beck, Ph.D.

Beck is director of the Beck Institute for Cognitive Therapy and Research in suburban Philadelphia. She is also a clinical assistant professor of psychology in the department of psychiatry at the University of Pennsylvania. Dr. Beck is the daughter and disciple of Aaron Beck, who developed cognitive therapy.

On Women and Panic

Women may be more likely than men to come in for treatment of panic disorder, rather than turning to alcohol and drugs.

On Treatment

Research shows that cognitive therapy is the most useful treatment. One of the big advantages of cognitive therapy is that the relapse rate is much less than with drug therapy. Patients who take medication often don't learn about panic disorder. They don't learn that their symptoms are not catastrophic, so it makes sense that there would be a higher relapse rate for patients being treated with medication.

The other advantage—for women—is that there are no side effects with cognitive therapy. Women of childbearing age have to be careful about taking medication.

The disadvantage of some medications (besides the risks of relapse and side effects) is that antianxiety medications like Xanax and Ativan are highly addictive. Medication can become a crutch; some patients on medication still think panic attacks are dangerous for them and need to always carry around Valium. They do this for years and years. It's disheartening; we are pleased when they finally get to us. They need to learn that their catastrophic imaginings won't come true.

On New Treatments

Much work is being done at Oxford University to attempt to shorten the number of cognitive therapy sessions. The standard is about 12 to 16 sessions for treatment of panic disorder. David Clark, Ph.D. at Oxford University has developed a seven-session treatment program. An important part of this program are self-help study manuals. People are working on these shorter sessions and patients can look forward to them in the future.

On Children and Adolescents

The treatment approach is similar to that for adults—get the child to really believe that his or her symptoms are not dangerous. Clinically, we see that cognitive therapy works for adolescents.

On Recovery

Patients today are getting diagnosed more quickly and more accurately. Therapists are more educated about proper treatment. In the past, many therapists spent years discussing the patient's childhood and current conflicts rather than focusing on catastrophic misinterpretations.

When a woman has a panic attack, she focuses on a small set of symptoms, like a fast heartbeat or difficulty breathing, which she fears will cause a catastrophe such as a heart attack in the next few seconds. If she feels dizzy, she thinks she will faint. If she experiences unreality, she fears she is going crazy. The symptoms are real but she misinterprets them as a catastrophe rather than realizing they are only symptoms of anxiety.

Cognitive therapy helps patients override an overreactive alarm system. Research (about ten studies in five countries) on cognitive therapy shows that between 80 and 90 percent of patients become panic-free by the end of 12 to 16 weeks of treatment and remain panic-free in follow-up studies. After therapy is over, patients may show some hypervigilance and hypersensitivity to symptoms for a number of months, although their symptoms decrease and they don't catastrophize as much. Maybe their bodies are easily set off, but as long as they realize that their symptoms aren't dangerous they get along just fine.

We consider a patient recovered when she is panic-free and no longer catastrophizes about the symptoms she notices and when she no longer fears having more panic attacks. It's important that patients lose their fear of panic attacks.

Edmund Bourne, Ph.D.

Bourne is former director of anxiety treatment centers in Santa Rosa and San Jose, California. He is currently a psychologist in Hawaii.

On Women and Panic

A large number of women with anxiety disorders seem to experience an aggravation of problems premenstrually. In some cases, a combination of natural progesterone and SSRI medications such as Paxil have been helpful. The fact that women with PMS often crave carbohydrates and sweets may indicate a deficiency in serotonin. These foods permit more tryptophan (an amino acid) to enter the brain. Tryptophan is naturally converted into serotonin. For some persons, supplemental tryptophan (in the form of 5-Hydroxy Tryptophan) is a natural alternative to SSRI medications. It's not as potent, but there are no side effects.

There are some cultural explanations for panic disorder in women. Factors in our society have traditionally allowed women to become housebound more easily than men, although that has changed in recent years. Women, increasingly, seek or need to be in the workforce while functioning as housekeepers and mothers; it is becoming less acceptable for them to stay home. Now I'm seeing a higher ratio of men struggling with agoraphobia. But our culture still gives more leeway for women to stay home and 75 to 80 percent of persons with agoraphobia are women.

Also, I see a number of agoraphobic clients with dependent personality disorders. Some people need to rely on someone else to feel good about themselves. They often need reassurance to make everyday decisions and are afraid to express their needs because they fear the loss of support or approval. Cognitive-behavioral therapy (CBT) helps them develop a sense of boundaries; it helps them to consider their own needs, not just the needs of their spouses and children. An important part of treating patients with dependent personality disorder and agoraphobia are specific homework assignments that lead to greater self-sufficiency and assertiveness. These assignments help such women to stand up for what they want and to say no to what they don't want.

The traditional female role is that of taking care of and relying on others. As gender roles evolve, becoming more equal, with each sex demonstrating aspects and qualities of the other gender, there will be changes in the role personality issues play in anxiety disorders.

On Treatment

In many cases, I prefer a strategy that combines cognitive-behavioral therapy and medication. Current research suggests that the combination is slightly superior to using either approach alone, especially for panic disorder, agoraphobia, and OCD.

With most clients, I begin with cognitive-behavioral therapy and basic education about the fact that panic attacks aren't dangerous, that they are aggravated through misinterpreting uncomfortable symptoms in terms of catastrophic thoughts.

To deal with the symptoms, patients need relaxation training, abdominal breathing training, and cognitive-restructuring of catastrophic thoughts. Patients with phobias benefit from these interventions combined with graded exposure.

If clients don't respond adequately to CBT strategies after a month or two, I encourage them to try medication. I prefer the newer SSRIs—Paxil, Zoloft, Luvox, or Serzone. These medications need to be started at a very low dose to minimize side effects. Prozac can be overstimulating to many persons with anxiety disorders. It is preferable for patients to take SSRIs for at least 18 months. Research indicates that when people take SSRIs for short periods of time, they are at greater risk of relapse. They tend to benefit more from medication if they stay with it.

I have found that when panic attacks are more severe or accompanied by depression, many clients may not have the capacity to practice the skills taught in CBT without the help of medication.

With anxiety disorders—especially panic disorder, agoraphobia, and OCD—there seems to be a neurobiological component that responds well to SSRI medications. SSRIs raise and normalize serotonin levels so the brain can function normally. Serotonin deficiencies are caused by trauma and/or chronic stress. Our stressful society certainly contributes to the problem. When people are subjected to many stressors over a period of time, their serotonin levels may become depleted. Deficiencies of serotonin in our culture seem to be widespread and contribute to a number of problems and illnesses, including panic disorder. Because of these deficiencies, a large number of adults in the United States are taking SSRIs. The pharmaceutical companies are working on developing new SSRIs with fewer side effects than existing medication.

Benzodiazepine medications have several problems. Although they provide symptom relief, once patients go off them, the risk of relapse (if there is no other treatment) is 100 percent. Certainly if patients have a severe problem and can't tolerate antidepressant medications, then I will recommend BZs, even on a long-term basis. However, if they don't practice cognitive-behavioral skills, exposure, and relaxation, if all they do is take BZs, they will likely relapse should they stop taking the medication.

On New Treatments

Interoceptive desensitization, which refers to the use of internal physiological stimuli, was developed in the late 1980s by David Barlow and came into use in the last mid-1990s. The technique was developed not to change the way people think, but to actually desensitize them to the specific symptoms of panic. During therapy sessions, patients hyperventilate, spin in a chair, or quickly walk up and down stairs to simulate various symptoms of panic. Repeated exposure to the physical symptoms of panic allows for desensitization.

It's helpful if patients can stop their catastrophic thoughts, but they may still be fearful of their bodily symptoms associated with panic. Interoceptive desensitization helps them overcome their fear of these symptoms. It's becoming a popular form of treatment.

On Adolescents

Young women, especially those who haven't yet acquired their own sense of identity, often experience a conflict between autonomy and dependency when they have to separate from their family. Many of them will marry, jumping from parents to a husband, if they are fearful of developing self-sufficiency and autonomy. A few years down the line, they may begin to feel trapped in their situation and (at that point) panic often sets in.

Entering adulthood is stressful for most women, regardless of how they handle separating from their family of origin. Therapy can help them develop a sense of self-sufficiency and autonomy. They can learn to be aware of and give precedence to their own needs.

On Recovery

A 100 percent cure isn't always possible, although patients with less severe problems are more likely to recover fully.

With patients who have more severe and chronic problems, it is more realistic to talk about managing symptoms and achieving a good quality of life. Approximately 50 percent of panic disorder patients don't fully recover, but with appropriate treatment they can manage symptoms well enough to have fulfilling and satisfying lives.

Beyond cognitive-behavioral therapy and medication, they need to address personality issues, such as perfectionism, excessive need for approval, dependency, or fear of abandonment.

In many cases, 10 to 12 weeks of CBT, even combined with appropriate medication, won't lead to long-term recovery unless patients also address their underlying personality and lifestyle issues. You can give a person all the Paxil and CBT in the world, but if she basically dislikes or is ashamed of herself, those measures likely won't be enough.

Donald Klein, M.D.

Klein is a professor of psychiatry at the Columbia University College of Physicians and Surgeons, and director of research at New York State Psychiatric Institute.

On Women and Panic

There's a relationship between PMS and panic disorder. During the second half of the menstrual cycle (after ovulation), women start producing progesterone, which is a respiratory stimulant that causes blood carbon dioxide to fall. Two or three days before menstruation begins, the progesterone cuts off; the carbon dioxide level rises and, I believe, triggers PMS. Women with PMS often have occasional panic attacks although they don't have panic disorder. Both PMS and panic disorder share the similarity of occurring during a rise in carbon dioxide (see discussion of false suffocation theory in Chapter 27), and both benefit from SSRIS like Prozac.

During pregnancy and childbirth, women are protected against panic disorder. High levels of progesterone during the last two trimesters of pregnancy lead to low levels of carbon dioxide, causing women with panic disorder to improve. During labor and delivery, extreme hyperventilation drops carbon dioxide to very low levels, so panic attacks are unlikely during that time.

On Treatment

SSRIS are outstanding. They really work and they're fast and cheap. But you have to start with a small dose. Starting with a normal therapeutic dose is a mistake that's frequently made. If you start with a usual dose, patients can get extremely jumpy. As far as relapse, it is not established that there's less relapse with CBT.

Drugs make it easier to treat anticipatory anxiety and avoidant behavior with exposure, which is a good technique. Because drugs block the panic, they facilitate other treatments. Exposure plus medication works better than exposure alone.

Patients may benefit from psychological techniques, but separation anxiety, which is prevalent in adult patients with panic disorder, doesn't require a psychological conflict; it can occur on its own although psychological experiences may exacerbate it. It's clear that a number of people have separation anxiety without any apparent causal conflict.

As far as relaxation techniques, I think they make things worse. When you try to get people with panic disorder to relax, they find it difficult; they fight it and don't like it. When they do relax, they breathe less deeply, so their carbon dioxide level rises. That's sufficient to trigger the alarm system in supersensitive people. For people with panic disorder, relaxation techniques are often counterproductive.

I don't think breathing retraining is very useful. We have evidence that during panic attacks, without training, people breathe abdominally. The diaphragm takes over. So why teach them this technique if it doesn't help to stop the attack?

Hyperventilation actually protects against getting a panic attack. People chronically hyperventilate to keep their blood carbon dioxide low. Then they are unlikely to trigger their carbon dioxide monitor.

On New Treatments

We are studying the effects of carbon monoxide. When people suffocate from carbon monoxide poisoning, they seem to die without panicking, even though suffocation should cause panic. Perhaps the reason that carbon monoxide does not cause panic is that it sabotages the alarm system. It's recently been shown that carbon monoxide is a neurotransmitter that may work as an antipanic agent. Work is currently in process to see if we can use carbon monoxide in small doses to block panic. One of the interesting aspects has to do with cigarettes. People with panic disorder are among the heaviest cigarette smokers. Cigarettes give them a dose of carbon monoxide and may dampen their anxiety.

We're also interested in depo-provera (progesterone), used for birth control. It's possible that it might be beneficial for preventing panic by keeping patients hyperventilating slightly. Women are less likely to panic when they have increased levels of progesterone. However, some case reports indicate just the opposite.

On Recovery

We are very optimistic about these patients and can really help them. They can have essentially normal lives. If they need treatment, it's no big deal. Some can get along without treatment.

There are long remissions but no cure. However, people can do very well. Some patients say they are OK for 12 years and then have a relapse. If they have a relapse they can use whatever worked before. They need to get help quickly so the secondary phobic fear doesn't develop.

Una McCann, M.D.

McCann is chief of the Unit on Anxiety Disorders at the National Institute of Mental Health.

On Women and Panic

I definitely think that, for some women, hormones play a big role in triggering panic disorder. Some women experience panic at times in their lives when there are changes in their hormonal balance. In the perimenopausal period (right before menopause), just when the ovaries begin to falter, women can become anxious or develop full-blown panic disorder. They wonder when this anxiety will diminish. Because the average age of onset for panic disorder is 24, it goes against common wisdom for women in their late 30s and early 40s to develop panic disorder. Although there may be major life changes at this time, the hormonal changes at menopause probably also play a role. In a recent case seen in our research program, a woman who developed panic disorder at the time of pre-menopause improved when she started taking estrogen, suggesting a hormonal cause for her anxiety. Does this mean that estrogen may help some women with panic disorder? Possibly, but the issue is complicated by the different formulations of the combination of the two hormones—estrogen and progesterone (with which estrogen is combined). Also, some women appear to get more anxious when taking estrogen. As yet, there have been no controlled studies evaluating the utility of estrogen for the treatment of perimenopausal anxiety. It's something we may see addressed in the near future.

There also appears to be a link between PMS and panic disorder. PMS has a significant anxiety component. Some of the symptoms of PMS are anxiety, mood swings, and a feeling of being on edge. As with perimenopause, there's a tremendous hormonal flux premenstrually. Like panic disorder, we don't know the exact cause of PMS. But studies have shown SSRIs to be effective in the treatment of PMS, just as they are with panic disorder.

Interestingly, hormonal changes during pregnancy can also trigger panic disorder or changes in anxiety. While some women show improvement during this time, others become worse.

Panic disorder impacts on a woman's role in society. Women are often responsible for the functioning of the household, for shopping, picking up the children from school—all the things wives and mothers are traditionally expected to do, plus a full-time job. If a woman develops agoraphobia as a complication of panic disorder, she can't perform her duties. Her illness will affect the household and family, too.

On Treatment

CBT and medication are the two treatments proved to be most effective for the treatment of panic disorder. It's not known if the combination is better than one alone but 70 to 90 percent of patients treated with either one or both will improve. Which treatment to choose should be a personal decision for the patient and therapist and treatment should be tailored to the patient.

On New Treatments

There are always new medications on the horizon. Certain drugs that are commonly approved for other disorders are now being tried in the treatment of panic disorder. There's hope for anticonvulsants and peptide antagonists, for example. One of the most promising of the latter drug type, currently under development, is a CRH antagonist—a drug that antagonizes naturally occurring stress hormones.

On Children and Adolescents

I don't know that there can be significant prevention. In some families, panic disorder is much more common, with mothers, sisters, and daughters developing the illness. Not just one gene, but probably several genes are the cause, in combination with environmental stresses. Once someone has those genes they are susceptible to the disorder. It would not be a great idea to shelter your daughters in an effort to prevent the development of panic disorder. Rather, if you have panic disorder, be open about your own symptoms and recovery. If your daughter has the disorder, take her for treatment immediately. Don't wait. With a young daughter, CBT is the way to go as the initial form of treatment.

On Recovery

We don't think there's a cure. You will always have your genes. But you can experience remission through treatment with CBT or medication, and stay symptom-free for some time. Someone with panic disorder can go months to years without a panic attack. When patients are panic-free, then associated symptoms like anticipatory anxiety and agoraphobia go away.

But if there is a stressful situation later in life, like severe illness in the family or divorce, symptoms can reemerge. Patients should then be treated with whatever worked the first time. Although patients can feel the symptoms when they return, they can squelch them before they're full-blown by using the techniques they have learned. If the panic attacks don't become full-blown, patients won't go downhill and probably won't have another attack for several more months.

Even if patients have minor symptoms, they are considered

recovered if they get their life back. It's analagous to someone
with migraine headaches who has found useful medication;
she'll have migraines once a month, whereas before she had
them once a week. Or like someone with type 2 (non-insulin-
dependent) diabetes whose symptoms are under control unless
challenged with a glucose load. Patients with panic disorder
will be under control unless they are challenged.

Katherine Shear, M.D.

Shear is director of the Anxiety Disorders Prevention Program
at the University of Pittsburgh.

On Women and Panic

In every culture and every species, females tend to be less com-
petitive, less aggressive, and less assertive than men. Lack of
assertiveness accompanies agoraphobia, and women tend to be
much more agoraphobic than men. And, of course, panic and
agoraphobia go together.

When women with panic disorder lack assertiveness, it is a
good idea for them to get some help. Women usually worry
about others' needs. They may be focused on helping their
family, while neglecting their own needs and not taking time
out to care for themselves. They need to put themselves into
the mix, without neglecting others.

Hormones may play a role in orienting women toward the
role of caretaker and nurturer. But like other biological pre-
dispositions, this can be modified. It's a question of deciding
you're going to change and working on it. You might not want
to change the nurturing role, but if the tendency is too strong,
to the exclusion of everything else, it can be a hazard.

Women might need some therapy to help alleviate this
problem of self-neglect. A lot of psychotherapy involves bringing to people's attention things they weren't aware of. Asking

the advice of friends or joining a support group can also be a good idea.

Social adversity also explains women's predisposition to anxiety and panic disorder. In general, women have less education and lower income than men. They can be exposed to domestic violence. Being a single mother with low income is a big stressor and is associated with anxiety disorders and depression.

On Treatment

CBT and medication are current standard treatments for panic disorder, although so far there are no studies to determine whether treatments are effective in the long term. CBT gives patients a sense of control. But medication is quite helpful for those who don't want to do CBT; they may find the homework exercises too time-consuming, for example. The SSRIs and the BZs are good medications with relatively few side effects.

For people with panic disorder who don't want to take medication or get involved with CBT, a form of psychotherapy called emotion-focused treatment may be an option. In emotion-focused therapy, the therapist helps the patient identify the emotions that triggered a panic attack. Identifying emotional reactions correctly helps a person to feel more in control and allows him or her to deal with the situation that triggered the emotion.

When the need to talk about a problem is as strong as the need to get the panic disorder taken care of, psychotherapy can help. Help solving the problem might also lessen panic attacks.

On Children and Adolescents

Managing a shy child or teenager requires gentle persuasion and a lot of support. Parents may need to be firm but they shouldn't be critical of children with a shy disposition. Instead they should use gentle encouragement to help their children overcome shyness.

In general, panic-prone individuals are fearful of bodily sensations. It's a good idea to give them reassurance that nothing terrible is happening, that they are not having a heart attack or dying.

On Recovery

Patients can expect to get a lot better. Sometimes they are symptom-free for long periods. If improvement can be considered recovery, then recovery is possible for most panic disorder patients.

Elke Zuercher-White, Ph.D.

Zuercher-White is on the staff of the Kaiser-Permanente Medical Group in South San Francisco. She is a pioneer in the use of group therapy to treat panic disorder.

On Women and Panic

One of the reasons more women than men develop panic disorder could be that they are more tuned in to their bodies. They feel sensations more, including those caused by hormonal changes. There is an increased incidence of panic at menopause and in the teenage years, but most often panic is first manifested in the 20s and 30s.

Research shows that agoraphobia is more prevalent in women, most likely because of cultural factors. It is more acceptable for women to be at home and not venture out so much. Men are traditionally outside the home, providing for their families.

On Treatment

Cognitive-behavioral therapy and medication are the most useful treatments. There are definite advantages to CBT but some people want or need medication, as well. For agoraphobia, the best treatment is in vivo exposure.

Treatment groups have many advantages. I run three types of groups: a new panickers group; a panic phobia group; and an anxiety group for seniors. Some of the work is psychoeducation, which is best dealt with in a group format. When it's done with one individual, it seems like lecturing. With the group, there are also the advantages of modeling and support from others. People don't feel as isolated and they like to help others.

On New Treatments

Shorter versions of CBT are being tried out. One of them, for instance, is four sessions long. It would be less costly and less time-consuming than the current 12 to 16 sessions.

On Children and Adolescents

In their early years, youngsters go through many changes that might threaten their sense of security and cause anxiety. The key is to help them recognize that, although panic attacks are uncomfortable, what they are experiencing is anxiety-related and not dangerous. Children and adolescents seem to make progress faster than adults. They are more flexible and their panic disorder hasn't yet become chronic.

On Recovery

The important point is overcoming the fear of panic attacks because there's no way to make sure they're gone for good. Mostly, fear is the ingredient that feeds the panic cycle. Symptoms can diminish and many patients can be panic-free, but the symptoms can come back. If patients can overcome their fear of the attacks, then repeat panic will, most likely, be an isolated event. If they become fearful again, or haven't gotten over their fear, then panic attacks may take a full-fledged form. Fear of the attacks and also fear of outside situations can often lead to agoraphobia.

Manuel Zane, M.D.

Zane developed contextual therapy and founded one of the country's first phobia clinics.

On Treatment

Panic disorder involves worrying about what can happen. The body reacts to this fear. Patients need to learn that they are reacting physically to whatever they imagine (What will happen to me? What will people say?) the same way they react to reality.

In reacting to scary thoughts, these patients become disorganized. Then, in an effort to get organized, they act compulsively, doing things like checking on something over and over. They do it to drive away their disorganizing panic and bring some control. When they realize it may appear crazy, they become more panicky and try to get away from it. But the minute they get anxious in their phobic situations, they act compulsively again. It scares them but they don't know any other way of dealing with their fear.

They need to talk to someone or take medication, though

I rarely use medication any longer. As we work, we always drop the medication and try to learn to deal with the panic. Patients have to learn to separate the bodily effects of imagination and reality.

On Recovery

The key is getting back to reality. It's something like dealing with a nightmare. When a person has nightmares, his or her mind conjures frightening things that the body then reacts to. The person gets back to reality by waking up. But while everyone has nightmares, not everyone has panic disorder. So patients don't understand that the process is similar. Once they get back to reality, they can get organized.

It's possible that women aren't as occupied during the day with reality; they have more time to think, imagine, and feel. Those who are more sensitive and imaginative are more likely to become phobic. It helps if they can learn to use their imaginations more constructively, but people with these vivid imaginations don't always find areas where they can be creative. Creativity can let them use their imaginations in a better way. Those who discover this often fare very well.

Claire Weekes, M.D.

Weekes was an Australian physician whose wisdom and compassion earned great respect from patients with anxiety. Although she is deceased, her ideas are still relevant and reassuring. We end this chapter with some of her thoughts.

On Recovery

The person practicing acceptance passes gradually from being terrified and dreading panic to disliking it, then from disliking to finding it no longer mattering. This does not mean that panic no longer comes. It takes time for no-longer-mattering to bring no panic. It is important to realize that panic can still flash and no longer matter. This is the beginning of recovery.[1]

We should not feel lesser human beings because we happen to be afraid in certain situations. Coping although frightened is true courage.[2]

Even when you can do things you previously could not do, memory may sometimes encourage that old demon, panic, to rattle his chains. However, the rattling gradually grows less and less as you cope with it the right way, until it finally fades and is only a thought without too much upsetting bodily reaction.[3]

When you can live in peace with the memory of what you have been through and if, when times of stress bring back your old symptoms, you can accept these and not let them upset you too much, not let them disrupt your life, then you can say you are cured.[4]

Recovery means that although symptoms can return under stress, there is a deep inner feeling of peace because the symptoms have come to no longer matter.[5]

For recovery, the sufferer must have, deep within himself, a special voice that says during any setback or dark moment, "It's all right, you've been here before. You know the way out. You can do it again. It works, you know it works!" That voice speaks with authority and brings comfort only when it has been earned by the sufferer himself, and it can be earned only by making the symptoms and experience that torture no longer matter. No-longer-mattering is the key.[6]

A Final Message

*N*ow that you have an understanding of your illness and the tools to help you recover, you are better able to take charge of your health and of your life. With the new information you have acquired, you can feel calmer and more in control.

You should feel a sense of relief knowing that you don't have some rare illness, that you aren't the only one with panic disorder. While we've tried to convey that message throughout this book, the media, too, have demonstrated the prevalence of panic disorder through recent prolific coverage of the illness. People who have long kept silent are pouring out their stories in newspaper and magazine accounts and on TV talk shows.

The public is listening. So are the experts. Lately, panic disorder, like other illnesses associated with women, has received greater attention and acknowledgment. The increased awareness and effort has led to concrete results that translate to more efficient diagnosis and more effective treatment.

We believe you have every reason to be optimistic. Remember, your symptoms aren't dangerous, panic disorder is highly treatable, and you can choose from many options. People with panic disorder can recover and have a good quality of life.

Here's a brief summary of specific reasons to feel hopeful.

- Behavior techniques will calm you.

- Cognitive techniques will reframe your thinking.

- Exposure and contextual therapy will help combat agoraphobia.

- Medication choices are available.

- Psychotherapy can help relieve emotional problems.

- Alternative therapies are available.

- Support groups abound.

- Clinics and therapists specialize in treating panic disorder.

The future will bring even more hope. Experts are working to develop new drugs and therapy that entails fewer sessions. Help, now accessible on the Internet, will become increasingly available. Exciting possibilities for recovery lie ahead.

Further Reading

Barlow, David H., and Jerome A. Cerny. *Psychological Treatment of Panic.* The Guilford Press, New York, 1988.

Beck, Aaron, and Gary Emery, with Ruth L. Greenberg, Ph.D. *Anxiety Disorders and Phobias.* HarperCollins, New York, 1987.

Benson, Herbert. *The Relaxation Response.* William Morrow and Co., New York, 1975.

———*The Wellness Book.* Simon and Schuster, New York, 1993.

Bourne, Edmund. *The Anxiety and Phobia Workbook.* New Harbinger Publications, Oakland, CA, 1995.

Burns, David. *Feeling Good: The New Mood Therapy.* William Morrow and Company, New York, 1980.

Gold, Mark. *The Good News About Panic, Anxiety, and Phobias.* Bantam Doubleday Dell, New York, 1989.

Gorman, Jack. *The New Psychiatry.* St. Martin's Press, New York, 1996.

Kramer, Peter. *Listening to Prozac.* Penguin Books, New York, 1993.

Mathews, Andrew M., Michael G. Gelder, and Derek W. Johnston. *Agoraphobia, Nature and Treatment.* The Guilford Press, New York, 1981.

Ross, Jerilyn. *Triumph Over Fear.* Bantam Books, New York, 1995.

Rowe, Clarence J. *An Outline of Psychiatry.* W. C. Brown Publishers, Dubuque, IA, 1989.

Sheehan, David V. *The Anxiety Disease.* Bantam Books, New York, 1983.

Smith, Manuel. *When I Say No, I Feel Guilty.* Bantam Doubleday Dell, New York, 1975.

Weekes, Claire. *Hope and Help for Your Nerves.* Bantam Books, New York, 1969.

———*More Help for Your Nerves.* Bantam Books, New York, 1984.

Zane, Manuel and Harry Milt. *Your Phobia.* American Psychiatric Press, Washington, D.C.,1984.

Zuercher-White, Elke. *An End to Panic.* New Harbinger Publications, Oakland, CA, 1995.

Appendix

*F*or brochures and journal articles, you can write to the Office of Scientific Information, NIMH, 5600 Fishers Lane, Room 7-99, Rockville, MD 20857. Or call (800) 64-PANIC for panic-related information or (888) ANXIETY for information on other anxiety-related disorders and phobias.

National Organizations

To get a referral to a mental health professional in your location, or to obtain information on self-help groups and other resources located near you, contact the following national organizations.

American Academy of Child and Adolescent Psychiatry
3615 Wisconsin Ave., NW
Washington, DC 20016
(202) 966-7300
Internet: http://www.aacap.org
(For referral information about child and adolescent psychiatrists)

American Mental Health Counselors
801 N. Fairfax St., Suite 304
Alexandria, VA 22314
(800) 326-2642
Internet: http://pie.org/amhc
(For referrals to counselors in your location)

American Psychiatric Association
Public Affairs Office, Suite 501
1400 K St., NW
Washington, DC 20005
(202) 682-6220
Internet: http://www.psych.org
(For referrals to psychiatrists in your location)

American Psychological Association
750 First St., NE
Washington, DC 20002
(202) 336-5800
Internet: http://www.helping.apa.org
(For referrals to psychologists in your location)

Anxiety Disorders Association of America
6000 Executive Blvd., Suite 513
Rockville, MD 20852
(301) 231-8368
Internet: http://www.cyberpsych.org/
(Call or write to receive a list of mental health professionals who treat anxiety disorders and a list of self-help groups in your area. Include a check or money order for $3 for postage and handling.)

Anxiety Support Foundation
2003 Grace Church Rd.
Silver Spring, MD 20910
(301) 608-0322
(Call or write to receive a list of mental health professionals
and support groups in your location.)

Association for Advancement of Behavior Therapy
305 Seventh Ave., 16th Floor
New York, NY 10001
(212) 647-1890
(Call or write to request a list of mental health professionals in
your state who use behavior therapy and/or CBT. Materials
include the brochure "Guidelines for Choosing a Behavior
Therapist." Include a check or money order for $5 for postage
and handling.)

Freedom From Fear
308 Seaview Ave.
Staten Island, NY 10305
(718) 351-1717
(Call or write for a free newsletter on anxiety disorders and a
referral list of treatment specialists.)

National Alliance for the Mentally Ill
200 N. Glebe Rd., Suite 1015
Arlington, VA 22203-3754
(800) 950-NAMI
Internet: http://www.nami.org
(For help in finding self-help groups in your location)

National Anxiety Foundation
3135 Custer Drive
Lexington, KY 40517-4001
(606) 272-7166
(NAF provides referrals to their members and other mental health professionals around the country. Include a check or money order for $10 for postage and handling.)

National Association of Social Workers
Clinical Registrar Office
750 First St., NE, Suite 700
Washington, DC 20002-4241
(800) 638-8799
Internet: http://www.naswdc.org
(For referrals to qualified clinical social workers in your location)

National Depressive and Manic-Depressive Association
730 N. Franklin, Suite 501
Chicago, IL 60610
(800) 826-3632
Internet: http://www.ndmda.org
(For a list of support groups in your location)

National Mental Health Association
1021 Prince St.
Alexandria, VA 22314-2971
(703) 684-7722 or (800) 969-NMHA
Internet: http://www. worldcorp.com/dc-online/nmha
(Call or write for a list of affiliated mental health organizations in your area who can provide resources and information about self-help groups, treatment professionals, and community clinics. Include a check or money order for $1 for postage and handling.)

National Panic/Anxiety Disorder News, Inc.
1718 Burgandy Pl.
Santa Rosa, CA 95403
(707) 527-5738
Internet: http://www.spiderweb.com/npadnews
(For referral sources and contacts for support groups)

Obsessive Compulsive Foundation
9 Depot St.
Milford, CT 06460
(203) 878-5669
Internet: http://pages.prodigy.com/alwillen/ocf.html
(For a list of mental health practitioners who specialize in treating OCD)

Self-Help Groups

The following lay organizations can provide additional referral information on national and local self-help groups. Several also provide monthly publications as well as guidelines and materials for starting a self-help group.

ABIL, Inc. (Agoraphobics Building Independent Lives)
3805 Cutshaw Ave., Suite 415
Richmond, VA 23230
(804) 353 3964
Internet: ABIL1996@aol.com
(National network of support groups)

A.I.M. (Agoraphobics in Motion)
1729 Crooks St.
Royal Oak, MI 48067-1306
(810) 547-0400
(20 groups nationally)

American Self-Help Clearinghouse
Northwest Covenant Medical Center
25 Pocono Rd.
Denville, NJ 07834
(800) 367-6724 (in NJ) or (201) 625-9565 (outside NJ)
Internet:http://www.cmhc.com/selfhelp
(National network)

National Mental Health Consumers' Self-Help Clearinghouse
1211 Chestnut Street, Suite 1000
Philadelphia, PA 19107
(800) 553-4539 or (215) 735-6082
Internet:http://www.libertynet.org/-mha/cl-house-html
(National network)

Phobics Anonymous
P.O. Box 1180
Palm Springs, CA 92263
(619) 322-COPE
(142 groups nationally)

Recovery, Inc.
802 N. Dearborn St.
Chicago, IL 60610
(312) 337-5661
(850 chapters nationally)

Research Programs

The following institutions have treatment research programs
and ongoing studies that are conducted with support from the
NIMH. Individuals with anxiety disorders, and their family
members, may be eligible to participate in these studies. Institutions are listed alphabetically by state and city.

California

University of California, Los Angeles
Anxiety Disorders Behavioral Program
Department of Psychology
Franz Hall, Room A225
405 Hilgard Ave.
Los Angeles, CA 90095-1563
(310) 206-9191

San Diego State University
Psychology Clinic
6363 Alvarado Ct. #103
San Diego, CA 92120
(619) 594-5134

Connecticut

Yale Anxiety Disorder Research Center
Connecticut Mental Health Center
34 Park St., Room 269
New Haven, CT 06519
(800) 536-0284 or (203) 789-6985 (in CT)

Yale University School of Medicine
West Haven VA Medical Center
Psychiatry 116A2
950 Campbell Ave.
West Haven, CT 06516
(203) 932-5711

Florida

University of Florida
Center for the Study of Emotion and Attention
P.O. Box 100165HSC
Gainesville, FL 32610
(352) 392-2439

Iowa

University of Iowa
Psychiatry Outpatient
University of Iowa Hospitals and Clinics
200 Hawkins Dr.
Iowa City, IA 52242-1000
(319) 353-6314

Maryland

The Johns Hopkins University
The Johns Hopkins Medical Institutions
Anxiety Disorders Clinic
600 N. Wolfe St., Meyer Room 115
Baltimore, MD 21287
(410) 955-5653

NIMH Anxiety Disorders Clinic
NIH Clinical Center
Building 10
4th Floor Outpatient Clinic
Bethesda, MD 20892-1368
(310) 496-7141

Massachusetts

Boston University
Center for Anxiety and Related Disorders
648 Beacon St., 6th Floor
Boston, MA 02215-2015
(617) 353-9610

Harvard University
Department of Psychology
33 Kirkland St.
Cambridge, MA 02138
(617) 495-3853

Michigan

University of Michigan
Anxiety Disorders Clinic
Med Inn C435
1500 E. Medical Center Dr.
Ann Arbor, MI 48109-0840
(313) 764-5348

Wayne State University
Depression/Schizophrenia/Anxiety Studies
2751 E. Jefferson, Suite 200
Detroit, MI 48207
(313) 993-3426

Missouri

Washington University
Department of Psychiatry
4940 Children's Place
St. Louis, MO 63110
(314) 362-7005

Nebraska

University of Nebraska, Lincoln
Psychological Consultation Center
116 Lyman
Department of Psychology
Lincoln, NE 68588-0308
(402) 472-2351

New York

Albert Einstein College of Medicine
Phobia, Stress, and Anxiety Clinic
Long Island Jewish Medical Center
Hillside Hospital
75-59 263rd St.
Glen Oaks, NY 11004
(718) 470-8442

The following institution has three programs:

Columbia University
New York State Psychiatric Institute
722 W. 168th St.
New York, NY 10032
(212) 960-2442
(212) 960-2438
(212) 960-2367

North Carolina

University of North Carolina, Chapel Hill
Department of Psychology
Davie Hall CB3270
Chapel Hill, NC 27599-3270
(919) 962-5082

Ohio

Wright State University School of Medicine
Anxiety and Affective Disorders Research Program
4100 W. Third St.
Dayton, OH 45428
(513) 267-5319

Kent State University
Department of Psychology
107A Kent Hall
Kent, OH 44242-0001
(330) 672-2266

Pennsylvania

University of Pittsburgh
Western Psychiatric Institute and Clinic
Anxiety Disorders Clinic
3811 O'Hara St.
Pittsburgh, PA 15213-2593
(412) 624-1000

Pennsylvania State University
Department of Psychology
The Stress and Anxiety Disorders Institute
541 Moore Building
University Park, PA 16802
(814) 863-6019

Rhode Island

Brown University/Butler Hospital
700 Butler Drive
Duncan Building
Box G-BH
Providence, RI 02906
(401) 444-1900

South Carolina

Medical University of South Carolina
Department of Psychiatry and Behavioral Sciences
Clinical Research Division
171 Ashley Ave.
Charleston, SC 29425
(800) 369-5472

Texas

University of Texas, Austin
Center for Cognitive Behavioral Therapy
2914 Kassarine Pass
Austin, TX 78704
(512) 404-9308

University of Texas Medical Branch
Department of Psychiatry and Behavioral Sciences
301 University Blvd.
Galveston, TX 77555-0429
(409) 772-0770

Washington

University of Washington
Department of Psychiatry
Harborview Medical Center
325 9th Ave.
Mail Stop 359911
Seattle, WA 98104
(206) 731-3404

(List courtesy of the Anxiety Disorders Education Program, National Institute of Mental Health)

References

Introduction
1. NIMH (National Institute of Mental Health), panic disorder statistics.
2. NIMH, Director, Frederick Goodwin.
3. NIMH panic disorder statistics.
4. NIMH panic disorder statistics.
5. NIMH panic disorder statistics.
6. NIH consensus statement.

Chapter 2: Understanding Jane
1. Kramer, Peter. *Listening to Prozac.* Penguin Books, New York, 1993, 287–288.
2. Ritter, Malcolm. "Inhibited Tots May Suffer Anxiety Later, Study Says." *The Record*, May 25, 1995.
3. Mathew, Wilson, et al. "Psychiatric Disorders in Adult Children of Alcoholics." *American Journal of Psychiatry*, May 1993, 150 (5), 793–800.
4. Barlow, David H., and Jerome A. Cerny. *Psychological Treatment of Panic.* The Guilford Press, New York, 1988, 16.
5. Ibid., 18.
6. Talan, Jamie. "The Realm of Freud May Lose a Territory." *The Record*, May 30, 1994.

Chapter 4: What Is Panic Disorder?
1. American Psychiatric Association. *Diagnostic and Statistical Manual of Mental Disorders*, 4th ed. American Psychiatric Association, Washington, DC, 1994, 395, 402–403.
2. NIMH statistics.
3. NIMH consensus statement.
4. NIMH statistics.
5. NIMH statistics.

6. Kaplan, Harold I., and Benjamin J. Sadock. *Synopsis of Psychiatry.* Williams and Wilkins, Baltimore, MD, 395.

7. Ibid.

8. NIMH statistics.

9. Kaplan, *Synopsis of Psychiatry,* 394.

10. NIMH Media Advisory.

11. NIMH statistics.

12. NIMH consensus statement, 17.

13. Gorman, Jack. *The New Psychiatry.* St. Martin's Press, New York, 1996.

14. Shear, M. Katherine, Arnold M. Cooper, Gerald L. Klerman, Fredric N. Busch, and Theodore Shapiro. "A Psychodynamic Model of Panic Disorder." *American Journal of Psychiatry,* June 1993, 150-156.

15. NIMH Panic Disorder Media Advisory.

16 Barlow, David, H., and Jerome A. Cerny. *Psychological Treatment of Panic.* The Guilford Press, New York, 1988, 22.

17. Goleman, Daniel. "Push Is On for Family Doctors to Spot Psychiatric Problems." *New York Times,* Dec. 14, 1994.

18. "Be Still My Beating Heart," *Vogue,* June 1997.

Chapter 6: Understanding Carol

1. Brody, Jane. "Helping the Depression-Prone to Quit Smoking." *New York Times,* Aug. 31, 1994, C9.

Chapter 8: The Connection Between Panic Disorder and Depression

1. "Let's Talk Facts About Depression." From the APA's *Let's Talk Facts About Mental Illnesses* pamphlet series, APA, 1988, 1989, rev. 1996.

2. Comprehensive Behavioral Healthcare, 1990 Bergen County Task Force. "A Cry for Help That's Dying to Be Heard" brochure. Lyndhurst, NJ.

Chapter 10: Understanding Anne

1. Keyl, Penelope M., and William W. Eaton. "Risk Factors for the Onset of Panic Disorder and Other Panic Attacks in a Prospective, Population-Based Study." *American Journal of Epidemiology,* 1990, vol. 131, no. 2, 302.

2. Ibid.

3. "Anxiety Drugs: When Long Use Is Right Use." *Medical Abstracts Newsletter,* July 1996, 8.

Chapter 12: The Connection Between Panic Disorder and Anxiety

1. Beck, Aaron, and Gary Emery, with Ruth L. Greenberg, Ph.D. *Anxiety Disorders and Phobias.* HarperCollins, New York, 1987, 82.

2. American Psychiatric Association. *Diagnostic and Statistical Manual of Mental Disorders,* 4th ed. American Psychiatric Association, Washington, DC, 1994.

3. Kaplan, Harold I., and Benjamin J. Sadock. *Synopsis of Psychiatry.* Williams and Wilkins, Baltimore, MD, 412.

4. Ibid., 391.

5. Beck. *Anxiety Disorders and Phobias.* 82.

6. Kaplan, *Synopsis of Psychiatry,* 396.

7. *Oxford Dictionary of Quotations*, 3rd ed., Oxford University Press, New York, 1979, 260.

8. Goleman, Daniel. "Early Onset Found for Panic Attacks." *New York Times*, Sept. 30, 1992, C12.

Chapter 14: Understanding Monica

1. Kendler, Neale, et al. "Childhood Parental Loss and Adult Psychopathology in Women: A Twin Study Perspective." *Archives of General Psychiatry*, 1992, 49 (2): 109–116.

2. NIMH fact sheet statistics.

3. NIMH fact sheet statistics.

Chapter 15: Monica's Recovery

1. Barlow, David H., and Jerome A. Cerny. *Psychological Treatment of Panic*. The Guilford Press, New York, 1988, 155.

2. Zane, Manuel, and Harry Milt. *Your Phobia*. American Psychiatric Press, Washington, DC, 1984, 242–244.

Chapter 16: The Connection Between Panic Disorder and Agoraphobia

1. Kaplan, Harold I., and Benjamin J. Sadock. *Synopsis of Psychiatry*. Williams and Wilkins, Baltimore, MD, 394.

2. Ibid., 397.

3. Beck, Aaron, and Gary Emery. *Anxiety Disorders and Phobias*. HarperCollins, New York, 140.

4. NIMH panic disorder facts.

5. *Harvard Mental Health Letter*, vol. 12, #10, April 1996, 2.

6. Kaplan, 395.

7. *Harvard Mental Health Letter*, vol. 12, #10, 3.

8. Kaplan, 394.

9. Ibid.

10. *Harvard Women's Health Watch*, October, 1995, 2.

11. Ibid.

12. Bourne, Edmund. *The Anxiety and Phobia Workbook*. New Harbinger Publications, 1995, Oakland, CA, 8.

13. Zane, Manuel, and Harry Milt. *Your Phobia*. American Psychiatric Press, 1984, 81–82.

14. Gold, Mark, M.D. *The Good News About Panic, Anxiety, and Phobias*. Bantam Doubleday Dell, New York, 1989, 73.

Chapter 17: Behavioral Techniques

1. Brody, Jane. "Doctors Miss Clues to Mental Disorders." *New York Times*, Dec. 14, 1994.

2. Silio, Chi Chi. *Answers To Your Questions About Panic Disorder*, produced by American Psychological Association Office of Public Affairs.

3. Bourne, Edmund. *The Anxiety and Phobia Workbook*. New Harbinger Publications, Oakland, CA, 1995, 69.

4. Flippin, Royce. "Slow Down, You Breathe Too Fast." *American Health*, June 1992, 72.
5. Ibid., 75.
6. Benson, Herbert. *The Relaxation Response*. William Morrow and Co., New York, 1975, 102.
7. Ibid., 19.
8. Ibid., 114–115.

Chapter 18: Cognitive Therapy

1. Rowe, Clarence J. *An Outline of Psychiatry*. Wm. C. Brown Publishers, Dubuque, IA, 1989, 334.
2. Benson, Herbert. *The Wellness Book*. Simon and Schuster, New York, 1993, 189.
3. Telch, Michael, et al. "Impact of Cognitive-Behavioral Treatment on Quality of Life in Panic Disorder Patients." *Journal of Consulting and Clinical Psychology*, vol. 63, #5, 1995, 823.
4. Brown, Timothy A., and David H. Barlow. "Long-Term Outcome in Cognitive-Behavioral Treatment of Panic Disorder: Clinical Predictors and Alternative Strategies for Assessment." *Journal of Consulting and Clinical Psychology*, 1995, 754.
5. Ibid.
6. Telch, Michael, et al. "Impact of Cognitive-Behavioral Treatment on Quality of Life in Panic Disorder Patients." *Journal of Consulting and Clinical Psychology*, vol. 63, #5, 1995, 828.
7. Brown, 764.
8. Weekes, Claire. *More Help For Your Nerves*. Doubleday, New York, 1969, 93–94.
9. Barlow, David H., and Jerome A. Cerny. *Psychological Treatment of Panic*. The Guilford Press, New York, 131–135.
10. Beck, Aaron, and Gary Emery with Ruth L. Greenberg, Ph.D. *Anxiety Disorders and Phobias*. HarperCollins, New York, 167.
11. Burns, David. *Feeling Good; The New Mood Therapy*. William Morrow and Company, New York, 1980, 29.
12. Zuercher-White, Elke. *An End to Panic*. New Harbinger Publications, Oakland, CA, 1995, 77.
13. Bourne, Edmund. *The Anxiety and Phobia Workbook*. New Harbinger Publications, Oakland, CA, 174.
14. Mathews, Andrew M., Michael G. Gelder, and Derek W. Johnston. *Agoraphobia, Nature and Treatment*. The Guilford Press, New York, 1981, 183.

Chapter 19: Medication

1. Barlow, David H., and Jerome A. Cerny. *Psychological Treatment of Panic*. The Guilford Press, New York, 41–42.
2. Gold, Mark, M.D. *The Good News About Panic, Anxiety, and Phobias*. Bantam Doubleday Dell, New York, 121.
3. Gorman, Jack. *The New Psychiatry*. St. Martin's Press, New York, 1996, 244.
4. Otto, Michael, and Mark Pollack. "Treatment Strategies for Panic Disorder: A Debate." *Harvard Review of Psychiatry*, 1994, 2: 166.
5. Zuercher-White, Elke. *An End to Panic*. New Harbinger Publications, Oakland, CA, 1995, 35.
6. Otto, 166.

7. Gold, 95.
8. Ibid., 216.
9. Otto, 167.
10. Ibid., 168–169.
11. *Harvard Women's Health Watch*, Feb. 1995, 6.
12. *American Health*, Dec. 1996, 21.
13. *"Mental Health, Does Therapy Help?" Consumer Reports*, Nov. 1995, 736.
14. Ibid.
15. Ibid.

Chapter 20: Exposure Therapy

1. Barlow, David. *Anxiety and Its Disorders*. The Guilford Press, New York, 1988, 430.
2. Ibid., 407.
3. Ibid., 408.
4. Barlow, David, and Michelle G. Craske. *Mastery of Your Anxiety and Panic*. Graywind Publishing, Albany, New York, 1989, 13–15.
5. Barlow, David H., and Jerome A. Cerny. *Psychological Treatment of Panic*. The Guilford Press, New York, 1988, 151–152.
6. Zuercher-White, Elke. *An End to Panic*. New Harbinger Publications, Oakland, CA, 1995, 151–154.

Chapter 21: Psychotherapy

1. "Mental Health, Does Therapy Help?" *Consumer Reports*, Nov. 1995, 739.
2. Goode, Erica E. "Does Therapy Work?" *U.S. News and World Report*, May 24, 1993, 63–64.
3. Shear, Katherine, et al. "Cognitive Behavioral Treatment Compared with Nonprescriptive Treatment of Panic Disorder," *Archives of General Psychiatry*, vol. 51, May 1994, 365, 399.
4. Zuercher-White, Elke. *An End to Panic*. New Harbinger Publications, Oakland, CA, 1995, 178.
5. Smith, Manuel. *When I Say No, I Feel Guilty*. Bantam Doubleday Dell, New York, 1975, 301–302.
6. Bourne, Edmund. *The Anxiety and Phobia Workbook*. New Harbinger Publications, Oakland, CA, 1995, 225.
7. Ibid., 301–302.
8. Ibid., 322.
9. Ibid., 319.
10. Ibid., 313.
11. Ibid., 29.

Chapter 22: Contextual Therapy

1. Zane, Manuel, and Harry Milt. *Your Phobia*. American Psychiatric Press, Washington, D.C.,1984, 28–29.
2. Ibid., 242–245.
3. Ibid., 149.
4. Ibid., 246–265.

Chapter 23: Support Groups

1. National Self-Help Clearinghouse. New York. Phone call to Audrey Gartner, Feb. 20, 1997.
2. Ibid.
3. Ibid.
4. "Mental Health, Does Therapy Help?" *Consumer Reports*, Nov. 1995, 738.
5. National Self-Help Clearinghouse brochure.
6. Barasch, Marc Ian. *The Healing Path.* Penguin Books, New York, 1993, 348.
7. Ibid., 346.
8. "The Self-Help Solution." *The Futurist*, May–June 1996.
9. Barasch, 347.
10. Yalom, Irvin D. *The Theory and Practice of Group Psychotherapy.* HarperCollins, New York, 1975, 3–17.
11. Ibid., 12.

Chapter 24: Humor

1. Wooten, Patty. "Humor: An Antidote to Stress," *Holistic Nursing Practice*, 1996, 10 (2) 52.
2. Cousins, Norman. *Anatomy of an Illness*, W. W. Norton, New York, 1979, 39–40.
3. Dossey, Larry. "Now You Are Fit to Live: Humor and Health." *Alternative Therapies*, vol. 1, no. 5, Sept. 1996, 9.
4. Ibid., p. 9.
5. Lally, Stephen. "Stress? Laugh It Off." *Washington Post*, Aug. 28, 1991.
6. Fry, William. "Medicinal Mirth." *Stanford Medicine*, Fall 1996.
7. Lally.
8. Benson, Herbert. *The Wellness Book.* Simon and Schuster, New York, 1993, 270.
9. Ibid., 269–270.
10. Wooten, 53.
11. Yovetich, Nancy. A., et al. "Benefits of Humor in Reduction of Threat-Induced Anxiety." *Psychological Reports*, 1990, 56, 66.
12. Fry.
13. Woods, Ralph. *The Modern Handbook of Humor.* McGraw Hill, New York, 1967, 494.
14. Benson, 270.
15. Klein, Allen. *The Healing Power of Humor.* J. P. Tarcher, Los Angeles, CA, 30.

Chapter 25: Spirituality

1. Bourne, Edmund. *The Anxiety and Phobia Workbook.* New Harbinger Publications, Oakland, CA, 1995, 392.
2. Williams III, Gurney. "The Healing Power of Prayer." *McCall's*, April 1996, 87.
3. Wallis, Claudia. "Faith & Healing." *Time*, June 24, 1996, 60.
4. Ibid.
5. Ibid.
6. Ibid.
7. Chute, Cindy. "Meditation Prevents Panic Attacks." *American Health*, July–Aug. 1996, 93.

8. Wallis, 61.
9. Ibid., 59–61.
10. Moore, Nancy G. "Spirituality in Medicine." *Alternative Therapies*, vol. 2, no. 6, Nov. 1996, 25.
11. Wallis, 61.
12. Moore, 25.
13. Ibid., 103.
14. Menahem, Sam. *When Therapy Isn't Enough*. Relaxed Books, Winfield, IL, 1995, 63.

Chapter 26: Choosing a Therapist
1. *American Health*, March 1997, 75.
2. Spiegel, David A. Boston University, reported on Fox TV, Channel 49, Nov. 24, 1996.
3. "Mental Health, Does Therapy Help?" *Consumer Reports*, November 1995, 735.
4. Ibid., 736.
5. Goode, Erica E. "Does Therapy Work?" *U.S. News and World Report*, May 24, 1993, 59.
6. Ibid., 59.
7. Ibid., 63.
8. Ibid., 61.

Chapter 27: New Findings
1. "Questionnaire May Help Predict Panic Attacks." *The Record*, Nov. 22, 1996, A23.
2. "Psychologists Predict Who Will Panic." *APA News*, Nov. 21, 1996, 1–2.
3. Brody, Jane E. "When Doctors Miss Clues to Mental Disorders." *New York Times*, Dec. 20, 1995, C10.
4. Goleman, Daniel. "Push Is On for Family Doctors to Spot Psychiatric Problems." *New York Times*, Dec. 14, 1994, C12.
5. Klein, Donald, M.D. "Panic Disorder and Agoraphobia: Hypothesis Hothouse." *Journal of Clinical Psychiatry* 1996; 57 (suppl. 6), 21–27.
6. Williams, Lena. "Can New York Make You Crazy." *New York Times*, April 13, 1997.
7. Goleman, Daniel. "Doctors Cite Gains in Treating Panic Attacks." *New York Times*, January 30, 1990.
8. Ritter, Malcolm. "Inhibited Tots May Suffer Anxiety Later, Study Says." *The Record*, May 25, 1995, A18.
9. Goleman, "Doctors Cite Gains in Treating Panic Attacks."
10. Goleman, Daniel. "Early Onset Found for Panic Attacks." *New York Times*, Sept. 30, 1992.
11. "Risks of Early Puberty." Health News, *The Record*, Feb. 13, 1997, SP-4.
12. Villeponteaux, V. A., R. B. Lydiard, M. T. Laraia, G. W. Stuart, and J. C. Ballenger. "The Effects of Pregnancy on Preexisting Panic Disorder." *Journal of Clinical Psychiatry*, June 1992, 53 (6): 201–203.

13. Klein, Donald F., Anne M. Skrobala, and Robin S. Garfinkel. "Preliminary Look at the Effects of Pregnancy on the Course of Panic Disorder." *Anxiety*, 1994–1995, 1:227–232.

14. Halle, M. T., and S. C. Dilsaver. "Comorbid Panic Disorder in Patients with Winter Depression." *American Journal of Psychiatry*, July 1993, 150 (7): 1108–1110.

15. Manu, P., T. J. Lane, and D. A. Matthews. "Chronic Fatigue and Chronic Fatigue Syndrome: Clinical Epidemiology and Aetiological Classification." Ciba Foundation Symposium, 1993; 173: 23–42.

16. Yanovski, S. Z., J. E. Nelson, B. K. Dubbert, and R. L. Spitzer. "Association of Binge Eating Disorder and Psychiatric Comorbidity in Obese Subjects." *American Journal of Psychiatry*, Oct. 1993, 150 (10): 1472–1479.

17. Kendler, K. S., C. MacLean, M. Neale, R. Kessler, A. Heath, and L. Eaves. "The Genetic Epidemiology of Bulimia Nervosa." *American Journal of Psychiatry*, Dec. 1991, 148 (12): 1627–1637.

18. Facchinetti, F., G. Romano, M. Fava, and A. R. Genazzani. "Lactate Infusion Induces Panic Attacks in Patients with Premenstrual Syndrome." *Psychosomatic Medicine*, May–June 1992, 54 (3), 288–296.

19. Walker, E. A., W. J. Katon, J. Hansom, J. Harrop-Griffiths, L. Holm, M. L. Jones, L. Hickok, and R. P. Jemelka. "Medical and Psychiatric Symptoms in Women with Childhood Sexual Abuse." *Psychosomatic Medicine*, Nov.–Dec. 1992, 54 (6), 658–664.

20. Pribor, E. F., and S. H. Dinwiddie. "Psychiatric Correlates of Incest in Childhood." *American Journal of Psychiatry*, Jan. 1992, 149 (1), 52–56.

21. Cordas, T. A., E. G. Rossi, M. Grinberg, V. Gentil, M. A. Bernik, G. Bellotti, and F. Pileggi. "Mitral Valve Prolapse and Panic Disorder." Arquiros Brasileiros de Cardiologia, Feb. 1991: 56 (2), 139–142.

22. *Baptist Medical Center Newsletter*, Montclair, NJ, spring 1989.

23. Goleman, Daniel. "Panic Attack Link to Suicide Questioned." *New York Times*, July 22, 1992, C12.

24. Goleman, Daniel. "Virtual Reality Conquers Fear of Heights." *New York Times*, June 21, 1995, C11.

25. Butler, Kate. "Too Good to Be True." *Networker*, Nov.–Dec. 1993, 19–31.

26. Shear, M. Katherine, Paul A. Pilkonis, Marylene Cloitre, and Andrew C. Leon. "Cognitive Behavioral Treatment Compared with Nonprescriptive Treatment of Panic Disorder." *Archives of General Psychiatry*, vol. 51, May 1994, 395–401.

Chapter 28: Words from the Experts

1. Weekes, Claire. *More Help for Your Nerves*. Doubleday, New York, 1969, 45.
2. Ibid., 41.
3. Ibid., 102.
4. Ibid., 113.
5. Ibid.
6. Ibid., 149–150

Index

About the Authors

*L*orna Weinstock is a licensed psychotherapist and Board Certified Diplomate in Clinical Social Work. She has been an Adjunct Assistant Professor at both Columbia University and New York University, as well as a senior clinician and training supervisor at Family Counseling Service of Ridgewood, New Jersey. She has a Certificate in Psychoanalytic Psychotherapy and is a Fellow of the New Jersey Society for Clinical Social Work. Ms. Weinstock runs workshops on stress reduction and anxiety disorders, and has lectured on these topics to the community. She has extensive experience in treating panic attack and other anxiety related disorders. Ms. Weinstock is in private practice in Bergen County, New Jersey.

Eleanor Gilman is a freelance writer with a special interest in health issues. She has written hundreds of articles for newspapers and for a variety of national magazines, including *Good Housekeeping*, *American Health*, *Woman's Day*, *Men's Health*, and *Modern Maturity*. She works as a writer for a family counseling agency and has taught numerous college writing courses. Ms. Gilman was recipient of the 1995 Equality, Dignity, and Independence Award presented by the National Easter Seal Society for her article, "Healing the Children," which appeared in *Family Circle* magazine.